MOON

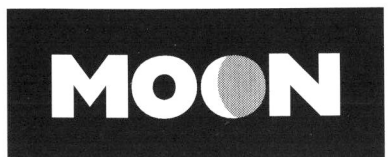

SPOTLIGHT

MAINE'S PENOBSCOT BAY & THE BLUE HILL PENINSULA

HILARY NANGLE

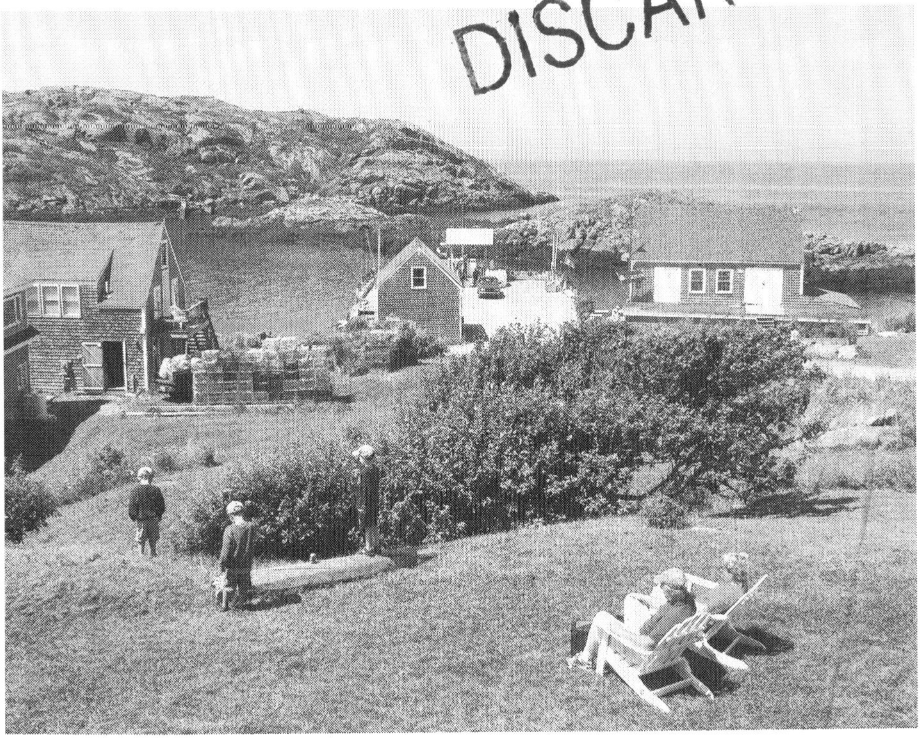

Contents

Penobscot Bay 8
Planning Your Time 10

Thomaston Area 11
Sights 11
  Montpelier 11
  Museum in the Streets 11
Events 12
Shopping 12
Camping 12
Food 12
Information and Services 12

Cushing Peninsula 13
Sights 13
  Broad Cove Church 14
  The Olson House 14

St. George Peninsula 15
Sights 15
  Marshall Point Lighthouse Museum... 15
Shopping 16
  Art 16
  Used Books 16
  General Store 16
Recreation 16
  Swimming and Beachcombing 16
  Sea Kayaking 17
  Excursion Boats 17
Accommodations 18
Food 19

Monhegan Island 20
  When to Go 22
  Other Points to Consider 22

Sights 22
  ◖ Monhegan Museum 22
  Artists' Studios 23
Recreation 23
  Hiking and Walking 23
  Bird-Watching 24
  Around-the-Island Tour 25
Accommodations 25
Food 25
Information and Services 26
Getting There and Around 26

Rockland 26
Sights 27
  ◖ The Farnsworth Art Museum
    and the Wyeth Center 27
  ◖ Owls Head Transportation
    Museum 28
  Maine Discovery Center 28
  Project Puffin Visitor Center 29
  ◖ Rockland Breakwater 29
  Sail Power & Steam Museum 29
  Main Street Historic District 29
  Flightseeing 30
  Excursion Train 30
Entertainment and Events 30
Shopping 30
  Galleries 30
  Wineries 31
Recreation 31
  Parks 31
  ◖ Owls Head Light State Park 31
  Swimming 31
  Golf 33
  Sea Kayaking 33
  Excursion Boats 33
  Maine State Ferry Service 33
  Bicycling 33

Accommodations..................33	Wine...........................50
Food............................34	Discount Shopping................50
Information and Services.........36	**Recreation**......................51
Getting Around...................36	Parks and Preserves..............51
	◖ Camden Hills State Park.........51
Vinalhaven and North Haven Islands...............37	Recreation Centers................53
	Bicycling and Sea Kayaking........53
Vinalhaven......................37	Hiking..........................53
Sights..........................38	Swimming.......................54
Entertainment....................39	Golf............................54
Shopping........................39	Day Sails and Excursions..........55
Parks and Preserves...............39	**Accommodations**..................55
Recreation.......................40	**Food**............................60
Accommodations..................41	**Information and Services**.........63
Food............................42	
Information and Services...........43	**Belfast**........................63
Getting Around...................43	**Sights**..........................63
North Haven.....................43	Historic Walking Tour..............63
Entertainment....................43	Bayside.........................64
Shopping........................44	Temple Heights..................64
Recreation.......................44	**Entertainment and Events**........64
Accommodations..................44	Entertainment...................64
Food............................45	Events..........................66
Information......................45	**Shopping**.......................66
Getting There....................45	Books..........................66
	Specialty Shops..................66
Greater Camden..............46	The Green Store.................67
Sights..........................46	**Recreation**......................67
Self-Guided Historical Tour..........46	Golf............................67
Old Conway Homestead and Cramer Museum..................46	Bicycling........................67
	Excursion Boats..................67
Vesper Hill......................46	Winter Sports...................68
Center for Maine Contemporary Art.............49	**Accommodations**..................68
	Food............................69
Entertainment....................49	**Information and Services**.........70
Festivals and Events.............49	
Shopping........................49	**Searsport Area**...............70
New and Old Books..............49	**Sights**.......................... 71
Dolls............................50	◖ Penobscot Marine Museum....... 71
Art, Crafts, and Gifts..............50	◖ Fort Knox...................... 71

- ◖ Penobscot Narrows Bridge
  and Observatory.................72
  BlueJacket Shipcrafters............72
- Shopping.........................73
- Recreation......................73
  - Parks............................73
  - Bicycling........................74
- Accommodations.................74
- Food.............................75
- Information and Services........75

Bucksport Area...............76

- Sights...........................76
  - Alamo Theatre 76
  - Bucksport Waterfront Walkway 76
  - H.O.M.E.........................76
  - Craig Brook National Fish Hatchery ..77
- Shopping........................77
- Recreation 77
  - Great Pond Mountain Conservation ..77
  - Canoeing........................77
  - Golf............................78
  - River Cruise....................78
- Accommodations.................78
- Food............................79
- Information and Services........79

Blue Hill Peninsula and Deer Isle 80

- Planning Your Time...............83

Blue Hill......................83

- Sights...........................83
  - ◖ Parson Fisher House 83
  - Historic Houses..................84
  - Bagaduce Music Lending Library.....84
  - Scenic Routes 84
- Entertainment 84
  - Music 84
- Events 85
- Shopping........................85
  - Antiques........................85
  - Books..........................85
  - Wine 85
- Parks and Recreation 85
  - ◖ Blue Hill Mountain 85
  - Blue Hill Heritage Trust...........85
  - Blue Hill Town Park 86
  - MERI Center....................86
  - Outfitter.......................87
- Accommodations.................87
- Food............................88
- Information and Services........89

Brooklin/Brooksville/ Sedgwick 90

- Sights...........................90
  - WoodenBoat Publications..........90
  - Historical Sights.................90
  - The Good Life Center............90
  - Four Season Farm................91
  - Scenic Routes 91
- Entertainment and Events........92
  - ◖ Flash! In the Pans Community
    Steel Band....................92
  - Brooksville Open Mic Nights........93
  - Eggemoggin Reach Regatta........93
- Shopping........................93
  - Antiques........................93
  - Artists' and Artisans' Galleries.......93
  - Wine and Gifts..................94
- Parks, Preserves,
  and Recreation.................95
  - ◖ Holbrook Island Sanctuary
    State Park 95
  - Swimming 95

Bicycling	95
Sailing	95
Picnicking	95

Accommodations 95

Food 96

Information and Services 97

Castine 97

History 97

Sights 98
 ◐ Castine Historic Tour 98

Entertainment and Events 100

Shopping 100
 Antiques and Galleries 100
 Books 100
 Furniture 100

Recreation 101
 Witherle Woods 101
 ◐ Sea Kayaking 101
 Swimming 101
 Golf 101

Excursion Boats 101

Accommodations 102

Food 102

Information and Services 104

Deer Isle 104

Sights 107
 ◐ Haystack Mountain School of Crafts 107
 Historic Houses and Museums 107

Pumpkin Island Light	109
Penobscot East Resource Center	109

Entertainment and Events 109

◐ **Art and Craft Galleries** 111
 North End of Deer Isle 111
 Deer Isle Village Area 111
 Sunshine Road 111
 Stonington 112

Shopping 112
 Antiques, Books, and Gifts 113
 Eclectic Shops 113

Recreation 113
 Parks and Preserves 113
 Sporting Outfitters and Guided Trips 115
 Guided Walks 115
 Sea Kayaking 116
 Swimming 116
 Golf and Tennis 116
 Excursion Boats 116
 ◐ Guided Island Tours 116

Accommodations 117

Food 119

Information and Services 120

Isle au Haut 121

◐ **Acadia National Park** 121
 Hiking 122

Other Recreation 122
 Biking 122
 Swimming 122

Accommodations and Food 122

Getting There 123

MAINE'S PENOBSCOT BAY & THE BLUE HILL PENINSULA

© HILARY NANGLE

PENOBSCOT BAY

The coastline edging island-studded Penobscot Bay is the image that lures many a vistor to Maine. The rugged and jagged coastline hides protected harbors and links fishing villages with comparatively cosmopolitan towns. Although the state considers this part of the Mid-Coast, this region has a different feel and view, one framed by coastal mountains in Camden and Lincolnville and accented by an abundance of islands.

From Thomaston through Searsport, no two towns are alike except that all are changing, as traditional industries give way to arts-and tourism-related businesses. Thomaston's Museum in the Streets, Rockland's art galleries, Camden's picturesque mountainside harbor, Lincolnville's pocket beach, Belfast's inviting downtown, Searsport's sea captains' homes, and Prospect's Fort Knox all invite exploration, as do offshore islands, many linked to the mainland by ferry.

From salty Port Clyde, take the mail boat to Monhegan, an offshore idyll known as the Artists' Island. From Rockland and Lincolnville Beach, car and passenger ferries depart to Vinalhaven, North Haven, Matinicus, and Islesboro. All are occupied year-round by hardy souls and joined in summer by less-hardy ones. Except for Matinicus, they're great day-trip destinations.

If what appeals to you about a ferry trip is traveling on the water, you can get a taste of the great age of sail by booking a three- or six-day cruise on one of the classic windjammer schooners berthed in Rockland, Rockport, and Camden. Or simply book a day sail or sea-kayak excursion.

© HILARY NANGLE

HIGHLIGHTS

◖ **Monhegan Museum:** View an impressive collection of masters at this museum adjacent to the lighthouse, then visit contemporary studios and see where artists find their inspiration by hiking island trails (page 22).

◖ **The Farnsworth Art Museum and the Wyeth Center:** Three generations of Wyeths are represented in this museum, which also boasts an excellent collection of works by Maine and American masters (page 27).

◖ **Owls Head Transportation Museum:** View a fabulous collection of vintage airplanes, automobiles, and even bicycles, many of which are flown, driven, or ridden during weekend special events (page 28).

◖ **Rockland Breakwater:** Take a walk on this nearly mile-long breakwater to the lighthouse at the end (open on weekends). It's an especially fine place to watch the windjammers sail in or out of Rockland Harbor (page 29).

◖ **Owls Head Light State Park:** The views of Penobscot Bay are spectacular, and it's a great place for a picnic lunch (page 31).

◖ **Camden Hills State Park:** If you have time, hike the moderate trail to the summit for a gull's-eye view over Camden Harbor and Penobscot Bay. If not, take the easy route and drive (page 51).

◖ **Penobscot Marine Museum:** Learn what life was *really* like during the Great Age of Sail in a town renowned for the number and quality of its sea captains (page 71).

◖ **Fort Knox:** A good restoration, frequent events, and secret passages to explore make this late-19th-century fort one of Maine's best (page 71).

◖ **Penobscot Narrows Bridge and Observatory:** On a clear day, the views from the 420-foot-high tower, one of only three in the world, extend from Mt. Katahdin to Cadillac Mountain (page 72).

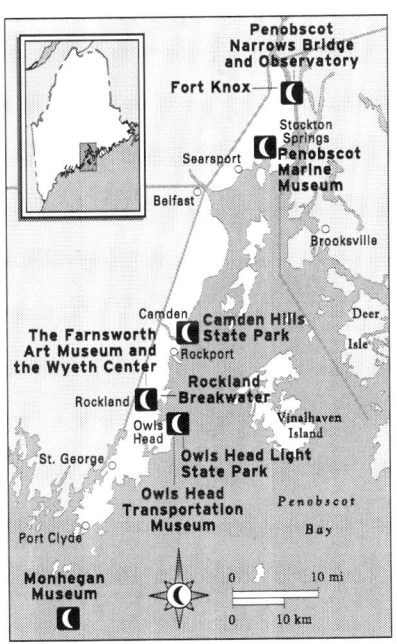

LOOK FOR ◖ TO FIND RECOMMENDED SIGHTS, ACTIVITIES, DINING, AND LODGING.

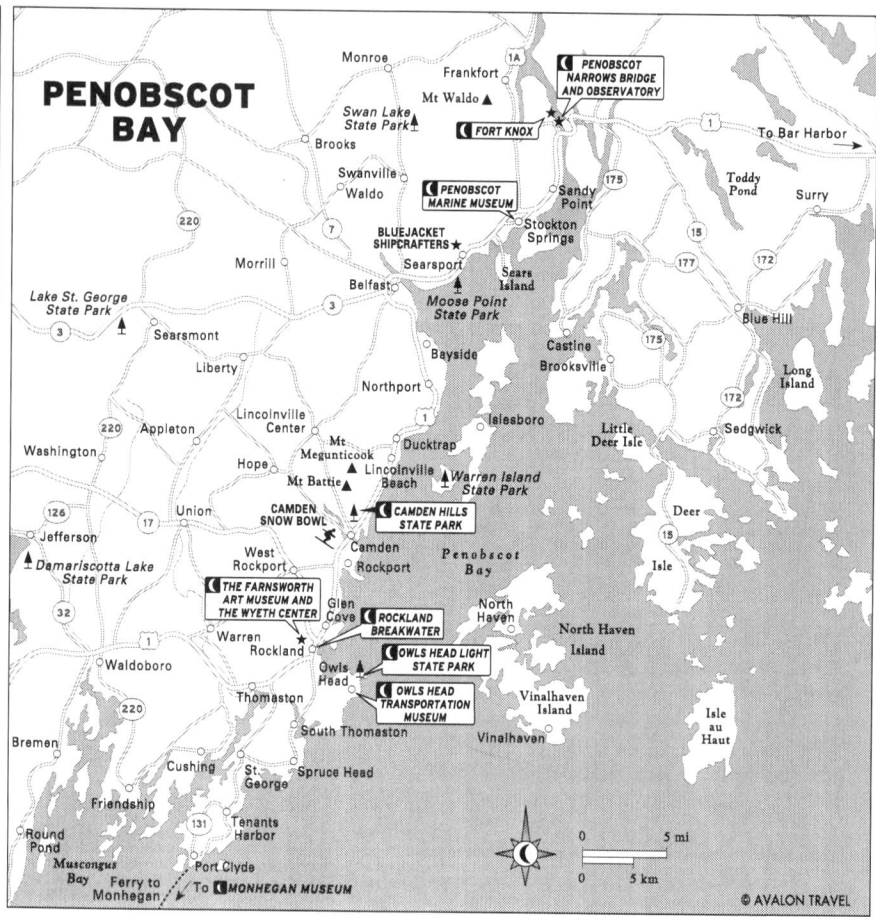

While it's easy to focus on the water, this region is rich in museums and art galleries, antiques and specialty shops, some of the state's nicest inns, and many of its better restaurants.

Most folks arrive in July and August, but autumn, when turning leaves color the hills and reflect in the sea, and the days remain warm and nights are cool, is an ideal season to visit, especially for leaf peepers who want to get off the beaten track. And in winter, when snow blankets the Camden Hills, you can ski while gazing out to Camden Harbor.

PLANNING YOUR TIME

To hit just the highlights, you'll need at least three days. If you want to relax a bit and enjoy the area, plan on 4–5 days. Make it a full week if you plan on overnighting on any of the offshore islands. In general, lodging is less expensive in Rockland, Belfast, and Searsport than it is in Camden. In any case, head for Monhegan or Vinalhaven on a good day and save the museums for inclement ones.

Two-lane Route 1 is the region's central artery, with veins running down the peninsula limbs.

Yes, traffic backs up, especially in Camden (and in Thomaston on the Fourth of July, when it's closed for a parade), but it rarely stops moving. If your destination is Rockland, take I-95 to Augusta and then Route 17 East; if it's Belfast or north, take I-95 to Augusta and then Route 3 East. Route 90 is a nifty bypass around Thomaston and Rockland, connecting Route 1 from Warren to Rockport. For a less direct route, the **Georges River Scenic Byway** is a 50-mile rural inland route, mostly along Route 131, between Port Clyde and Liberty. It parallels the coast, but it meanders through farmlands and tiny villages, and by lakes and rivers, with antiques shops and farmstands along the way. It's simply gorgeous in autumn.

Thomaston Area

Thomaston is a little gem of a town, and getting more so each year thanks to the razing of the old Maine State Prison. It's also the gateway to two lovely fingers of land bordering the St. George River and jutting into the Gulf of Maine—the Cushing and St. George Peninsulas.

In 1605, British adventurer Captain George Waymouth sailed up the river now named after him (the St. George River was originally called the Georges River). A way station for Plymouth traders as early as 1630, Thomaston was incorporated in 1777 and officially named after General John Thomas, a Revolutionary War hero.

Industry began with the production of lime, which was used for plaster. A growing demand for plaster, and the frequency with which the wooden boats were destroyed by fire while carrying loads of extremely flammable lime, spurred the growth of shipbuilding and its related infrastructure. Thomaston's slogan became "the town that went to sea."

Seeing the sleepy harborfront today, it's hard to visualize the booming era when dozens of tall-masted wooden ships slid down the ways. But the town's architecture is a testament and tribute to the prosperous past. All those splendid homes on Main and Knox Streets were funded by wealthy shipowners and shipmasters who well understood how to occupy the idle hands of off-duty carpenters.

SIGHTS
Montpelier
As you head north out of Thomaston on Route 1, you'll come face to face with an imposing colonial hilltop mansion at the junction with Route 131 South. (Behind it, unfortunately, is the rather ugly outline of a huge cement plant.) Dedicated to the memory of General Henry Knox, president George Washington's secretary of war, Montpelier (Rtes. 1 and 131, Thomaston, 207/354-8062, www.generalknoxmuseum.org, 10 A.M.–3:30 P.M. Tues.–Sat. late May–mid-Oct., $7 adults, $6 seniors, $4 children 5–13, $18 per family) is a 1930s replica of Knox's original Thomaston home. The mansion today contains Knox family furnishings and other period antiques—all described with great enthusiasm during the hour-long tours. A gift shop run by the Friends of Montpelier carries books and other relevant items. Concerts, lectures, and special events occur here periodically throughout the summer; General Knox's birthday is celebrated with considerable fanfare in July.

Museum in the Streets
Montpelier is the starting point for a walking, cycling, or, if you must, driving tour (about three miles) of nearly 70 sites in Thomaston's National Historic District. Pick up a copy of the tour brochure at one of the local businesses. Included are lots of stories behind the facades of the handsome 19th-century homes that line Main and Knox Streets; the architecture here

is nothing short of spectacular. Much of this history is also recounted in the Museum in the Streets, a walking tour taking in 25 informative plaques illustrated with old photos throughout town.

EVENTS

Thomaston's **Fourth of July,** an old-fashioned hometown celebration reminiscent of a Norman Rockwell painting, draws huge crowds. A spiffy parade—with bands, veterans, kids, and pets—starts off the morning (11 A.M.), followed by races, craft and food booths, and lots more. If you need to get *through* Thomaston on the Fourth of July, do it well before the parade or well after noon; the marchers go right down Main Street (Rte. 1), and gridlock forces a detour.

SHOPPING

Thomaston has a block-long shopping street (on Rte. 1), with ample free parking out back behind the stores.

If you arrive at Marti Reed's **Personal Book Shop** (78 Main St., Thomaston, 207/354-8058) at the right time, you're likely to run into local writers' groups that gather frequently to swap tips and gossip. That's just the kind of place this is—an independent bookstore with a warm, nurturing feel. Not to mention a dog and cat in residence.

The **Maine State Prison Showroom Outlet** (Main St./Rte. 1, corner of Wadsworth St., Thomaston, 207/354-3131) markets the handiwork of inmate craftsmen. Some of the souvenirs verge on kitsch; the bargains are wooden bar stools, toys (including dollhouses), and chopping boards. You'll need to carry your purchases with you; prison-made goods cannot be shipped.

High-end 17th- and 18th-century American furniture and accessories are the stock-in-trade of **David C. Morey American Antiques** (161 Main St., 207/354-6033).

At the southern end of Thomaston, in a renovated chicken barn, is **Thomaston Place Auction Gallery** (51 Atlantic Hwy./Rte. 1, Thomaston, 207/354-8141 or 888/834-5538, www.thomastonauction.com), the home of Kaja Veilleux, a longtime dealer, appraiser, and auctioneer. Auctions occur frequently, with previews beforehand.

Just south of Thomaston is **Lie-Nielsen Toolworks** (Rte. 1, Warren, 800/327-2520, www.lie-nielsen.com), crafting heirloom-quality hand tools for connoisseurs; tours available.

CAMPING

The best campground is on the Thomaston/Cushing town line at **Saltwater Farm Campground** (Wadsworth St./Cushing Rd., Cushing, 207/354-6735, www.saltwaterfarmcampground.com), a 35-acre Good Sam park 1.5 miles south of Route 1. Thirty-seven open and wooded tent and RV sites ($35–45) overlook the St. George River. Cabins go for $70 a day. Facilities include a bathhouse, pool, hot tub, laundry facilities, store, and a play area. The river is tidal, so swimming is best near high tide; otherwise you're dealing with mudflats.

FOOD

Call to verify days and hours of operation.

Often overlooked by visitors (but certainly not by locals) is casual **Thomaston Café and Bakery** (154 Main St./Rte. 1, Thomaston, 207/354-8589, www.thomastoncafe.com, 7 A.M.–2 P.M. Mon.–Thurs., 7 A.M.–2 P.M. and 5:30–8 P.M. Fri.–Sat., 8:30 A.M.–1:30 P.M. Sun.). German-born chef Herb Peters and his wife, Eleanor, produce superb pastries, breads, and desserts (eat here or take out). Everything's homemade, there are children's options, and the café uses only organic poultry. Try the incredible wild-mushroom hash. Dinner entrées are $16–24. Beer and wine only; reservations essential.

INFORMATION AND SERVICES

The **Rockland-Thomaston Area Chamber of Commerce** (Gateway Center,

Rockland, 207/596-0376 or 800/562-2529, www.therealmaine.com) is the area's best resource.

The **Thomaston Public Library** (42 Main St., Thomaston, 207/354-2453) occupies part of the Greek Revival Thomaston Academy.

Cushing Peninsula

Cushing's recorded history goes back at least as far as 1605, when someone named "Abr [maybe Abraham] King"—presumably a member of explorer George Waymouth's crew—inscribed his name here on a ledge (now private property). Since 1789, settlers' saltwater farms have sustained many generations, and the active Cushing Historical Society keeps the memories and memorabilia from fading away. But the outside world knows little of this. Cushing is better known as "Wyeth country," the terrain depicted by the famous artistic dynasty of N. C., Andrew, and Jamie Wyeth (and assorted talented other relatives).

If you're an Andrew Wyeth fan, visiting Cushing will give you the feeling of walking through his paintings. The flavor of his Maine work is here—rolling fields, wildflower meadows, rocky tidal coves, broad vistas, character-filled farmhouses, and some well-hidden summer enclaves.

SIGHTS

Cushing's town boundary begins 1.3 miles south of Route 1 (take Wadsworth Street at the Maine State Prison Showroom Outlet). Two miles farther, you'll pass giant wooden sculptures in the yard of the late artist **Bernard Langlais,** who died in 1977.

Six miles from Route 1 is the **A. S. Fales**

The Olson House inspired many of Andrew Wyeth's works.

BEANHOLE BEANS

"To be happy in New England," wrote one Joseph P. MacCarthy at the turn of the 20th century, "you must select the Puritans for your ancestors...[and] eat beans on Saturday night." There is no better way to confirm the latter requirement than to attend a "beanhole" bean supper – a real-live legacy of colonial times, with dinner baked in a hole in the ground.

Generally scheduled, appropriately, for a Saturday night (check local newspapers), a beanhole bean supper demands plenty of preparation from its hosts – and a secret ingredient or two. (Don't even think about trying to pry the recipe out of the cooks.) The supper always includes hot dogs, cole slaw, relishes, home-baked breads, and homemade desserts, but the beans are the star attraction. (Typically, the suppers are also alcohol-free.) Not only are they feasts; they're also bargains, never setting you back more than about $8.

The beans at the Broad Cove Church's annual mid-July beanhole bean supper, served family-style at long picnic tables, are legendary – attracting nearly 200 eager diners. Minus the secrets, here's what happens:

Early Friday morning: Church volunteers load 10 pounds of dry pea and soldier (yellow-eye) beans into each of four large kettles and add water to cover. The beans are left to soak and soften for 6-7 hours. Two or three volunteers uncover the churchyard's four rock-lined beanholes (each about three feet deep), fill the holes with hardwood kindling, ignite the wood, and keep the fires burning until late afternoon, when the wood is reduced to red-hot coals.

Early Friday afternoon: The veteran chefs parboil the beans and stir in the seasonings. Typical additions are brown sugar, molasses, mustard, salt, pepper, and salt pork (much of the secret is in the exact proportions). When the beans are precooked to the cooks' satisfaction, the kettle lids are secured with wire and the pots are lugged outdoors.

Friday midafternoon: With the beans ready to go underground, some of the hot coals are quickly shoveled out of the pits. The kettles are lowered into the pits and the coals replaced around the sides of the kettles and atop their lids. The pits are covered with heavy sheet metal and topped with a thick layer of sand and a tarpaulin. The round-the-clock baking begins, and no one peeks before it's finished.

Saturday midafternoon: Even the veterans start getting nervous just before the pits are uncovered. Was the seasoning right? Did too much water cook away? Did the beans dry out? Not to worry, though – failures just don't happen here.

Saturday night: When a pot is excavated for the first of three seatings (about 5 P.M.), the line is already long. The chefs check their handiwork and the supper begins. No one seems to mind waiting for the second and third seatings – while others eat, a sing-along gets under way in the church, keeping everyone entertained.

---

and Son Store (locally, just Fales's Store), Cushing's heart and soul—source of fuel, film, gossip, and groceries. Built in 1889, the store has been in the Fales family ever since. You might want to pick up lunch while here. Just beyond the store, take the left fork, continuing down the peninsula toward the Broad Cove Church and the Olson House.

Broad Cove Church

Andrew Wyeth aficionados will recognize the Broad Cove Church as one of his subjects—alongside Cushing Road en route to the Olson House. It's open most days, so step inside and admire the classic New England architecture. The church is also well known as the site of one of the region's best beanhole bean suppers, held on a Saturday mid-July and attracting several hundred appreciative diners. Bear left at the fork after Fales's Store; the church is 0.4 mile farther, on the right.

The Olson House

Many an art lover makes the pilgrimage to the Olson House (11 A.M.–4 P.M. daily late May–mid-Oct., $5), a famous icon near the end of Hathorn Point Road. The early-19th-century farmhouse appears in Andrew Wyeth's 1948 painting *Christina's World* (which hangs in New York's Museum of Modern Art), his best-known image of the disabled Christina Olson, who died in 1968. In 1991, two philanthropists donated the Olson House to the Farnsworth Art Museum in Rockland (a $12 combination ticket includes Farnsworth museum admission), which has retained the house's sparse, lonely, and almost mystical ambience. The clapboards outside remain unpainted, the interior walls bear only a few Wyeth prints (hung close to the settings they depict), and it is easy to sense Wyeth's inspiration for chronicling this place. From Route 1 in Thomaston, at the Maine State Prison Showroom Outlet, turn onto Wadsworth Street and go six miles to Fales's Store. Take the left fork after the store, go 1.5 miles, and turn left onto Hathorn Point Road. Go another 1.9 miles to the house.

St. George Peninsula

Even though the Cushing and St. George Peninsulas face each other across the St. George River, they differ dramatically. Cushing is far more rural, seemingly less approachable—with little access to the surrounding waters; St. George has a slew of things to do and see, and places to sleep and eat, plus shore access in various spots along the peninsula.

The St. George Peninsula is actually better known by some of the villages scattered along its length: **Tenants Harbor, Port Clyde, Wiley's Corner, Spruce Head**—plus the smaller neighborhoods of Martinsville, Smalleytown, Glenmere, Long Cove, Hart's Neck, and Clark Island. Each has a distinct personality, determined partly by the different ethnic groups—primarily Brits, Swedes, and Finns—who arrived to work the granite quarries in the 19th century. Wander through the Seaview Cemetery in Tenants Harbor and you'll see the story: row after row of gravestones with names from across the sea.

A more famous former visitor was 19th-century novelist Sarah Orne Jewett, who holed up in an old schoolhouse in Martinsville, paid a weekly rental of $0.50, and wrote *The Country of the Pointed Firs,* a tale about "Dunnet's Landing" (Tenants Harbor).

Today the picturesque peninsula has saltwater farms, tidy hamlets, a striking lighthouse, spruce-edged tidal coves, an active yachting harbor, and, at the tip, a tiny fishing village (Port Clyde), which serves as a springboard to offshore Monhegan Island.

Port Clyde is likely the best-known community here. (Fortunately, it's no longer called by its unappealing 18th-century name—Herring Gut.) George Waymouth explored Port Clyde's nearby islands in 1605, but you'd never suspect its long tradition. It's a sleepy place, with a general store, low-key inns, a few galleries, and pricey parking.

SIGHTS
Marshall Point Lighthouse Museum
Not many settings can compare with the spectacular locale of the Marshall Point Lighthouse Museum (Marshall Point Rd., Port Clyde, 207/372-6450, www.marshallpoint.org, 1–5 P.M. Sun.–Fri., 10 A.M.–5 P.M. Sat., late May–mid-Oct., free), a distinctive 1857 lighthouse and park overlooking Port Clyde, the harbor islands, and the passing lobster-boat fleet. Bring a picnic and let the kids run on the lawn (but keep them well back from the shoreline). The tiny museum, in the 1895 keeper's house, displays lighthouse and local memorabilia. The grounds are accessible year-round. Take Route 131 to Port Clyde and watch for signs to the museum.

In the keeper's house at Marshall Point Lighthouse, at the tip of the St. George Peninsula, is a small museum.

SHOPPING
Art
The St. George Peninsula has been attracting artists for decades, and galleries pepper the peninsula. Some have been here for years, others started yesterday; most are worth a stop, so keep an eye out for their signs. In early August, a number of renowned artists usually coordinate an open-studio weekend.

Overlooking the reversing falls in downtown South Thomaston, **The Old Post Office Gallery** (Rte. 73, South Thomaston, 207/594-9396, www.artofthesea.com) has 11 rooms filled with marine art and antiques: ship models, prints, paintings, sculpture, scrimshaw, and jewelry.

Used Books
Drive up to the small parking area at **Lobster Lane Book Shop** (Island Rd., Spruce Head, 207/594-7520), and you'll see license plates from everywhere. The tiny shop, in a crammed but well-organized shed that's been here since the 1960s, has 50,000 or so treasures for used-book fans. For a few dollars, you can stock up on a summer's worth of reading. The shop is just under a mile east of Route 73, with eye-catching vistas in several directions (except, of course, when Spruce Head's infamous fog sets in).

General Store
Despite periodic ownership changes, **Port Clyde General Store** (Rte. 131, Port Clyde, 207/372-6543) remains a characterful destination, a two-century-old country store with ever-increasing upscale touches. Stock up on groceries, pick up a newspaper, order breakfast or a pizza, or buy a sweatshirt (you may need it on the Monhegan boat). Current owner Linda Bean has gussified it even more and added a shop upstairs, and also operates **The Dip Net** out back.

RECREATION
Swimming and Beachcombing
Drift Inn Beach, on Drift Inn Beach Road

(also called Candy's Cove Road), isn't a big deal as beaches go, but it's the best public one on the peninsula, so it gets busy on hot days. The name comes from the Drift Inn, an early-20th-century summer hotel. Drift Inn Beach Road parallels Route 131, and the parking lot is accessible from both roads. Heading south on the peninsula, about 3.5 miles after the junction with Route 73, turn left at Drift Inn Beach Road. The sign frequently disappears; watch for an imposing square granite house and a red farmhouse on your left, turn, then continue 0.2 mile.

Sea Kayaking

The St. George Peninsula is especially popular for sea kayaking, with plenty of islands to add interest and shelter. **Port Clyde Kayaks** (Rte. 131, Port Clyde, 207/372-8128, www.portclydekayaks.com) offers 2.5-hour ($55) and four-hour ($79) guided tours around the tip of the peninsula, taking in Marshall Point lighthouse and the islands. Other options include full moon and sunset tours. Ask about multi-day camping or bed-and-breakfast tours.

If you have kayaking experience, you can launch on the ramp just before the causeway that links the mainland with Spruce Head Island, in Spruce Head (Island Rd., off Rte. 73). Parking is limited. A great paddle goes clockwise around Spruce Head Island and nearby Whitehead (there's a lighthouse on its southeastern shore) and Norton Islands. Duck in for lunch at Waterman's Beach Lobster. Around new moon and full moon, plan your schedule to avoid low tide near the Spruce Head causeway, or you may become mired in mudflats.

Excursion Boats

The best boating experience on this peninsula is a passenger-ferry trip from Port Clyde to offshore **Monhegan Island**—for a day, overnight, or longer. Perhaps because the private ferry company has a monopoly on this harbor, the trip isn't cheap, and parking adds

For fresh seafood and the best harbor views, visit the Port Clyde General Store.

The Monhegan-Thomaston Boat Line ferries passengers to Monhegan Island and also offers scenic cruises.

to the cost, but it's a "must" excursion, so try to factor it into the budget. Port Clyde is the nearest mainland harbor to Monhegan; this service operates all year. **Monhegan-Thomaston Boat Line** (Port Clyde, 207/372-8848, www.monheganboat.com) uses two boats, the *Laura B.* (70 minutes each way) and the newer *Elizabeth Ann* (50 minutes). Round-trip tickets are $32 adults, $18 children 2–12. (Leave your bicycle in Port Clyde; you won't need it on the island.) Reservations are essential in summer, especially for the 10:30 A.M. boat; a $5 per person fee holds the reservation until 75 minutes before departure, so you have to get to the dock early. No deposit is needed for other boats, but show up 30 minutes before departure. Parking in Port Clyde is $4 a day. If a summer day trip is all you can manage, aim for the first or second boat and return on the last one; don't go just for the boat ride.

During the summer, the Monhegan–Thomaston Boat Line also offers 2.5-hour sightseeing cruises, on a varied schedule, including a Puffin/Nature Cruise and Lighthouse Cruise. Each costs $25 adults, $10 children.

ACCOMMODATIONS

Rates noted are for peak season.

Inns

The dreamy island-dotted, oceanfront setting complements **The East Wind Inn** (Mechanic St., Tenants Harbor, 207/372-6366 or 800/241-8439, www.eastwindinn.com, $118–226), the perfect rendition of an old-fashioned country inn—some parts of it more old-fashioned than others. Built in 1860 and originally used as a sail loft, it has a huge veranda, a cozy parlor, harbor-view rooms, and a quiet dining room with a creditable New England menu. Rooms are divided between the main inn, some with shared bath, and the spiffed-up 19th-century Meeting House, a former sea captain's home, which also has one apartment. All rates include a full breakfast. The water-view dining room is open to the public daily for breakfast (7:30–9:30 A.M., to 10 A.M. in July–Aug.) and dinner

(5:30–8:30 P.M., to 9:30 P.M. in July–Aug.). Dinner entrées are $17–26. Reservations are wise. Lunch is available in summer at a dockside take-out. Children are welcome; pets are $15 per visit. The inn is open all year; the dining room is open April–November.

Bed-and-Breakfasts

In the center of South Thomaston village but overlooking the reversing falls on the tidal Wessaweskeag River, the 1830 **Weskeag at the Water** (14 Elm St., Rte. 73, South Thomaston, 207/596-6676 or 800/596-5576, www.weskeag.com, $125–150) has nine rooms, of which four have in-room private baths; one has a whirlpool tub. This place is especially relaxing; congenial innkeepers Gray and Lynne Smith provide guests with games, puzzles, books, a huge video library, a great deck, and a lawn stretching to the river. Bring your sea kayaks and bicycles. It's 1.5 miles from the Owls Head Transportation Museum (the Smiths love vintage cars) and a few more miles from the restaurants of downtown Rockland. It's open all year.

If you stay at the **Ocean House** (Rte. 131, Port Clyde, 207/372-6691 or 800/269-6691, www.oceanhousehotel.com, $110–145), you can plan to roll out of bed, eat breakfast, and head down the hill to the Monhegan boat. Several of the 10 unpretentious rooms (seven with private bath) have great harbor views. No credit cards.

Smack-dab in the middle of Port Clyde, the **Seaside Inn** (5 Cold Storage Rd., Port Clyde, 207/372-0700 or 800/279-5041, www.seasideportclyde.com, $99–159) is an unfussy 1850s sea captain's home with both private and shared baths. A 1st-floor library has books, puzzles, TV, and a fireplace. Rates include a full breakfast.

Every room has a view of Owl's Head Harbor at the **Trinity on the Ocean Bed and Breakfast** (20 Ocean Ave., Owl's Head, 207/596-0071, www.trinityontheocean.com, $180–220), an oceanfront bed-and-breakfast that's within walking distance of Primo restaurant. Hosts Steve and Donna Belyea are Rockland natives, so they know the area well, and they like to share their finds. Donna made the quilts topping the beds in the three guest rooms, each named after a Maine windjammer. A full breakfast is served either inside or on the ocean-view deck.

Camping

The third generation now operates **Lobster Buoy Campsites** (280 Waterman's Beach Rd., South Thomaston, 207/596-7546, www.lobsterbuoycampsites.com, $22–32), an oceanfront campground with 40 sites, 28 with water and electric, all with fire ring and picnic table. You can launch a canoe or kayak from the small sand beach. Most sites are in an open field, and Lookout Beach is reserved for tenting. Every morning in July and August, homemade doughnuts are sold in the office.

FOOD

Call to verify days and hours of operation.

Local Flavors

Don't be surprised to see the handful of tables occupied at the **Keag Store** (Rte. 73, Village Center, South Thomaston, 207/596-6810, 6 A.M.–9 P.M. Mon.–Sat., 7 A.M.–8 P.M. Sun.), one of the most popular lunch stops in the area. (Keag, by the way, is pronounced GIG—short for "Wessaweskeag.") Roast-turkey sandwiches with stuffing are a big draw, as is the pizza, which verges on the greasy but compensates with its flavor—no designer toppings, just good pizza. Order it all to go and head across the street to the public wharf, where you can hang out and observe all the comings and goings.

Casual Dining

The decidedly old-fashioned **Craignair Inn Restaurant** (Clark Island Rd., off Rte. 71, Spruce Head, 207/594-7644, www.craignair.com), built in 1928 to house granite workers, serves dinner in its water-view dining room daily except Sunday, entrées $16–26. Seafood is the specialty. Also in the Main Inn and Vestry Annex are rooms, some with shared baths ($110–153 with breakfast).

Waterman's Beach Lobster provides a front-row table on Penobscot Bay.

Lobster in the Rough

These open-air lobster wharves are the best places in the area to get down and dirty and manhandle a steamed or boiled lobster.

Poking right into Wheeler's Bay, **Miller's Lobster Company** (Eagle Quarry Rd., off Rte. 73, Spruce Head, 207/594-7406, www.millerslobster.com, 11 A.M.–7 P.M. daily) is the quintessential lobster pound, a well-run operation that draws crowds all summer long. Lobster rolls, steamed clams, crabmeat rolls, homemade pies—the works. Even hot dogs if you need them. Several picnic tables are under cover for chilly or rainy weather. BYOB.

A broad view of islands in the Mussel Ridge Channel is the bonanza at **Waterman's Beach Lobster** (343 Waterman's Beach Rd., South Thomaston, 207/596-7819, www.watermansbeachlobster.com, 11 A.M.–7 P.M. Wed.–Sun.). This tiny operation has a big reputation: It's won a James Beard Award. It turns out lobster, clam, and mussel dinners, fat lobster and crabmeat rolls, and superb pies (and hot dogs and grilled cheese). Step up to the window and place your order. Service can be slow, but why rush with a view like this? Choose a good day; there's no real shelter from bad weather. BYOB; no credit cards. Next door to the Blue Lupin B&B, the wharf is on a side road off Route 73 between Spruce Head Village and South Thomaston; watch for signs on Route 73.

Monhegan Island

Eleven or so miles from the mainland lies a unique island community with gritty lobstermen, close-knit families, a longstanding summertime artists' colony, no cars, astonishingly beautiful scenery, and some of the best birdwatching on the Eastern Seaboard. Until the 1980s, the island had only radiophones and generator power; with the arrival of electricity and real phones, the pace has quickened a bit—but not much. Welcome to Monhegan Island.

But first a cautionary note: Monhegan has remained idyllic largely because generations of residents, part-timers, and visitors have been ultrasensitive to its fragility. When you buy your ferry ticket, you'll receive a copy of the regulations, all very reasonable, and the captain of your ferry will repeat them. *Heed them or don't go.*

Many of the regulations have been developed by The Monhegan Associates, an island land trust founded in the 1960s by Theodore Edison, son of the inventor. Firmly committed to preservation of the island in as natural a state as possible, the group maintains and marks the trails, sponsors natural-history talks, and insists that no construction be allowed beyond the village limits.

The origin of the name Monhegan remains up in the air; it's either a Maliseet or Micmac name meaning "out-to-sea island" or an adaptation of the name of a French explorer's daughter. In any case, Monhegan caught the attention of Europeans after English explorer John Smith stopped by in 1614, but the island had already been noticed by earlier adventurers, including John Cabot, Giovanni da Verrazzano, and George Waymouth. Legend even has it that Monhegan fishermen sent dried fish to Plimoth Plantation during the Pilgrims' first winter on Cape Cod. Captain Smith returned home and carried on about Monhegan, snagging the attention of intrepid souls who established a fishing/trading outpost here in 1625. Monhegan has been settled continuously since 1674, with fishing as the economic base.

In the 1880s, lured by the spectacular setting and artist Robert Henri's enthusiastic reports, gangs of artists began arriving, lugging their easels here and there to capture the surf, the light, the tidy cottages, the magnificent headlands, fishing boats, even the islanders' craggy features. American, German, French, and British artists have long (and continue to) come here; well-known signatures associated with Monhegan include Rockwell Kent, George Bellows, Edward Hopper, James Fitzgerald, Andrew Winter, Alice Kent Stoddard, Reuben Tam, William Kienbusch, and Jamie Wyeth.

Officially called Monhegan Plantation, the island has about 75 year-rounders. Several hundred others summer here. A handful of students attend the tiny school through eighth grade; high-schoolers have to pack up and move "inshore" to the mainland during the school year.

At the schoolhouse, the biggest social event of the year is the Christmas party, when everyone brings casseroles, salads, and desserts to complement a big beef roast. Kids perform their Christmas play, Santa shows up with presents, and dozens of adults look on approvingly. The islanders turn out en masse for almost every special event at the school, and the adults treat the island kids almost like common property, feeling free to praise or chastise them any time it seems appropriate—a phenomenon unique to isolated island communities.

> **TEN RULES FOR MONHEGAN VISITORS**
>
> 1. Smoking is banned everywhere except in the village.
> 2. Rock climbing is not allowed on the wild headlands on the back side of the island.
> 3. Preserve the island's wild state – do not remove flowers or lichens.
> 4. Bicycles and strollers are not allowed on island trails.
> 5. Camping and campfires are forbidden islandwide.
> 6. Swim only at Swim Beach, just south of the ferry landing – if your innards can stand the shock. Wait for the incoming tide, when the water is warmest (and this warmth is relative). It's wise not to swim alone.
> 7. Dogs must be leashed; carry a pooper-scooper to remove their waste.
> 8. Be respectful of private property; stay on the trails. (As the island visitors guide puts it, "Monhegan is a village, not a theme park.")
> 9. If you're staying overnight, bring a flashlight; the village paths are very dark.
> 10. Carry the island trail map when you go exploring; you'll need it.
>
> A strong suggestion: Carry a trash bag, use it, and take it off the island when you leave.

For years, Monhegan's lobster-fishing season—a legislatively sanctioned period—perversely began on December 1 (locally known as Trap Day), but in 2007 that was moved forward to October 1, making it possible for visitors to view the action. An air of nervous anticipation surrounds the dozen or so lobstermen after midnight the day before as they prepare to steam out to set their traps on the ocean floor. Of course, with less competition from mainland fishermen that time of year, and a supply of lobsters fattening up since the previous June, there's a ready market for their catch. But success still depends on a smooth "setting." Meetings are held daily during the month beforehand to make sure everyone will be ready to "set" together. The season ends on June 25.

March brings the annual town meeting, an important community event that draws every able-bodied soul and then some.

Almost within spitting distance of Monhegan's dock (but you'll still need a boat) is whale-shaped **Manana Island,** once the home of an ex–New Yorker named Ray Phillips. Known as the Hermit of Manana, Phillips lived a solitary sheepherding existence on this barren island for more than half a century until his death in 1975. His story had spread so far afield that even the *New York Times* ran a front-page obituary when he died. (Photos and clippings are displayed in the Monhegan Museum.) In summer, youngsters with skiffs often hang around the harbor, particularly Fish Beach and Swim Beach, and you can usually talk one of them into taking you over, for a fee. (Don't try to talk them down too much or they may not return to pick you up.) Some curious inscriptions on Manana (marked with a yellow X near the boat landing) have led archaeologists to claim that Vikings even made it here, but cooler heads attribute the markings to Mother Nature.

One last note: Monhegan isn't for the mobility impaired. There's no public transportation, and roads are rough and hilly.

When to Go

If a day trip is all your schedule will allow, visit Monhegan between Memorial Day weekend and mid-October, when ferries from Port Clyde, New Harbor, and Boothbay Harbor operate daily, allowing 5–8 hours on the island—time enough to do an extensive trail loop, visit the museum and handful of shops, and picnic on the rocks. Other months, there's only one ferry a day from Port Clyde (only three a week Nov.–Apr.), so you'll need to spend the night—not a hardship, but definitely requiring planning.

Almost any time of year, but especially in spring, fog can blanket the island, curtailing photography and swimming (although usually not the ferries). A spectacular sunny day can't be beat, but don't be deterred by fog, which lends an air of mystery you won't forget. Rain, of course, is another matter; some island trails can be perilous even in a misty drizzle.

Other Points to Consider

Monhegan has no bank, but there are a couple of ATMs. Credit cards are not accepted everywhere. Personal checks, travelers checks, or cash will do. The few public telephones in the village require phone credit cards.

The only public restroom unconnected to a restaurant or lodging is on Horn Hill, at the southern end of the village (near the Monhegan House), and it will cost you $1 to use it. Outrageous, perhaps, but the restroom was installed to protect the woods and trails and deter day-trippers from bothering innkeepers. Unfortunately, the fee inspires some people to spurn these facilities and head for the woods. Please spend the dollar and preserve the island.

SIGHTS

Monhegan is a getaway destination, a relaxing place for self-starters, so don't anticipate organized entertainment beyond the occasional lecture or narrated nature tour. Bring sturdy shoes (maybe even an extra pair in case trails are wet), a windbreaker, binoculars, a camera, and perhaps a sketchpad or a journal. If you're staying overnight, bring a flashlight for negotiating the unlighted island walkways, even in the village. For rainy days, bring a book. (If you forget, there's an amazingly good library.) In winter, bring ice skates for use on the Ice Pond.

◖ Monhegan Museum

The National Historic Register **Monhegan Lighthouse**—activated in July 1824 and automated in 1959—stands at the island's highest point, Lighthouse Hill, an exposed summit that's also home to the Monhegan Historical

Climb Lighthouse Hill to the Monhegan Museum for panoramic views over the village and Manana Island, beyond.

and Cultural Museum (207/596-7003, www.monheganmuseum.org, 11:30 A.M.–3:30 P.M. daily July–Aug., 12:30–2:30 P.M. daily June and Sept.) in the former keeper's house and adjacent buildings. Overseen by the Monhegan Historical and Cultural Museum Association, the museum contains an antique kitchen, lobstering exhibits, and a fine collection of paintings by noted and not-so-noted artists. Two outbuildings have tools and gear connected with fishing and ice-cutting, traditional island industries. The assistant lightkeeper's house, recently restored top to bottom as a handsome art gallery, provides a climate-controlled environment for the museum's impressive art collection. A volunteer usually is on hand to answer questions. The museum also owns two buildings designed and built by Rockwell Kent and later owned by James Fitzgerald. The house is maintained as a historic house museum; Fitzgerald's works are displayed in the studio. Both are open on a limited basis. Admission is technically free, but donations are encouraged.

Artists' Studios

Nearly 20 artists' studios are open to the public during the summer (usually July and August), but not all at once. At least five are open most days—most in the afternoon (Monday has the fewest choices). Sometimes it's tight timewise for day-trippers who also want to hike the trails, but most of the studios are relatively close to the ferry landing. An annually updated map-schedule details locations, days, and times. It's posted on bulletin boards in the village and is available at lodgings and shops.

Two group galleries worth a visit are **Winter Works,** a craft co-op, and **Lupine Gallery** (207/594-8131), with works by Monhegan artists and artists' supplies.

RECREATION
Hiking and Walking

Just over a half mile wide and 1.7 miles long, barely a square mile in area, Monhegan has 18 numbered hiking trails, most easy to moderate, covering about 11 miles. All are described in the *Monhegan Associates Trail Map* (www.

On Monhegan Island, it seems nearly every place you turn, there are artists capturing the iconic scenes.

monheganassociates.org), available at mainland ferry offices and island shops and lodgings or on the website. (The map is not to scale, so the hikes can take longer than you think.)

The footing is uneven everywhere, so Monhegan can present major obstacles to those with disabilities, even on the well-worn but unpaved village roads. Maintain an especially healthy respect for the ocean here, and don't venture too close; through the years, rogue waves on the island's backside have claimed victims young and old.

A relatively easy **day-tripper loop,** with a couple of moderate sections along the backside of the island, takes in several of Monhegan's finest features starting at the southern end of the village, opposite the church. To appreciate it, allow at least two hours. From the Main Road, go up Horn Hill, following signs for the **Burnthead Trail** (no. 4). Cross the island to the **Cliff Trail** (no. 1). Turn north on the Cliff Trail, following the dramatic headlands on the island's backside. There are lots of great picnic rocks in this area. Continue to Squeaker Cove, where the surf is the wildest, but be cautious.

Then watch for signs to the **Cathedral Woods Trail** (no. 11), carpeted with pine needles and leading back to the village.

When you get back to Main Road, detour up the **Whitehead Trail** (no. 7) to the museum. If you're spending the night and feeling energetic, consider circumnavigating the island via the **Cliff Trail** (nos. 1 and 1-A). Allow at least 5-6 hours for this route; don't rush it.

Bird-Watching

One of the East Coast's best bird-watching sites during spring and fall migrations, Monhegan is a migrant trap for exhausted creatures winging their way north or south. Avid bird-watchers come here to add rare and unusual species to their life lists, and some devotees return year after year. No bird-watcher should arrive, however, without a copy of the superb *Birder's Guide to Maine*.

Predicting exact bird-migration dates can be dicey, since wind and weather aberrations can skew the schedule. Generally, the best times are mid- to late May and most of September, into early October. If you plan to spend a night (or more) on the island during migration seasons, don't try to wing it—reserve a room well in advance.

Around-the-Island Tour
On most days, the Balmy Days excursion boat makes a half-hour circuit around the island 2–2:30 P.M. for a nominal fee. Ask at the ferry dock.

ACCOMMODATIONS
Rates noted are for peak season.

The island has a variety of lodgings from rustic to comfortable, but none are luxurious. Pickup trucks of dubious vintage meet all the ferries and transport luggage to the lodgings. For cottage renters, Monhegan Trucking charges a small fee for each piece of luggage. Rates are quoted for peak season.

Best lodging is the ◖ **Island Inn** (207/596-0371, www.islandinnmonhegan.com, $165–395), an imposing three-story hotel, dating from 1816, that commands a prime chunk of real estate overlooking the harbor. Most rooms have been updated, but retain the simplicity of another era, with painted floors, antique oak furnishings, and comfy beds covered with white down duvets. Just try to resist the siren song of the Adirondack chairs on the expansive veranda and lawns overlooking the ferry landing. Rates for the 32 harbor- and meadow-view rooms and suites (most with private baths) include full breakfast. Add $4 per person daily gratuity and $5 per person for a one-night stay.

In the heart of the village, **Monhegan House** (207/594-7983 or 800/599-7983, www.monheganhouse.com, $77–81 s, $135–165), built in 1870, is a large four-story building with 33 rooms. All but one suite ($215) have shared baths, not always on the same floor as your room. Don't miss the looseleaf notebook in the lobby. Labeled *A Monhegan Novel,* it's the ultimate in shaggy-dog sagas, created by a long string of guests since 1992. Rates include breakfast. There may be a $5 per person surcharge for one-night stays. Children are welcome: Ages 4–12 are $18, ages 13 and older are $28. It's open late May–Columbus Day.

A more modernized hostelry, **Shining Sails** (207/596-0041, www.shiningsails.com, $140–210) lacks the quaintness of the other inns, but the rooms and efficiencies are very comfortable, convenient to the dock, stay open all year, and have private baths. Breakfast (included only in season) is continental. "Well-supervised" children are welcome. An additional four apartments are in a separate building ($165–230). Shining Sails also manages more than two dozen weekly-rental cottages and apartments, with rates beginning around $800/week in season.

The funkiest lodging, and not for everyone, is **The Trailing Yew** (207/596-0440 or 800/592-2520, www.trailingyew.com, $170). Spread among five rustic buildings are 35 rooms, most with shared baths (averaging five rooms per bath and not always in the same building) and lighted with kerosene (about 12 have electricity). Rates include breakfast, dinner, taxes, and gratuities; kids are $45 and up, depending on age. The old-fashioned, low-key 50-seat dining room is open to the public for dinner at 5:45 P.M., served family-style by reservation, and for breakfast at 7:45 A.M. Bring a sleeping bag in spring or fall; rooms are unheated. No credit cards.

FOOD
Most visitors don't arrive on Monhegan expecting gourmet cuisine. Everything is quite casual, and food is hearty and ample. None of the eateries have liquor licenses, so buy beer or wine at one of the stores or the Barnacle Café, or bring it from the mainland. All of the restaurants and food sources are in or close to the village. In most cases hours change frequently, so call first.

Prepared foods, varying from pastries to sandwiches and salads, are available from **Barnacle Café** (207/596-0371), under the same ownership as the nearby Island Inn; **The Novelty,** behind and operated by The Monhegan House; **Carina** (207/594-0837), a boutique grocery; and the **Monhegan Store**.

Casual Dining
The restaurant at the **Island Inn,** open to the public for breakfast and dinner (opens at

6 P.M.), has an excellent dinner menu with creative entrées that range $15–27. It's also open for lunch Thursday–Sunday.

Islanders and visitors flock to the **Monhegan House Café,** overlooking the village, for breakfast and dinner (entrées $13–20).

Lobster in the Rough

You can't get much rougher for lobster in the rough than **Fish House Fish** (on Fish Beach, www.fishbeachmonhegan.com, 11:30 A.M.–7 P.M. daily). Lobster and crabmeat rolls, locally smoked fish, and homemade stews and chowders are on the menu as well as fresh lobster. Take it to the picnic tables on the beach and enjoy.

INFORMATION AND SERVICES

Several free brochures and flyers, revised annually, will answer most questions about planning a day trip or overnight visit to Monhegan. Ferries supply visitors with the *Visitor's Guide to Monhegan Island* and sell the Monhegan Associates Trail Map ($1). Both are also available at island shops, galleries, and lodgings. Info also is available at www.monhegan.com and www.monhegan.info.

Monhegan's pleasant little library, the Jackie and Edward Library, was named after two children who drowned in the surf in the 1920s. The fiction collection is especially extensive, and it's open to everyone.

Also check the Rope Shed, the community bulletin board next to the meadow, right in the village. Monhegan's version of a bush telegraph, it's where everyone posts flyers and notices about nature walks, lectures, excursions, and other special events. You'll also see the current Monhegan Artists Studio Locations map.

GETTING THERE AND AROUND

Ferries travel year-round to Monhegan from Port Clyde, at the end of the St. George Peninsula. Seasonal service to the island is provided from New Harbor by Hardy Boat Cruises and from Boothbay Harbor by Balmy Days Cruises.

Part of the daily routine for many islanders and summer folk is a stroll to the harbor when the ferry comes in, so don't be surprised to see a good-size welcoming party when you arrive. You're the live entertainment.

Monhegan's only vehicles are a handful of pickup trucks owned by local lobstermen and lil' ol' trucks used by Monhegan Trucking. If you're staying a night or longer and your luggage is too heavy to carry, they'll be waiting when you arrive at the island wharf.

Rockland

A "Share the Pride" campaign—kicked off in the 1980s to boost sagging civic self-esteem and the local economy—was the first step in the transformation of Rockland. Once a run-down county seat best known for the aroma of its fish-packing plants, the city has undergone a sea change, most of it for the better. The expansion of the Farnsworth Museum of American Art and the addition of its Wyeth Center was a catalyst. Benches and plants line Main Street (Rte. 1), stores offer appealing wares, coffeehouses and more than a dozen art galleries attract a diverse clientele, and Rockland Harbor is home to more windjammer cruise schooners than neighboring Camden (which had long claimed the title "Windjammer Capital"). If you haven't been to Rockland in the last decade, prepare to be astonished.

Foresighted entrepreneurs had seen the potential of the bayside location in the late 1700s and established a tiny settlement here called "Shore Village" (or "the Shore"). Today's commercial-fishing fleet is one of the few reminders of Rockland's past, when multimasted schooners lined the wharves, some to load volatile cargoes of lime destined to become building material for cities all along the eastern seaboard, others to head northeast—toward the storm-racked Grand Banks and the lucrative cod fishery there. Such hazardous pursuits meant an early demise for many a local seafarer, but Rockland's 5,000 or so residents were enjoying their prosperity in the late 1840s. The settlement was home to more than two dozen shipyards and dozens of lime kilns, was enjoying a construction boom, and boasted a newspaper and regular steamship service. By 1854, Rockland had become a city.

Today, Rockland remains a commercial hub—with Knox County's only shopping plazas (no malls, but the big-box stores have arrived), a fishing fleet that heads far offshore, and ferries that connect nearby islands. Rockland also claims the title of "Lobster Capital of the World," thanks to Knox County's shipment nationally and internationally of 10 million pounds of lobster each year. (The weathervane atop the police and fire department building is a giant copper lobster.)

With just more than 8,000 souls, Rockland is more year-round community than tourist town. But visitors pour in during two big summer festivals—the North Atlantic Blues Festival in mid-July and the Maine Lobster Festival in early August. Highlight of the Lobster Festival is King Neptune's coronation of the Maine Sea Goddess—carefully selected from a bevy of local young women—who then sails off with him to his watery domain.

SIGHTS
◀ The Farnsworth Art Museum and the Wyeth Center

Anchoring downtown Rockland is the nationally respected Farnsworth Art Museum (16 Museum St., 207/596-6457, www.farnsworthmuseum.org), established in 1948 through a trust fund set up by Rocklander Lucy Farnsworth. With an ample checkbook, the first curator, Robert Bellows, toured the country, accumulating a splendid collection of 19th- and 20th-century Maine-related American art, the basis for the permanent "Maine in America" exhibition.

The 6,000-piece collection today includes work by Fitz Hugh Lane, Gilbert Stuart, Eastman Johnson, Childe Hassam, John Marin, Maurice Prendergast, Rockwell Kent, George Bellows, and Marsden Hartley. Best known are the paintings by three generations of the Wyeth family (local summer residents) and sculpture by Louise Nevelson, who grew up in Rockland. Sculpture, jewelry, and paintings by Nevelson form the core of the 3rd-floor Nevelson-Berliawsky Gallery for 20th Century Art. (The only larger Nevelson collection is in New York's Whitney Museum of American Art.) The Wyeth Center, across Union Street in a former church, contains the work of Andrew, N. C., and Jamie Wyeth. The 6,000-square-foot Jamien Morehouse Wing hosts rotating exhibits.

In the Farnsworth's library—a grand, high-ceilinged oasis akin to an English gentleman's reading room—browsers and researchers can explore an extensive collection of art books and magazines. The museum's education department annually sponsors hundreds of lectures, concerts, art classes for all ages, poetry readings, and field trips. Most are open to nonmembers; some require an extra fee. A glitzy gift shop stocks posters, prints, notecards, imported gift items, and art games for children.

Next door to the museum is the mid-19th-century Greek Revival **Farnsworth Homestead,** with original high-Victorian furnishings. Looking as though William Farnsworth's family just took off for the day, the house has been preserved rather than restored.

The Farnsworth also owns the **Olson House,** 14 miles away in nearby Cushing, where the whole landscape looks like a Wyeth diorama. Pick up a map at the museum to help you find the house; it's definitely worth the side trip.

The Farnsworth ($12 adults, $10 seniors and students 17 and older, free children 16 and under and Rockland residents) is open year-round, including summer holidays. Farnsworth hours are 10 A.M.–5 P.M. daily (to 8 P.M. Wed.) in summer, 10 A.M.–5 P.M. Wednesday–Sunday in winter. Call the museum for its current definition of summer and winter. The Homestead (10 A.M.–5 P.M. daily) and the Olson House (11 A.M.–4 P.M. daily) are open late May–mid-October. Note: Admission is free on Wednesdays after 5 P.M.

◖ Owls Head Transportation Museum

Don't miss this place, even if you're not an old-vehicle buff. A generous endowment has made the Owls Head Transportation Museum (Rte. 73, Owls Head, 207/594-4418, www.ohtm.org, 10 A.M.–4 P.M. daily Nov.–Mar., $10 adults, $8 seniors, free children under 18, special events are extra), a premier facility for celebrating wings and wheels; it draws more than 75,000 visitors a year. Scads of eager volunteers help restore the vehicles and keep them running. On weekends May–October, the museum sponsors air shows (often including aerobatic displays) and car and truck meets for hundreds of enthusiasts. The season highlight is the annual rally and aerobatic show (early August), when more than 300 vehicles gather for two days of festivities. Want your own vintage vehicle? Attend the antique, classic, and special-interest auto auction (third Sunday in August). The gift shop carries transportation-related items. If the kids get bored (unlikely), there's a play area outside, with picnic tables. In winter, groomed cross-country-skiing trails wind through the museum's 60-acre site. (Ask for a map at the information desk.)

Maine Discovery Center

The headliner at the Maine Discovery Center (1 Park Dr.) is the **Maine Lighthouse Museum** (207/594-3301, www.mainelighthousemuseum.com, 9 A.M.–5 P.M. Mon.–Fri., 10 A.M.–4 P.M. Sat.–Sun. late May–mid-Oct., closed Sun.–Wed. in winter, $5 adults, $4 seniors, free children under 12), home to the nation's largest collection of Fresnel lenses, along with a boatload-plus of lighthouse-, Coast Guard–, and maritime-related artifacts. On view are foghorns, ships' bells, nautical books and photographs, marine instruments, ship models, scrimshaw, and so much more.

The Owls Head Transportation Museum is a must for fans of vintage wings and wheels and is often the site of air shows.

Project Puffin Visitor Center

If you can't manage a trip to see the puffins, Audubon's Project Puffin Visitor Center (311 Main St., 207/596-5566 or 877/478-3346, www.projectpuffin.org, 10 A.M.–5 P.M. daily, to 7 P.M. Wed., June 1–Oct. 31; call for off-season hours) will bring them to you. Live videos of nesting puffins are just one of the highlights of the center, which also includes interactive exhibits, a gallery, and films, all highlighting successful efforts to restore and protect these clowns of the sea.

◖ Rockland Breakwater

Protecting the harbor from wind-driven waves, the 4,346-foot-long Rockland Breakwater took 18 years to build, with 697,000 tons of locally quarried granite. In the late 19th century, it was piled up, chunk by chunk, from a base 175 feet wide on the harbor floor (60 feet below the surface) to the 43-foot-wide cap. The Breakwater Light—now automated—was built in 1902 and added to the National Historic Register in 1981. The city of Rockland owns the keeper's house, but it's maintained by the Friends of the Rockland Breakwater Lighthouse (www.rocklandlighthouse.com). Member volunteers usually open the lighthouse to the public 9 A.M.–5 P.M. Saturday and Sunday late May–mid-October and for special events. The breakwater provides unique vantage points for photographers, and a place to picnic or catch sea breezes or fish on a hot day, but it is extremely dangerous during storms. Anyone on the breakwater risks being washed into the sea or struck by lightning (ask the local hospital staff: it *has* happened!). Do not take chances when the weather is iffy.

To reach the breakwater, take Route 1 North to Waldo Avenue and turn right. Take the next right onto Samoset Road and drive to the end to **Marie Reed Memorial Park** (tiny beach, benches, limited parking). Or go to the Samoset Resort and take the path to the breakwater from there.

Sail Power & Steam Museum

Opened in 2009, the Sail Power & Steam

A nearly mile-long breakwater connects the Samoset Resort to the lighthouse marking Rockland's harbor.

Museum (Sharp's Point South, 75 Mechanic St., 207/701-7626, www.sailpowerandsteammuseum.org, 10 A.M.–4 P.M. Wed.–Sat., noon–4 P.M. Sun.) is Captain Jim Sharp's labor of love. Built on the grounds of the former Snow Shipyard, the museum displays highlight Rockland's maritime heritage and include half-models of boats used by shipbuilders in the 19th century, vintage photos, tools of the trade, and other artifacts. Docked nearby is *The Reckord,* a 1914 Norwegian freighter that's used by Sharp for harbor tours.

Main Street Historic District

Rocklanders are justly proud of their Main Street Historic District, lined with 19th- and early-20th-century Greek and Colonial Revival structures, as well as examples of mansard and Italianate architecture. Most now house retail shops on the ground floor; upper floors have offices, artists' studios, and apartments. The chamber of commerce has a map and details.

Flightseeing

Get a gull's-eye view of Coastal Maine riding in an R-44 Raven chopper with **Scenic Helicopters of Maine** (207/596-7006 or 866/596-7006, www.scenic-helicopters.com). Rates begin at $75 per person, minimum two people, for an introductory flight over Rockland and Owl's Head. Flights depart from a heliport on Route 1 at the Thomaston/Rockland line.

For something a bit quieter, soar and swoop on a glider ride with **Spirit Soaring** (207/319-9514, www.spiritsoaring.org). Rates begin at $120 for a half-hour ride over coastal Penobscot Bay. It operates from Knox County Regional Airport in Owls Head, just south of Rockland.

Excursion Train

Ride in restored vintage railcars on the scenic **Maine Eastern Railroad** (207/596-6725 or 800/637-2457, www.maineeasternrailroad.com), operating between Rockland and Brunswick with stops in Wiscasset and Bath. The train operates late May–early November, with special holiday trains in December. Adult fares are $40 round-trip, $25 one-way; seniors $35/$25; children 5–15 $20/$15; family rate $100/$75, covering two adults and two kids. Packages with lodging, meals, and theater are available.

ENTERTAINMENT AND EVENTS

Stop by the **Lincoln Street Center for Arts and Education** (24 Lincoln St., 207/594-6490, www.lincolnstreetcenter.org), a community arts center with exhibitions, performances, and classes, to see what's on the schedule.

The historic **Strand Theater** (339 Main St., 207/594-7266, www.rocklandstrand.com), opened in 1923, underwent an extensive restoration in 2005. Films as well as live entertainment are scheduled. It's also the venue for many **Bay Chamber Concerts** (207/236-2823 or 888/707-2770, www.baychamberconcerts.org) events.

If you're a film buff, you might want to see what the **Saltwater Film Society** (www.saltwaterfilmsociety.org) has on its schedule.

Arts in Rockland (www.artsinrockland.com) coordinates an Art Walk every Wednesday evening in June, July, and August, as well as other special arts events.

In mid-July, the **North Atlantic Blues Festival** means a weekend of festivities featuring big names in blues. Thousands of fans jam Harbor Park for the nonstop music.

August's **Maine Lobster Festival** is a five-day lobster extravaganza, with live entertainment, the Maine Sea Goddess pageant, a lobster-crate race, craft booths, boat rides, a parade, lobster dinners, and megacrowds (the hotels are full for miles in either direction). Tons of lobsters bite the dust during the weekend—despite annual protests by the People for the Ethical Treatment of Animals. (The protests, however, seem only to increase the crowds.)

SHOPPING
Galleries

Piggybacking on the fame of the Farnsworth Museum, or at least working symbiotically, art galleries line Rockland's main and many side streets. Ask around and look around. During the summer, many of them coordinate monthly openings (usually a Wednesday evening) so you can meander and munch (and sip) from one gallery to another.

Across from the Farnsworth's side entrance, the **Caldbeck Gallery** (12 Elm St., 207/594-5935, www.caldbeck.com) has gained a top-notch reputation as a "must-see" (and "must-be-seen") space. Featuring the work of contemporary Maine artists, the gallery mounts more than half a dozen solo and group shows each year, May–September.

Eric Hopkins Gallery (21 Winter St., 207/594-1996, www.erichopkins.com) shows the North Haven artist's colorful aerial-view paintings.

Archipelago (386 Main St., 207/596-0701), on the ground floor of the Island Institute (a nonprofit steward of Maine's 4,617 offshore islands), is an attractive retail outlet for talented craftspeople from 14 year-round islands.

Other eminently browsable downtown Rockland galleries are **Harbor Square Gallery** (374 Main St., 207/594-8700 or 877/594-8700, www.harborsquaregallery.com), **Landing Gallery** (8 Elm St., 888/394-2787), **Playing with Fire! Glassworks & Gallery** (497 Main St., 207/594-7805, www.playingwithfireglassworks.com) and **Nan Mulford Gallery** (313 Main St., 207/594-8481, www.mulfordgallery.com). All are within steps of each other.

Wineries

Head inland on Route 17 and then noodle off on the back roads to discover not one but two wineries. At **Sweetgrass Farm Winery and Distillery** (347 Carroll Rd., Union, 207/785-3024, www.sweetgrasswinery.com, 11 A.M.–5 P.M. daily late May–late Dec.), owner Keith Bodine uses Maine-grown fruits to produce both wines and spirits, and he is eager to show interested folks how. Bring a picnic to enjoy while hiking the winery's trails. Carroll Road is between Shepard Hill Road and North Union Road, both north off Route 17 west of Route 131.

Nearby is **Savage Oakes** (174 Barrett Hill Rd., Union, 207/785-5261, www.savageoakes.com, 11 A.M.–5 P.M. daily, mid-May–late Oct.), where Elmer and Holly Savage and their sons have added winemaking to their second-generation Belted Galloway cattle farm. They grow nine varieties of grapes, both red and white, and produce more than a half dozen wines. Barrett Hill Road is off Route 17 directly opposite Route 131 South.

RECREATION
Parks
◖ OWLS HEAD LIGHT STATE PARK

On Route 73, about 1.5 miles past the junction of Routes 1 and 73, you'll reach North Shore Road in the town of Owls Head. Turn left, toward Owls Head Light State Park. Standing 3.6 miles from this turn, Owls Head Light occupies a dramatic promontory with panoramic views over Rockland Harbor and Penobscot Bay. Don't miss it. The keeper's house and the light tower are off-limits, but the park surrounding the tower has easy walking paths, picnic tables, and a pebbly beach where you can sunbathe or check out Rockland Harbor's boating traffic. (If it's foggy or rainy, don't climb the steps toward the light tower: The view evaporates in the fog, the access ramp can be slippery, and the foghorn is dangerously deafening.) Follow signs to reach the park. From North Shore Road, turn left onto Main Street, then left onto Lighthouse Road, and continue along Owls Head Harbor to the parking area. This is also a particularly pleasant bike route—about 10 miles round-trip from downtown Rockland—although, once again, the roadside shoulders are poor along the Owls Head stretch.

HARBOR PARK

If you're looking for a park with more commotion than quiet green space, spend some time at Harbor Park. Boats, cars, and delivery vehicles come and go, and you can corner a picnic table, a bench, or a patch of grass and watch all the action. During the holidays, a lobster trap Christmas tree presides over the park. Public restrooms (open late May–mid-October) are available. The park is just off Main Street.

Swimming

Lucia Beach is the local name for **Birch Point Beach State Park,** one of the best-kept secrets in the area. In Owls Head, just south of Rockland—and not far from Owls Head Light—the spruce-lined sand crescent (free; outhouses but no other facilities) has rocks, shells, tide pools, and very chilly water. There's ample room for a moderate-size crowd, although parking and turnaround space can get a bit tight on the access road. From downtown Rockland, take Route 73 one mile to North Shore Drive (on your left). Take the next right, Ash Point Drive, and continue past Knox County Regional Airport to Dublin Road. Turn right, go 0.8 mile, then turn left onto Ballyhac Road (opposite the airport landing lights). Go another 0.8 mile, fork left, and continue 0.4 mile to the parking area.

WINDJAMMING

In 1936, Camden became the home of the "cruise schooner" (sometimes called "dude schooner") trade when Captain Frank Swift restored a creaky wooden vessel and offered sailing vacations to paying passengers. He kept at it for 25 years, gradually adding other boats to the fleet – and the rest, as they say, is history. Windjammers have become big business on the Maine coast, with Camden and Rockland sparring for the title of Windjammer Capital. Rockland wrested it from Camden in the mid-1990s and, so far, has held on to it.

Named for their ability to "jam" into the wind when they carried freight up and down the New England coast, windjammers trigger images of the Great Age of Sail. Most are rigged as schooners, with two or three soaring wooden masts; their lengths range from 64 to 132 feet. Nine are National Historic Landmarks; four were built for the trade.

These windjammers head out for 3-6 days, late May-mid-October, tucking into coves and harbors around Penobscot Bay and its islands. The mostly engineless craft set their itineraries by the wind, propelled by stiff breezes to Buck's Harbor, North Haven, and Deer Isle. Everything's totally informal, geared for relaxing.

You're aboard for the experience, not for luxury, so expect basic accommodations with few frills, although newer vessels were built with passenger trade in mind and tend to be a bit more comfy. Down below, cabins typically are small and basic, with paper-thin walls – sort of a campground afloat (earplugs are often available for light sleepers). It may not sound romantic, but be aware that the captains keep track of post-cruise marriages. Most boats have shared showers and toilets. If you're Type-A, given to pacing, don't inflict yourself on the cruising crowd; if you're flexible and ready for whatever, go ahead and sign on. You can help with the sails, eat, curl up with a book, inhale salt air, shoot photos, eat, sunbathe, bird-watch, eat, chat up fellow passengers, sleep, eat, or just settle back and enjoy spectacular sailing you'll never forget.

When you book a cruise, you'll receive all the details and directions, but for a typical six-day trip, you arrive at the boat by 7 P.M. for the captain's call to meet your fellow passengers. You sleep aboard at the dock that night and then depart midmorning Monday and spend five nights and days cruising Penobscot Bay, following the wind, the weather, and the whims of the captain. (Many of the windjammers have no engines, only a motorized yawlboat used as a pusher and a water taxi.) You might anchor in a deserted cove and explore the shore, or you might pull into a harbor and hike, shop, and bar-hop. Then it's back to the boat for chow – windjammer cooks are legendary for creating three hearty, all-you-can-eat meals daily, including at least one lobster feast! When the cruise ends, most passengers find it hard to leave.

On the summer cruising schedule, several weeks coincide with special windjammer events, so you'll need to book a berth far in advance for these: mid-June (Boothbay Harbor's Windjammer Days), July Fourth week (Great Schooner Race), Labor Day weekend (Camden's Windjammer Weekend), and the second week in September (WoodenBoat Sail-In).

Most windjammers offering three- to six-day sails out of Camden, Rockland, and Rockport are members of the **Maine Windjammer Association** (800/807-9463, www.sailmainecoast.com), a one-stop resource for vessel and schedule information. Rates for most schooners begin around $650 for a four-day cruise.

If frigid ocean water doesn't appeal, head for freshwater **Chickawaukee Lake,** on Route 17, two miles inland from downtown Rockland. Don't expect to be alone, though; on hot days, **Johnson Memorial Park**'s pocket-size sand patch is a major attraction. A lifeguard holds forth, and there are restrooms, picnic tables, a snack bar, and a boat-launch ramp. (In winter, iceboats, snowmobiles, and ice-fishing shacks take over the lake.) A signposted bicycle path runs alongside the busy highway, making the park an easy pedal from town.

Golf

The semi-private **Rockland Golf Club** (606 Old County Rd., 207/594-9322, www.rocklandgolf.com, Apr.–Oct.) is an 18-hole course 0.2 mile northeast of Route 17.

For an 18-hole course in an unsurpassed waterfront setting (but with steep rental and greens fees), tee off at the **Samoset Resort** (220 Warrenton St., Rockport, 207/594-2511 or 800/341-1650, www.samoset.com).

Sea Kayaking

Veteran Maine Guide and naturalist Mark DiGirolamo is the sparkplug behind **Breakwater Kayak** (Rockland Public Landing, 207/596-6895 or 877/559-8800, www.breakwaterkayak.com), which has a full range of tours, even multiday ones. A two-hour Rockland Harbor tour (usually offered three times a day at the height of summer) is $50, and the all-day Owls Head Lighthouse tour is $100, including lunch. Reservations are advisable. This outfit is particularly eco-sensitive—Mark has a degree in environmental science—definitely worth supporting. Maine Audubon often taps Mark to lead natural-history field trips. Dress warmly for these tours and be sure to bring a filled water bottle.

Excursion Boats

Marine biologist Captain Bob Pratt is the skipper of *A Morning in Maine* (207/594-1844 or 207/691-7245 seasonal boat phone, www.amorninginmaine.com), a classic 55-foot ketch designed by noted naval architect R. D. (Pete) Culler and built by Concordia Yachts. From June through October, *Morning* departs from the middle pier at the Rockland Public Landing three times daily for two-hour sails ($30), with plenty of knowledgeable commentary from Captain Pratt. A 6 P.M. sunset sail is available in July and August. Inquire about boat-and-breakfast overnights, which run $500 per couple and include a sail, lobster dinner, overnight on the boat, and continental breakfast.

Watch Captain Steve Hale set and haul lobster traps during a 1.25-hour cruise aboard the *Captain Jack* (Rockland Harbor, 207/594-1048, www.captainjacklobstertours.com), a 30-foot working lobster boat. Cruises depart up to seven times daily, Monday–Saturday May–September; $25 adults, $15 children under 12. Note: There are no toilets aboard. Captain Jack offers a lobster-roll lunch cruise for $45 per person. Reservation required; minimum two people for a trip.

Maine State Ferry Service

Car and passenger ferries service the islands of Vinalhaven, North Haven, and Matinicus. The Vinalhaven and North Haven routes make fantastic day trips (especially with a bike), or you can spend the night; the Matinicus ferry is much less predictable and island services are few.

Bicycling

Rentals ($20), sales, repair, and coffee are provided by **Bikesenjava** (481 Main St., 207/596-1004, www.haybikesenjava.com).

ACCOMMODATIONS

Rates noted are for peak season.

If you're planning an overnight stay in the Rockland area the first weekend in August—during the Maine Lobster Festival—*be sure* to make reservations well in advance. Festival attendance runs close to 100,000, No Vacancy signs extend from Waldoboro to Belfast, and there just aren't enough beds or campsites to go around.

Samoset Resort

The 221-acre waterfront Samoset Resort (220 Warrenton St., Rockport, 207/594-2511 or 800/341-1650, www.samoset.com) straddles the boundary between Rockland and Rockport, the next town to the north. Built on the ashes of a classic 19th-century summer hotel, the Samoset is a top-of-the-line modern resort with knockout ocean views from most of its 178 rooms and suites, all refurbished in

2007 (rates begin around $270), plus 72 separate town houses. Rooms have all the expected bells and whistles, and facilities include indoor and outdoor pools, fitness center, lighted tennis courts, children's day camp ($35, including lunch, ages 5–12), golf simulator, and a fabulous 18-hole waterfront golf course.

Bed-and-Breakfasts

These bed-and-breakfasts are in Rockland's historic district, within easy walking distance of downtown attractions and restaurants, and are members of the **Historic Inns of Rockland Maine** (www.historicinnsofrockland.com), which coordinates the January Pies on Parade event.

Most elegant is ◖ **The Berry Manor Inn** (81 Talbot Ave., 207/596-7696 or 800/774-5692, www.berrymanorinn.com, $165–265), on a quiet side street a few blocks from downtown. Cheryl Michaelsen and Michael LaPosta have totally restored the manse built in 1898 by wealthy Rocklander Charles Berry as a wedding gift for his wife (thoughtful fellow). High ceilings and wonderful Victorian architectural touches are everywhere, especially in the enormous front hall and two parlors. Guest rooms and suites are spread between the main house and adjacent carriage house. Most have gas fireplaces and whirlpool tubs. All have air-conditioning, flat-screen TV-DVD, and Wi-Fi. A guest pantry is stocked with free soda and juices and sweets—not that you'll be hungry after the extravagant breakfast.

Opened in 1996, the **Captain Lindsey House Inn** (5 Lindsey St., 207/596-7950 or 800/523-2145, www.lindseyhouse.com, $171–211) is more like a boutique hotel than a bed-and-breakfast. The Barnes family gutted the 1835 brick structure and restored it dramatically, adding such modernities as phones, air-conditioning, Wi-Fi, and TV. The decor is strikingly handsome, not at all fussy or frilly. Don't miss the 1926 safe in the front hall or the hidden-from-the-street garden patio—not to mention the antiques from everywhere that fill the nine comfortable rooms. It's smack downtown, and a few rooms have glimpses of the water. Rates include an extensive hot-and-cold breakfast buffet and afternoon refreshments.

The Limerock Inn (96 Limerock St., 207/594-2257 or 800/546-3762, www.limerockinn.com, $149–229) is a lovely painted lady. The 1890s Queen Anne mansion, with wraparound porch and turret, is listed on the National Historic Register. Each of the eight rooms has its own distinctive flavor—such as the Turret Room with a wedding canopy bed and the Island Cottage Room with a private deck overlooking the back gardens. All are elegantly furnished with an emphasis on guest comfort. Three have whirlpool tubs, one a fireplace; there's Wi-Fi throughout. Breakfast is a treat.

Traveling with Fido and the kiddos? Check into the kid- and pet-friendly **Granite Inn** (546 Main St., Rockland, 800/386-9036, www.oldgraniteinn.com, $150–215), where you can practically roll out of bed and onto an island ferry.

FOOD

Call to verify days and hours of operation.

Local Flavors

A winner for creative breakfasts and lunches is **The Brown Bag** (606 Main St., 207/596-6372 or 800/287-6372, bakery 207/596-6392, 7 A.M.–2:30 P.M., bakery to 4 P.M., Mon.–Sat.). It's *the* place for breakfast, especially weekends, with fantastic baked goods and a full blackboard of other options. Order at the counter; no table service. Find it at the junction of Routes 1 and 17.

Holding down the other end of Main Street is the **Brass Compass Café** (305 Main St., 207/596-5960, 5 A.M.–3 P.M. daily, to 9 P.M. Fri.–Sat.), a great choice for Maine fare. The portions are big, the prices are small, and most of the ingredients are locally sourced. In 2009, celebrity chef Bobby Flay challenged chef-owner Lynn Archer to a lobster club throwdown. Sit indoors or on the dog-friendly patio.

Hot diggity dog! Backed up against an outside wall of The Brown Bag is a longstanding Rockland lunch landmark—**Wasses Hot Dogs** (2 N. Main St., 207/594-7472, 10:30–6 P.M. Mon.–Sat., 11 A.M.–4 P.M. Sun.), source of great chili dogs and creative ice cream (in waffle cones). This onetime lunch wagon is now a permanent modular building—only for takeout, though. It's open all year.

Lots of Rockland-watchers credit Maine's first bookstore-café, **Rock City Books and Coffee** (328 Main St., 207/594-4123, www.rockcitycoffee.com, 6:30 A.M.–8 P.M. Mon.–Sat., from 7 A.M. Sun.), with sparking the designer-food renaissance in town. The menu has expanded greatly since the original coffee, tea, and treats to include frozen drinks, soups, salads, sandwiches, and wraps (including rockin' breakfast wraps, served until 11 A.M.), and plenty of vegetarian choices. Order at the counter and then peruse the shelves of more than 10,000 carefully selected new and "gently used" books while you wait. Frequently there is weekend entertainment.

Scratch-made bread, pastries, and grab-and-go sandwiches have made **Atlantic Baking Co.** (351 Main St., 207/596-0505, www.atlanticbakingco.com, 7 A.M.–6 P.M. Mon.–Sat., 8 A.M.–4 P.M. Sun.) a popular spot for a quick, informal lunch. There are plenty of tables to enjoy your treats, or take it to the waterfront park.

Even closer to Harbor Park is **Sweets & Meats Market** (218 Main St., Rockland, 207/594-2070, www.sweetsandmeatsmarket.com), with a nice selection of sandwiches, including a vegan option, as well as cheeses, meats, and baked goods; there's indoor seating and free Wi-Fi.

If you're craving a decent breakfast or lunch and are up for a little foray "down the peninsula," head for the **Owls Head General Store** (2 S. Shore Dr., Owls Head, 207/596-6038, 6 A.M.–7 P.M. Mon.–Sat., 8 A.M.–3 P.M. Sun.), where the atmosphere is friendly and definitely contagious. If you get lost, the helpful staff will steer you the right way, and they will even take your photograph in front of the store. Despite all the competition from lobster-in-the-rough places, the lobster roll here is among the best around, and more than one critic has proclaimed the burgers the state's best.

The **Rockland Farmers Market** gets underway 9 A.M.–1 P.M. each Thursday June–September at Harbor Park, on Rockland's Public Landing. Wares from more than a dozen vendors include produce, chocolates, crafts, syrup, poultry, mushrooms, baked goods, and cheeses. Every week, there's a special event—music, dancers, lectures, special giveaways, and occasionally a llama or goat for the kids to pet.

Ethnic Fare

Ask local pooh-bah chefs where they go on their night off, and the answer often is Keiko Suzuki Steinberger's **Suzuki's Sushi Bar** (419 Main St., 207/596-7447, www.suzukisushi.com, 11 A.M.–2:30 P.M. and 5–8:30 P.M. Tues.–Sat.). The food matches the decor, simple yet sophisticated. Sashimi, nigiri, *maki*, and *temaki* choices range $6–10; hot entrées are $11–18. Both hot and cold sake are served, or try a sake-tume, made with gin or vodka, sake, and ume plum. Reservations are essential.

Cassoulet! Moules Provençal! Steak tartare! Chefs Lynette Mosher and Robert Krajewski have created a delicious pocket of France in downtown Rockland at **Lily Bistro** (421 Main St., Rockland, 207/594-4141, www.lilybistromaine.com, 5–9:30 P.M. daily). Most entrées range $16–20.

A small dining area decorated in avocado and gold is the appropriate setting for the Cal-Mex food dished out at **Sunfire Mexican Grill** (488 Main St., 207/594-6196, 11 A.M.–3 P.M. Tues.–Wed., 11 A.M.–3 P.M. and 5–8 P.M. Thurs.–Sat.). You'll find all the usuals, from tacos ($2.95) to a chipotle shrimp tostada ($11.75). Everything is prepared fresh on-site.

When you're *really* famished, the place to go (maybe) is **Conte's Fish Market and Restaurant** (Harbor Park, off Main St., Rockland, no phone), where portions are humongous and prices are not ($10–20). John Conte moved here from New York in 1995, bringing his family's century-old restaurant tradition. Specialties are pasta and seafood—Italian all the way, loaded with garlic. The decor is wildly funky—fishnets, marine relics, old books, even stacks of canned plum tomatoes. Menus are handwritten on paper-towel rolls and in-your-face at the door (order before you sit down), table coverings are yesterday's newspapers, and Edith Piaf chansons or operatic arias sometimes play in the background. Eccentric, unpredictable, not spotless, and definitely not for everyone. Bring your sense of humor and don't be put off by the exterior or the attitude; there's life behind the doors. Beer and wine only. No credit cards. It's open at 4 P.M. daily for dinner, all year (usually, but maybe not). Note: As of early 2010, Conte's future was uncertain; ask locally.

Casual Dining

Big flavors come out of the tiny kitchen at **Café Miranda** (15 Oak St., 207/594-2034, www.cafemiranda.com, 5:30–9 P.M. daily). The menu is overwhelming in size and hard to read, even harder to digest are the flavor contrasts, which will make your brain spin. When it works, it shines, but when it doesn't, it can be painful. Service is irregular. Entrées are $18–27, but many of the appetizers ($6.50–12.50) are enough for a meal. Fresh-from-the-brick-oven focaccia comes with everything. If you sit at the counter, you can watch chef Kerry Altiero's creations emerging from the oven. Beer and wine only. Reservations are essential throughout the summer and on weekends off-season. Patio dining in season.

At the end of a day exploring Rockland, it's hard to beat ◖ **In Good Company** (415 Main St., 207/593-9110, from 4:30 P.M. Tues.–Sun., $5–18), a chic and casual wine and tapas bar. Sit at the bar and watch chef-owner Melody Wolfertz, a Culinary Institute of America grad, concoct her creative tapas-style selection of small and large plates. Always a pleasure, and the staff is accommodating and helpful.

Destination Dining

Arriving in Rockland trailing a James Beard Award–winning reputation, chef Melissa Kelly opened **Primo** (Rte. 73, 207/596-0770, www.primorestaurant.com, 5:30–10 P.M. Wed.–Sun.) in the spring of 2000 and hasn't had time to breathe. Since then, she's gone on to open two other restaurants and in 2007 expanded this one in an air-conditioned Victorian home. Fresh local ingredients (many from the restaurant's gardens) are a high priority, and unusual fish specials appear every day. Appetizers are especially imaginative; entrée range is $24–42, but a bar menu with lighter fare and a nightly special also is available ($10–20). Kelly's partner Price Kushner produces an impressive range of breads and desserts. Reservations are essential, usually at least a week ahead on midsummer weekends—and you still may have to wait when you get there. Closed January–May.

INFORMATION AND SERVICES

Information

For information visit the **Penobscot Bay Regional Chamber of Commerce** (Gateway Center, 207/596-0376 or 800/562-2529, www.therealmaine.com, 9 A.M.–5 P.M. Mon.–Fri., 10 A.M.–2 P.M. Sat.) or **Rockland Public Library** (80 Union St., 207/594-0310, www.rocklandlibrary.org).

Public Restrooms

You'll find public restrooms at the Gateway Center; the Knox County Court House, at Union and Masonic Streets; the Rockland Recreation Center, across from the courthouse, next to the playground, at Union and Limerock Streets; the Rockland Public Library; and the Maine State Ferry Service terminal.

GETTING AROUND

All Aboard Trolley Co. (207/594-9300 or 866/594-9300, www.aatrolley.com) offers 40-minute narrated sightseeing tours of downtown Rockland ($8 adults, free children under 12) departing from the Penobscot Bay Regional Chamber of Commerce at the Gateway Center about six times daily.

Vinalhaven and North Haven Islands

Vinalhaven and neighboring North Haven have been known as the Fox Islands ever since 1603, when English explorer Martin Pring sailed these waters and allegedly spotted gray foxes in his search for sustenance. Nowadays, you'll find reference to that name only on nautical charts, identifying the passage between the two islands as the Fox Islands Thorofare—and there's nary a fox in sight.

Each island has its own distinct personality. To generalize, Vinalhaven is the largest and busiest, while North Haven is sedate and exclusive.

VINALHAVEN

Five miles wide, 7.5 miles long, and covering 10,000 acres, Vinalhaven is 13 miles off the coast of Rockland—a 75-minute ferry trip. The shoreline has so many zigs and zags that no place on the island is more than a mile from water.

The island is famed for its granite. The first blocks headed for Boston around 1826, and within a few decades quarrymen arrived from as far away as Britain and Finland to wrestle out and shape the incredibly resistant stone. Schooners, barges, and "stone sloops" left Carver's Harbor carrying mighty cargoes of granite destined for government and commercial buildings in Boston, New York, and Washington, D.C. In the 1880s, nearly 4,000 people lived on Vinalhaven, North Haven, and Hurricane Island. After World War I, demand declined, granite gave way to concrete and steel, and the industry petered out and died. But Vinalhaven has left its mark in ornate columns, paving blocks, and curbstones in communities as far west as Kansas City.

With a full-time population of about 1,300 souls, Vinalhaven is a serious working community, not primarily a playground. Nearly 600 island residents depend on the lobster and

Working boats far outnumber pleasure craft in Vinalhaven's Carver's Harbor.

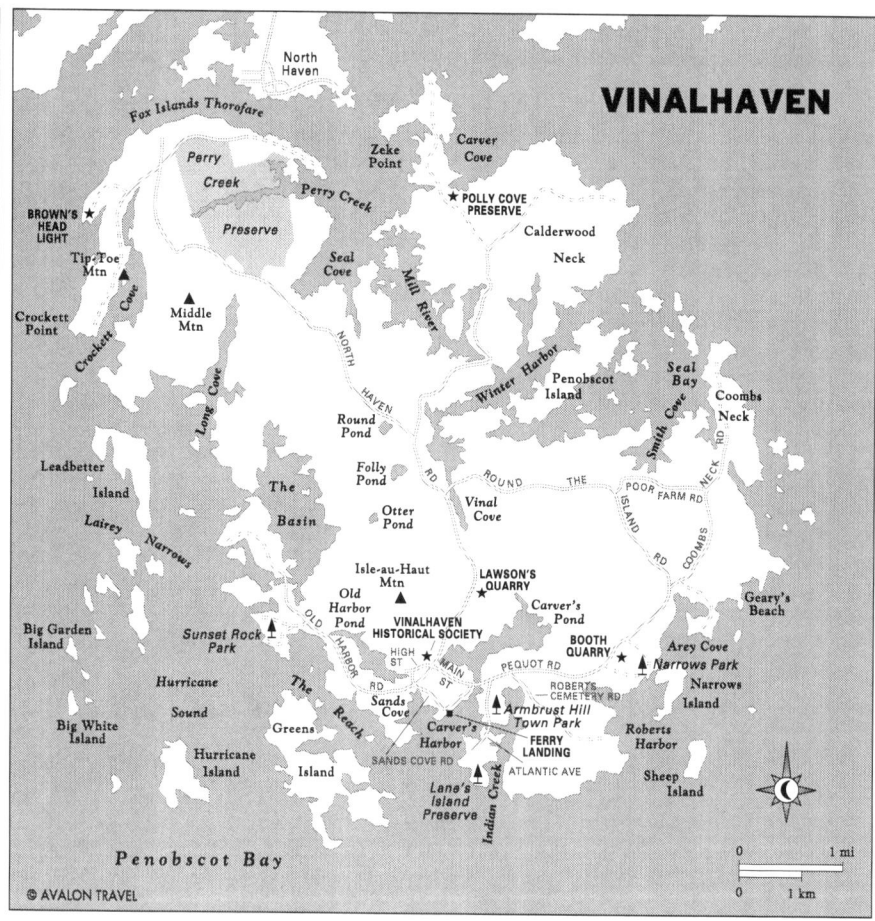

fishing industry. Shopkeepers cater to locals as well as visitors, and increasing numbers of artists and artisans work away in their studios. For day-trippers, there's plenty to do—shopping, picnicking, hiking, biking, swimming—but an overnight stay provides a chance to sense the unique rhythm of life on a year-round island.

Sights

One Main Street landmark that's hard to miss is the three-story cupola-topped **Odd Fellows Hall,** a Victorian behemoth with American flag motifs on the lower windows and assorted gewgaws in the upper ones. Artist Robert Indiana, who first arrived as a visitor in 1969, owns the structure, built in 1885 for the IOOF Star of Hope Lodge. It's not open to the public.

At the top of the hill just beyond Main Street (corner of School and E. Main Sts.) is a greenish-blue replica **galamander,** a massive reminder of Vinalhaven's late-19th-century granite-quarrying era. Galamanders, hitched to oxen or horses, carried the stone from island quarries to the finishing shops. (By the way, the origin of the name remains unexplained.) Next to the galamander is a colorful wooden bandstand, site of very popular evening band concerts held sporadically during the summer.

The **Vinalhaven Historical Society** (207/863-4410, www.vinalhavenhistoricalsociety.org, noon–5 P.M. daily July and Aug. or by appt., free) operates a delightful museum in the onetime town hall on High Street, just east of Carver's Cemetery. The building itself has a tale, having been floated across the bay from Rockland, where it served as a Universalist church. The museum's documents and artifacts on the granite industry are particularly intriguing, and special summer exhibits add to the interest. Donations are welcomed. At the museum, request a copy of *A Self-Guided Walking Tour of the Town of Vinalhaven and Its Granite-Quarrying History,* a handy little brochure that details 17 intown locations related to the late-19th and early-20th-century industry.

Built in 1832 and now owned by the town of Vinalhaven, **Brown's Head Light** guards the southern entrance to the Fox Islands Thorofare. To reach the grounds (no access to the light itself; the keeper's house is a private residence for the town manager), take the North Haven Road about six miles, at which point you'll see a left-side view of the Camden Hills. Continue about another mile to the second road on the left, Crockett River Road. Turn and take the second road on the right, continuing past the Brown's Head Cemetery to the hill overlooking the lighthouse.

Entertainment

No one visits Vinalhaven for nightlife, but concerts (Fox Island series and others), films, and lectures (most organized by the Vinalhaven Land Trust or the Vinalhaven Historical Society) are frequent. Check *The Wind* to see what's on the docket during your visit.

The Saturday-morning anything-goes flea markets are an island must, as much for the browsing and buying as for the gossip.

Brown's Head Light marks the entrance to the Fox Islands Thorofare.

Shopping

Vinalhaven's shops change regularly, but here are a few that have withstood the test of time. **The Paper Store** (Vinal's News Stand, Main St., 207/863-4826) carries newspapers, gifts, film, maps, and odds and ends. **Five Elements Gallery + Studio** (Main St., 207/863-2262) is filled with artist-owner Alison Thibault's jewelry creations and other finds. **New Era Gallery** (Main St., 207/863-9351, www.neweragallery.com) has a well-chosen selection of art in varied media representing primarily island artisans. Don't miss the sculpture garden. A few doors away is **Second Hand Prose,** a used books store run by the Friends of the Vinalhaven Public Library. On the stretch of road between the ferry dock and downtown, **Vinalhaven Candy Co.** (Harbor Wharf, 33 West Main St., 207/863-2031) is a pleaser for both kids and adults.

Parks and Preserves

Vinalhaven is loaded with wonderful hikes and

walks, some deliberately unpublicized. Since the mid-1980s, the foresighted **Vinalhaven Land Trust** (207/863-2543, www.vinalhavenlandtrust.org) has expanded the opportunities. When you reach the island, pick up maps at the land trust's office at **Skoog Memorial Park** (Sands Cove Road, west of the ferry terminal) or inquire at the town office or the Paper Store. The trust also offers a seasonal series of educational walks and talks.

Some hiking options are the Perry Creek Preserve (terrific loop trail), Middle Mountain Park, Tip-Toe Mountain, Polly Cove Preserve, Isle au Haut Mountain, Arey's Neck Woods, Huber Preserve, and Sunset Rock Park.

The Maine chapter of the **Nature Conservancy** (207/729-5181) owns or manages several islands and island clusters near Vinalhaven. **Big Garden** (formerly owned by Charles and Anne Morrow Lindbergh) and **Big White Islands** are easily accessible and great for shoreline picnics if you have your own boat. Other Conservancy holdings in this area are fragile environments, mostly nesting islands off-limits mid-March–mid-August. Contact the Conservancy for specifics.

No, you're not on the moors of Devon, but you could be fooled in the 45-acre **Lane's Island Preserve,** one of the Nature Conservancy's most-used island preserves. Masses of low-lying ferns, rugosa roses, and berry bushes cover the granite outcrops of this sanctuary—and a foggy day makes it even more moorlike and mystical, a Brontë novel setting. The best (albeit busiest) time to come is early August, when you can compete with the birds for blackberries, raspberries, and blueberries. Easy trails wind past old stone walls, an aged cemetery, and along the surf-pounded shore. The preserve is a 20-minute walk (or five-minute bike ride) from Vinalhaven's ferry landing. Set off to the right on Main Street, through the village. Turn right onto Water Street and then right on Atlantic Avenue. Continue across the causeway on Lane's Island Road and left over a salt marsh to the preserve. The large white house on the harbor side of Lane's Island is privately owned.

Next to the ferry landing in Carver's Harbor is **Grimes Park,** a wooded vest-pocket retreat with a splendid view of the harbor. Owned by the American Legion, the 2.5-acre park is perfect for picnics or for hanging out (especially in good weather) between boats.

Just behind the Island Community Medical Center, close to downtown, is 30-acre **Armbrust Hill Town Park,** once the site of granite-quarrying operations. Still pockmarked with quarry pits, the park has beautifully landscaped walking paths and native flowers, shrubs, and trees—much of it thanks to late island resident Betty Roberts, who made this a lifelong endeavor. From the back of the medical center, follow the trail to the summit for a southerly view of Matinicus and other offshore islands. If you're with children, be especially careful about straying onto side paths, which go perilously close to old quarry holes. Before the walk, lower the children's energy level at the large playground off to the left of the trail.

Recreation
SWIMMING

Abandoned quarries are all over the island, and most are on private property, but two town-owned ones are easy to reach from the ferry landing. **Lawson's Quarry,** on the North Haven Road, is one mile from downtown on the North Haven Road; **Booth Quarry** is 1.6 miles from downtown via East Main Street. Both are signposted. You'll see plenty of sunbathers on the rocks and swimmers on a hot day, but there are no lifeguards, so swimming is at your own risk. There are no restrooms or changing rooms. *Note:* Pets and soap are not allowed in the water; camping, fires, and alcohol are not allowed in the quarry areas.

Down the side road beyond Booth Quarry is **Narrows Park,** a town-owned space looking out toward Narrows Island, Isle au Haut, and, on a clear day, Mount Desert Island.

For saltwater swimming, take East Main

Street 2.4 miles from downtown to a crossroads, where you'll see a whimsical bit of local folk art—the Coke lady sculpture. Turn right (east) and go a half mile to **Geary's Beach** (also called **State Beach**), where you can picnic and scour the shoreline for shells and sea glass.

BICYCLING

Even though Vinalhaven's 40 or so miles of public roads are narrow, winding, and poorly shouldered, they're relatively level, so a bicycle is a fine way to tour the island. Bring your own, preferably a hybrid or mountain bike, or rent one at the **Tidewater Motel** (207/863-4618) on Main Street ($15 per day). A wide selection of rental bikes is available on the mainland in Rockport at **Maine Sport Outfitters** (Rte. 1, Rockport, 207/236-8797 or 888/236-8796), but you have to pay extra to bring a bike on the ferry.

A 10-mile, 2.5-hour bicycle route begins on Main Street and goes clockwise out the North Haven Road (rough pavement), past Lawson's Quarry, to Round the Island Road (some sections are dirt), then Poor Farm Road to Geary's Beach and back to Main Street via Pequot Road and School Street. Carry a picnic and enjoy it on Lane's Island; stop for a swim in one of the quarries; or detour down to Brown's Head Light. If you're here for the day, keep track of the time so you don't miss the ferry.

Far more rewarding view-wise, and far shorter, is the one-way-and-back pedal out the Old Harbor Road to The Basin, which is rich in bird and wildlife and serves as a seal nursery. There's also a nice trail at the road's end to The Basin's shorefront and across to an island; ask Phil at the Tidewater Motel for directions.

SEA KAYAKING

Sea kayak rentals are available at the Tidewater Motel for $25 per day including delivery. A guide can be arranged, but it's not necessary to have one to poke around the harbor or, even better, paddle through The Basin, which is especially popular with bird- and wildlife-watchers.

BIRD- AND WILDLIFE-WATCHING

Expert bird guide **John Drury** (207/596-1841, $280) takes bird- and wildlife-watchers on 3.5-hour cruises to spy gannets, Arctic terns, puffins, eagles, and seals. Sightings have even included minke whales and albatross.

Accommodations

If you're planning on staying overnight, don't even consider arriving in summer without reservations. If you're going for the day, pay attention to the ferry schedule and allow enough time to get back to the boat. Islanders may be able to find you a bed in a pinch, but don't count on it. The island has no campsites. Rates listed are for peak season.

Your feet practically touch the water when you spend the night at the ◖ **Tidewater Motel and Gathering Space** (12 Main St., Carver's Harbor, 207/863-4618, www.tidewatermotel.com, $165–295), a well-maintained motel in two buildings cantilevered over the harbor. Owned by Phil and Elaine Crossman (she operates the New Era Gallery down the street), the 19-room motel was built by Phil's parents in 1970. It's the perfect place to sit on the deck and watch the lobster boats do their thing. Be aware, though, that commercial fishermen are early risers, and lobster-boat engines can rev up as early as 4:30 on a summer morning—all part of the pace of Vinalhaven. Phil is practically a one-man chamber of commerce. He can recommend hikes and other activities and, since he maintains the island's calendar of events, he always knows what's happening and when. A continental breakfast and use of bicycles are included in the rates; rental sea kayaks are available. Kids 10 and under are free; seven units are efficiencies. It's open all year. Also on the premises is **Island Spirits,** a small gourmet-foods store stocked with wines, beers, cheeses, breads, and other goodies, even picnic baskets to pack it all in. About once a month, the motel hosts a wine tasting in the 2nd-floor Gathering Space, overlooking the harbor. If

The Tidewater Motel hangs over Vinalhaven's Carver's Harbor, delivering guests a front-row seat on the action.

you want to get a better sense of island life, pick up a copy of Phil's book *Away Happens,* a collection of humorous essays about island living. You can see a sample from it on the motel's website.

Also convenient to downtown is **The Libby House** (Water St., 207/863-4696, www.libbyhouse1869.com, $75–140), with a two-bedroom apartment and five rooms, three sharing one bath. No breakfast.

Food

Hours listed are for peak season. Expect reduced hours and fewer days of operation at other times.

Baked bean suppers are regularly held at a couple of island locations. Check *The Wind.*

On the harborfront a few minutes walk from the ferry terminal is **Greet's Eats,** a fair-weather takeout for lobster and crab rolls as well as burgers and hot dogs.

The island's best breakfast place is **Surfside** (Harbor Wharf, 207/863-2767, 4 A.M.–1:30 P.M. Mon.–Fri., 4–11 A.M. Sat.–Sun.).

Eat inside or on the wharf. The fishcakes earn their raves and are always available on Sundays. It *may* also be open for dinner.

In the morning, **Island Coffee House** (30 Main St., 207/863-4311, 4 A.M.–noon Mon.–Sat., 5–11 A.M. Sun.) serves scrumptious baked goods. In the evening it morphs into **The Pizza Pit** (4–8 P.M. Thurs.–Sun.) serving pizza, wings, pastas, quesadillas, and similar fare; BYOB.

Craving a cappuccino or latte? Vinalhaven's student-run **ARCafé** (39 High St., 207/863-4191, 7 A.M.–6:30 P.M. Mon.–Fri., 10 A.M.–4 P.M. Sat.), next door to the historical society, is the island's best coffee source and provides free Internet access.

Good lunch options are the **Harbor Gawker** (Main St., 207/863-9365, 11 A.M.–8 P.M. Mon.–Sat.), a local landmark since 1975, but now with a nice indoor dining area; **Trickerville Sandwich Shop** (Atlantic St., 207/863-9344, 5 A.M.–4 P.M. Mon.–Sat., 11 A.M.–4 P.M. Sun.), with a few tables inside and out, but no views (lobster dinners served some evenings, ask); and **The Sand Bar** (Main St., 207/863-4500, 11 A.M.–9 P.M. Tues.–Sun.), which has a full bar as well as a good menu of pub-style favorites, soups, salads, and pizza.

For casual dining, book a table at **The Haven Restaurant** (Main St., 207/863-4969), with two options: Harborside (Tues.–Sat., seatings at 6 and 8:15 P.M.) delivers on its name and serves a creative menu that changes nightly. Streetside (6:30–9 P.M., closed Tues.) doesn't take reservations and serves pub-style fare. The restaurant is a one-woman show, and Torry Pratt doubles as a popular local caterer, so it's wise to call.

Newer on the scene is **64 Main** (64 Main St., 207/863-4464, 5:30–9 P.M. Wed.–Sat.), where chef Brett Ackerman draws on his experience at New York City's Union Square Café to create updated versions of vaguely familiar classics. Entrées run $16–20.

Information and Services

Vinalhaven Chamber of Commerce (www.vinalhaven.org) produces a useful little flyer-map showing locations in the Carver's Harbor area. Also helpful for trip planning is a guidebook published by Phil Crossman at the Tidewater Motel (207/863-4618, $3.50). On the island, pick up a copy of Vinalhaven's weekly newsletter, *The Wind,* named after the island's original newspaper, first published in 1884. It's loaded with island flavor: news items, public-supper announcements, editorials, and ads. A year's subscription is $50; free single copies are available at most downtown locales.

Check out the Vinalhaven Public Library (E. Main and Chestnut Sts., 207/863-4401).

Public restrooms are at the ferry landing and the town office (weekdays only).

Getting Around

I can't emphasize this enough: Don't bring a car unless it is absolutely necessary. If you're coming over for a day trip, you can get to parks and quarries, shops, restaurants, and the historical society museum on foot. If you want to explore farther, a bicycle is an excellent option, or you can rent a car or reserve a taxi through the Tidewater Motel (207/863-4618), or Phil will meet you at the ferry landing. Call well ahead to reserve.

NORTH HAVEN

Eight miles long by three miles wide, North Haven is 12 miles off the coast of Rockland—an hour by ferry. The island has sedate summer homes, open fields where hundreds of sheep once grazed, about 350 year-round residents, a yacht club called the Casino, and a village gift shop that's been here since 1954.

Originally called North Island, North Haven had much the same settlement history as Vinalhaven, but, being smaller (about 5,280 acres) and more fertile, it has developed—or not developed—differently. In 1846, North Haven was incorporated and severed politically from Vinalhaven, and by the late 1800s, the Boston summer crowd began buying traditional island homes, building tastefully unpretentious new ones, and settling in for a whole season of sailing and socializing. Several generations later, "summer folk" now come for weeks rather than months, often rotating the schedules among slews of siblings. Informality remains the key, though—now more than ever.

The island has two distinct hamlets—North Haven Village, on the Fox Islands Thorofare, where the state ferry arrives, and Pulpit Harbor, particularly popular with the yachting set. The village is easily explored on foot in a morning.

North Haven doesn't offer a lot for the day visitor, and islanders tend not to welcome them with open arms.

Entertainment

Waterman's Community Center (Main St., 207/867-2100, www.watermans.org) provides a place for island residents and visitors to gather for entertainment, events, and even coffee and gossip. It's home to North Haven Arts & Enrichment. Check the schedule on its website to see what's planned.

North Haven's ferry dock is smack downtown.

Shopping

Fanning out from the ferry landing is a delightful cluster of substantial year-round clapboard homes—a marked contrast to the weathered-shingle cottages typical of so many island communities. It won't take long to stroll and shop Main Street.

Anchoring the handful of "downtown" shops and galleries is the **North Haven Gift Shop** (Main St., 207/867-4444), a rabbit warren of rooms that June Hopkins has been running since 1954. You'll have no problem spending money here—everything's tastefully selected, from the pottery to the notecards to the books, jewelry, and gourmet condiments. One room is a gallery with work by Maine artists.

Next door (connected via an elevated corridor) is the **Eric Hopkins Gallery** (Main St., 207/867-2229), owned by June Hopkins's son, a mega-talented painter who's gained repute far beyond Maine. If you can't spring for an original (figure on several thousand dollars), his distinctive work—luminous bird's-eye views of island, sea, and forest—now appears also on notecards, postcards, T-shirts, and one-of-a-kind sweaters. It's open by chance or appointment.

On the main floor of the four-story early-20th-century Calderwood Hall is **North Island Fiber Shop** (Main St.), a huge draw for knitters and hookers. It sells all-natural Maine-made yarns as well as wonderful creations, including quilts, throws, baskets, even candles and pottery, all crafted by Maine artists and artisans. Upstairs is **Herb Parsons Gallery.**

Recreation

North Haven has about 25 miles of paved roads that are conducive to bicycling, but, just as on most other islands, they are narrow, winding, and nearly shoulderless. Starting near the ferry landing in North Haven Village, take South Shore Road eastward, perhaps stopping en route for a picnic at town-owned Mullin's Head Park (also spelled Mullen Head) on the southeast corner of the island. Then follow the road around, counterclockwise, to North Shore Road and Pulpit Harbor.

Accommodations

Within walking distance of the ferry is **Nebo**

Renowned artist Eric Hopkins maintains a gallery on North Haven.

Lodge (11 Mullins La., 207/867-2007, www.nebolodge.com, $125–250). Nine rooms (four year-round), some with shared baths, are decorated with island art and many have rugs by Angela Adams. There's Wi-Fi throughout. Rates include a full breakfast and use of inn bikes.

Food

Stop into **Waterman's Coffee Shop** (Waterman Center, 207/867-2100, 7 A.M.–4 P.M. Mon.–Sat., 11:30 A.M.–4 P.M. Sun.) for coffee and sweets and local news.

For a casual meal, on the deck, inside, or take-away (if you've come for the morning, pick up a sandwich for the return ferry), slip into **Sip Ahoy** (207/867-2060, 11 A.M.–11 P.M. daily). For a sit-down meal with a view, head for the **Coal Wharf at H. P. Blake's** (Main St., 207/867-4739, 11 A.M.–11 P.M. daily July–Aug.); it's at Brown's Boatyard. Dinner also is available at **Nebo Lodge** (11 Mullins La., 207/867-2007, www.nebolodge.com).

Information

The best source of information about North Haven is the North Haven Town Office (Upper Main St., 207/867-4433, www.northhavenmaine.org).

GETTING THERE

The Maine State Ferry Service (207/596-2202, www.exploremaine.com) operates six round-trips daily between Rockland and Vinalhaven (75-minute crossing) in summer and three round-trips between Rockland and North Haven (70-minute crossing). Round-trip tickets are $17.50 adults, $8.50 children. Both ferries take cars ($49.50 round-trip, plus $14 reservation fee), but a bicycle ($16.50 round-trip per adult bike, $9.50 per child bike) will do fine unless you have the time or inclination to see every corner of the island. Getting car space on the ferry during midsummer can be a frustrating—and complicated—experience, so *avoid taking a car to the island*. Give yourself time to find a parking space and perhaps to walk from it to the terminal. If you leave a car at the Rockland lot (space is limited and availability varies), it's $10 per 24 hours or $50 per week. You can also park on some of Rockland's side streets and walk, or, for a day trip, in the city lot between Main Street and the water or Harbor Park.

No official ferry service travels between Vinalhaven and North Haven, even though the two islands are almost within spitting distance. Fortunately, the J. O. Brown and Sons boat shop on North Haven provides shuttles 7 A.M.–5 P.M. Call the boat shop (207/867-4621) to arrange a pickup on the Vinalhaven side. Fee is $5 per person round trip. (A handy outdoor pay phone is at the north end of Vinalhaven—at the end of the North Haven Road.) Don't let anyone convince you to return to Rockland for the ferry to North Haven.

Penobscot Island Air (207/596-7500, www.penobscotislandair.net) flies twice daily to Vinalhaven and North Haven, weather permitting, from Knox County Regional Airport in Owls Head, just south of Rockland. Seat availability is dependent on mail volume.

Greater Camden

Camden, flanked by **Rockport** to the south and **Lincolnville** to the north, is one of the Mid-Coast's—even Maine's—prime destinations.

Camden (pop. 5,300), the better known of the three, typifies Maine nationwide, even worldwide, on calendars and postcards, in photo books, you name it. Much of its appeal is its drop-dead-gorgeous setting—a deeply indented harbor with parks, a waterfall, and a dramatic backdrop of low mountains. That harbor is a summer-long madhouse, jammed with dinghies, kayaks, windjammers, megayachts, minor yachts, and a handful of fishing craft.

Driven apart by a local squabble in 1891, Camden and Rockport (pop. 3,500) have been separate towns for more than a century, but they're inextricably linked. They share school and sewer systems and an often-hyphenated partnership. On Union Street, just off Route 1, a white wooden arch reads Camden on one side and Rockport on the other. Rockport has a much lower profile, and its harbor is relatively peaceful—with yachts, lobster boats, and a single windjammer schooner.

Two distinct enclaves make up Lincolnville (pop. 2,000): oceanfront Lincolnville Beach ("the Beach") and, about five miles inland, Lincolnville Center ("the Center"). Lincolnville is laid-back and mostly rural; the major activity center is a short strip of shops and restaurants at the Beach, and few visitors realize there's anything else.

SIGHTS
Self-Guided Historical Tour

Historic Downtown Camden is an illustrated map and brochure detailing historical sites and businesses in and around downtown. To cover it all, you'll want a car or bike; to cover segments and really appreciate the architecture, don your walking shoes. Pick up a copy of the brochure at the chamber of commerce.

Old Conway Homestead and Cramer Museum

Just inside the Camden town line from Rockport, the Old Conway Homestead and Cramer Museum (Conway Rd., Camden, 207/236-2257, www.crmuseum.org, 11 A.M.–3 P.M. Tues.–Fri. July–Aug., $5 adults, $2 children) is a six-building complex owned and run by the Camden-Rockport Historical Society. The 18th-century Cape-style Conway House, on the National Register of Historic Places, contains fascinating construction details and period furnishings; in the barn are carriages and farm tools. Two other buildings—a blacksmith shop and a 19th-century sap house used for making maple syrup—have been moved to the grounds and restored. In the contemporary Mary Meeker Cramer Museum (named for the prime benefactor) are displays from the historical society's collection of ship models, old documents, and period clothing. For local color, don't miss the Victorian outhouse. Also here is an education center for workshops and seminars. The museum and sap house are also open for maple-syrup demonstrations on Maine Maple Sunday (fourth Sunday in March).

Vesper Hill

Built and donated to the community by a local benefactor, the rustic open-air **Vesper Hill Children's Chapel** is dedicated to the world's children. Overlooking Penobscot Bay and surrounded by gardens and lawns, the nondenominational chapel is an almost mystical oasis in a busy tourist region. Except during weddings or memorial services, there's seldom a crowd, and if you're lucky, you might have the place to yourself. From Central Street in downtown Rockport, take Russell Avenue east to Calderwood Lane (fourth street on right). On Calderwood, take the second right (Chapel St.) after the

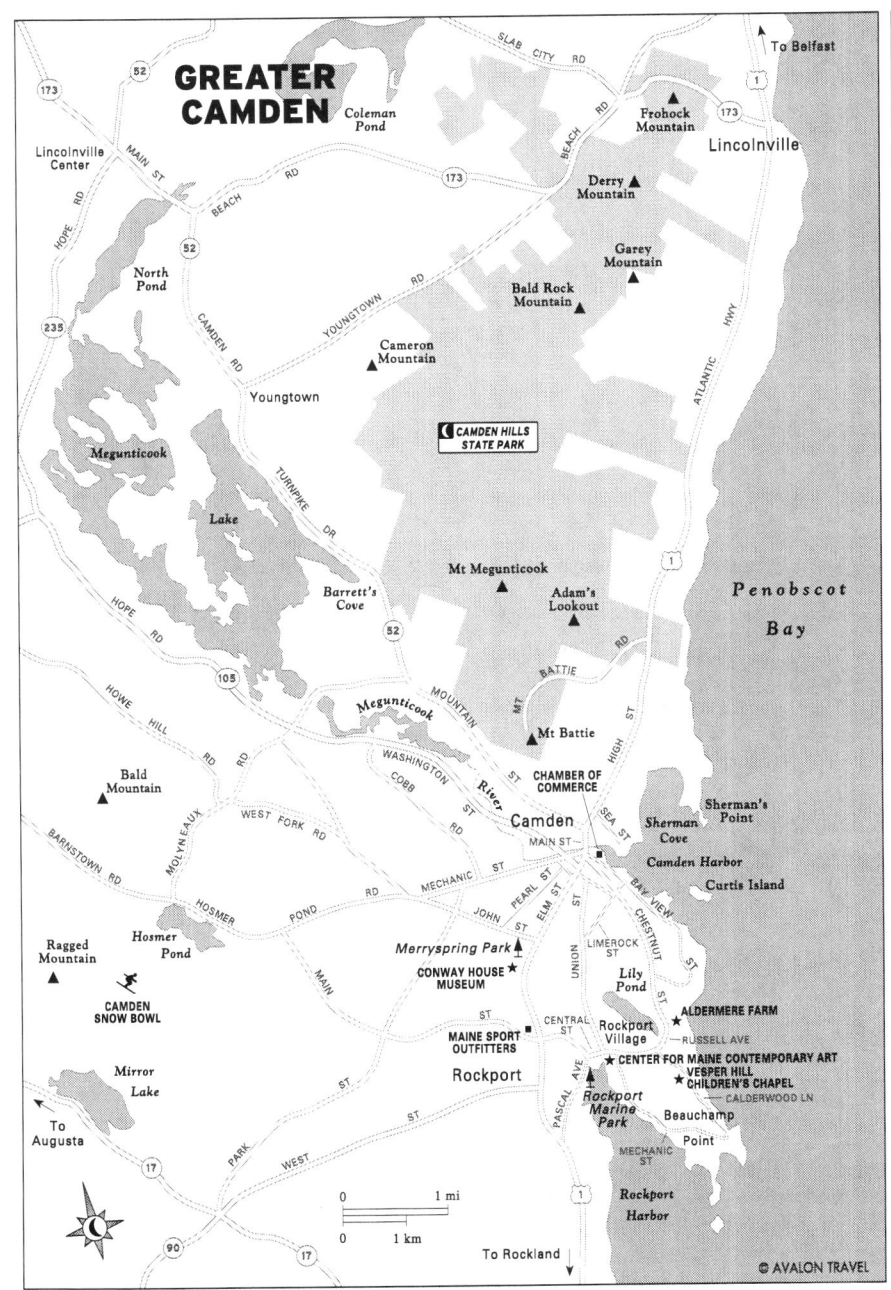

ISLESBORO

Lying three miles offshore from Lincolnville Beach, via 20-minute car ferry, is 12-mile-long Islesboro, a year-round community with a population of about 600 – beefed up annually by a sedate summer colony. Car ferries are frequent enough to make Islesboro an ideal day-trip destination – and that's the choice of most visitors, partly because food options are few and overnight lodging isn't available. The only camping is on nearby Warren Island State Park – and you have to have your own boat to get there.

The best way to get an island overview is to do an end-to-end auto or bike tour. Pick up an island map at the ferry terminal and explore, heading down to Dark Harbor and Town Beach at the island's bottom then up to Pripet and Turtle Head at its top. You won't see all the huge "cottages" tucked down long driveways, and you won't absorb island life and its rhythms, but you'll scratch the surface of what Islesboro is about.

En route, you'll pass exclusive summer estates, workaday homes, spectacular seaside vistas, a smattering of shops, and the **Historical Society Museum** (388 Main St., 207/734-6744, 12:30-4:30 P.M. Sat.-Wed., July-Aug. and by appt.). On the up-island circuit, watch for a tiny marker on the west side of the road (0.8 mile north of the Islesboro Historical Society building). It commemorates the 1780 total eclipse witnessed here – the first recorded in North America. At the time, British loyalists still held Islesboro, but they temporarily suspended hostilities, allowing Harvard astronomers to lug their instruments to the island and document the eclipse.

Allow time before the return ferry to visit the **Sailors' Memorial Museum,** a town-owned museum filled with seafaring memorabilia and allegedly home to a benevolent ghost or two. It's in the keeper's house adjacent to **Grindle Point Light** (207/734-2253, www.lighthouse.cc/grindle), built in 1850, rebuilt in 1875, and now automated.

The car ferry *Margaret Chase Smith* (207/789-5611, Islesboro 207/734-6935, www.exploremaine.org) departs Lincolnville Beach almost every hour on the hour, 8 or 9 A.M. to 5 P.M., and Islesboro on the half hour, 7:30 A.M.-4:30 P.M. Round-trip fares are $25 for car, $8.50 adults, $3.25 children, $7 adult bicycles, and $4 child bikes. Reservations are $5 extra. A slightly reduced schedule prevails late October-early May. The 20-minute trip crosses a stunning three-mile stretch of Penobscot Bay, with views of islands and the Camden Hills. In summer, avoid the biggest bottlenecks: Friday afternoon (to Islesboro), and Sunday afternoon and Monday holiday afternoons (from Islesboro). The *Smith* remains on Islesboro overnight, so don't miss the last run to Lincolnville Beach.

(private) golf course. If the sign is down, look for a boulder with Vesper Hill carved in it. From downtown Camden, take Chestnut Street to just past Aldermere Farm; turn left at Calderwood Lane and take the second right after the golf course.

Aldermere Farm (20 Russell Ave., Rockport, 207/236-2739, www.aldermere.org), by the way, is the home of America's original herd of Belted Galloway cattle—Angus-like beef cattle with a wide white midriff. First imported from Scotland in 1953, the breed now shows up in pastures all over the United States. The animals' startling "Oreo-cookie" hide pattern never fails to halt passersby—especially in spring and early summer, when the calves join their mothers in the pastures. Maine Coast Heritage Trust, a state conservation organization based in Brunswick, owns the 136-acre farm. Call for information on tours or other events.

Center for Maine Contemporary Art

Once a local firehouse, this attractive building has been totally rehabbed to provide display space for the work of Maine's best contemporary artists. The nonprofit Center for Maine Contemporary Art (62 Russell Ave., Rockport, 207/236-2875, www.artsmaine.org, 10 A.M.–5 P.M. Tues.–Sat., 1–5 P.M. Sun., $5) mounts as many as a dozen shows each summer, along with special lectures, a wildly popular art auction (early August), an annual juried art exhibition featuring more than 100 selections, and an annual juried craft show (mid-October) spotlighting several dozen artisans. An exceptional gift shop carries high-end crafts.

ENTERTAINMENT

At 8 P.M. Wednesday and Thursday in July and August, and once a month the rest of the year, **Bay Chamber Concerts** (207/236-2823 or 888/707-2770, www.baychamberconcerts.org) draw sell-out audiences to the beautifully restored (and air-conditioned) Rockport Opera House and Rockland's Strand Theatre. Founded in the 1960s as a classical series, the summer concerts feature a resident quartet, prominent guest artists, and outstanding programs. It has expanded to include world music, jazz, and dance. The first week in August ("Next Generation Week") is devoted to classes and concerts for and by talented teenagers. Seats are reserved for summer concerts ($25–34 adults, $8 children 18 and younger, plus $5 processing fee per order); open seating is the rule in winter, when tickets are less expensive and programs vary from classical to pops to jazz. (Season tickets and flex passes are available.)

The beautifully renovated **Camden Opera House** (29 Elm St., Camden, 207/236-7963, box office 207/236-4884, www.camdenoperahouse.com) is the site of many performances by renowned performers.

The Lincolnville Band, one of the oldest town bands in the country, often plays in the park's Bicentennial Bandstand, built to commemorate the town's 200th birthday.

FESTIVALS AND EVENTS

One weekend in February is given over to the **Camden Conference,** an annual three-day foreign-affairs conference with nationally and internationally known speakers. The first weekend in February marks the **National Toboggan Championships,** two days of races and fun at the nation's only wooden toboggan chute at the Camden Snow Bowl.

The third Thursday of July is **House and Garden Day,** when you can take a self-guided tour (10 A.M.–4:30 P.M.) of significant homes and gardens in Camden and Rockport. Proceeds benefit the Camden Garden Club. **HarborArts,** on the third weekend in July, draws dozens of artists and craftspeople displaying and selling their wares at the Camden Amphitheatre, Harbor Park.

Labor Day weekend is also known as **Windjammer Weekend** here, with cruises, windjammer open houses, fireworks, and all kinds of live entertainment in and around Camden Harbor. Twenty top artisans open their studios for the annual **Country Roads Artists and Artisans Tour** in September.

Dozens of artists and craftspeople display and sell their wares at the **Fall Festival and Arts and Crafts Show,** the first weekend in October at the Camden Amphitheatre, Harbor Park.

A who's who of entrepreneurs show up for the annual **PopTech** conference in late October.

Christmas by the Sea is a family-oriented early-December weekend featuring open houses, special sales, concerts, and a visit from Santa Claus.

SHOPPING
New and Old Books

The Owl and Turtle Bookshop (32 Washington St., Camden, 207/236-4769 or 800/876-4769), one of Maine's best independent new-books stores, has thousands of books and a wonderful children's room. It's just off Main Street in the Knox Mill Center.

Another source for books and a whole lot more is **Sherman's** (Main St., Camden, 207/236-2223), part of a small Maine chain.

If you want a good read at a great price, **Stone Soup Books** (33 Main St., Camden, no phone), a tiny 2nd-floor shop across from the Lord Camden Inn, is Camden's best source for contemporary used fiction.

Dolls

Antique and hand-crafted museum-quality dolls and doll houses fill **Lucy's Doll House** (49 Bay View St., Camden, 207/236-4122).

Art, Crafts, and Gifts

You'll need to wander the streets to take in all the gift and craft shops, particularly in Camden. Some are obvious; others are tucked away on side streets and back alleys. Explore.

A downtown Camden landmark since 1940, **The Smiling Cow** (41 Main St., Camden, 207/236-3351 or 800/646-6169) is as good a place as any to pick up Maine souvenirs—a few slightly kitschy, but most reasonably tasteful. Before or after shopping here, head for the rear balcony for coffee and a knockout view of the harbor and the Megunticook River waterfall.

Also downtown is **Ducktrap Bay Trading Co.** (37 Bayview St., Camden, 207/236-9568), source of decoys, wildlife, and marine art and other fine craft.

Just off Route 90, less than two miles from the Rockport intersection with Route 1, is **Carver Hill Gallery** (264 Meadow St., Rockport, 207/236-0745, www.carverhillgallery.com), exhibiting fine art and craft in a center-chimney cape, barn, and gardens.

At **Danica Candleworks** (Rte. 90, West Rockport, 207/236-3060), owner Erik Laustsen learned the hand-dipping trade from his Danish relatives.

The **Messler Gallery** (25 Mill St., Rockport, 207/594-5611), just off Route 90 and on the campus of the Center for Furniture Craftsmanship, presents rotating shows that focus on woodworking.

Handsome dark wood buildings 0.2 mile north of the Beach are home to **Windsor Chairmakers** (Rte. 1, Lincolnville, 207/789-5188 or 800/789-5188). You can observe the operation, browse the display area, or order some of the well-made chairs, cabinets, and tables.

Professional boatbuilder Walt Simmons has branched out into decoys and wildlife carvings, and they're just as outstanding as his boats. Walt and his wife, Karen, run **Duck Trap Decoys** (Duck Trap Rd., Lincolnville, 207/789-5363), a gallery-shop that also features the work of nearly five dozen other woodcarvers.

It's a lot easier to get soft, wonderful handwoven and hand-dyed **Swans Island Blankets** (231 Rte. 1, Northport, 297/338-9691) since the company moved its sales operation off the island near Mount Desert to the mainland, just 2.7 miles north of Lincolnville Beach. Such quality comes at a sky-high price.

Wine

Gaze out the backdoor of the **Cellardoor Vineyard** (367 Youngtown Rd., Lincolnville, 207/763-44778, www.mainewine.com), and it's possible to convince yourself you're in Sonoma Valley. Tucked in the folds of the rolling hills, just inland of Lincolnville Beach, Cellardoor occupies a farmhouse and barn overlooking six acres of grapes. Inside the barn, the retail shop offers free tastings, and you can pick up cheeses and other munchies for an impromptu picnic on the deck. The winery also has a retail shop at the intersection of Route 1 and 90 in Rockport.

Discount Shopping

How could anyone resist a thrift shop with the name **Heavenly Threads** (57 Elm St./Rte. 1, Camden, 207/236-3203)? Established by Camden's community-oriented First Congregational Church (next door to the shop), Heavenly Threads carries high-quality preowned clothing, books, and jewelry. It's staffed by volunteers, with proceeds going to such local ecumenical causes as Meals on Wheels.

RECREATION
Parks and Preserves

For more than a century, the Camden-Rockport area has benefited from the providence of conscientious year-round and summertime conservationists. Thanks to their benevolence, countless acres of fragile habitat, woodlands, and scenic viewpoints have been preserved. Nowadays, the most active organization is the **Coastal Mountains Land Trust** (CMLT, 101 Mt. Battie St., Camden, 207/236-7091, www.coastalmountains.org), founded in 1986. It has protected nearly 6,000 acres. Maps and information about trails open to the public are available from CMLT. Check the website for guided hikes and other events.

A Rockland-based group, **The Georges River Land Trust** (207/594-5166, www.grlt.org), whose territory covers the Georges (St. George) River watershed, is the steward for The Georges Highland Path, a low-impact hiking trail that reaches Rockport and Camden from the back side of the surrounding hills.

(CAMDEN HILLS STATE PARK

A five-minute drive and a small fee gets you to the top of **Mt. Battie,** centerpiece of 5,650-acre Camden Hills State Park (Belfast Rd./Rte. 1, 207/236-3109, www.parksandlands.com, $4.50 nonresident adults, $3 resident adults, $1.50 nonresident seniors, free resident seniors, $1 children 5–11) and the best place to understand why Camden is "where the mountains meet the sea." The summit panorama is breathtaking, and reputedly the inspiration for Edna St. Vincent Millay's poem "Renascence" (a bronze plaque marks the spot); information boards identify the offshore islands. Climb the summit's stone tower for an even better view. The 20 miles of hiking trails (some for every ability) include two popular routes up Mt. Battie—an easy hour-long hike from the base parking lot (Nature Trail) and a more

Camden Harbor Park was designed by Frederick Law Olmsted in 1931 and is now listed on the National Register of Historic Places.

strenuous 45-minute one from the top of Mt. Battie Street in Camden (Mt. Battie Trail). Or drive up the paved Mt. Battie Auto Road. The park has plenty of space for picnics. In winter, ice climbers use a rock wall near the Maiden's Cliff Trail, reached via Route 52 (Mountain St.). The park entrance is two miles north of downtown Camden. Request a free trail map. The park is open mid-May–mid-October. Hiking trails are accessible all year, weather permitting.

MERRYSPRING PARK

Straddling the Camden-Rockport boundary, .66-acre Merryspring Park (Conway Rd., Camden, 207/236-2239, www.merryspring.org) is a magnet for nature lovers. More than a dozen well-marked trails wind through woodlands, berry thickets, and wildflowers; near the preserve's parking area are lily, rose, and herb gardens. Admission is free, but donations are welcomed. Also free are family programs. Special programs (fee charged) include lectures, workshops, and demonstrations. The entrance is on Conway Road, 0.3 mile off Route 1, at the southern end of Camden. Trails are open dawn to dusk daily.

INTOWN PARKS

Just behind the Camden Public Library is the **Camden Amphitheatre** (also called the Bok Amphitheatre, after a local benefactor), a sylvan spot resembling a set for *A Midsummer Night's Dream* (which, yes, has been performed here). Concerts, weddings, and all kinds of other events take place in the park. Across Atlantic Avenue, sloping to the harbor, is **Camden Harbor Park,** with benches, a couple of monuments, and some of the best waterfront views in town. The noted landscape firm of Frederick Law Olmsted designed the park in 1931 and it is listed on the National Register of Historic Places. Both the park and amphitheatre were restored to their original splendor in 2004.

Rockport's in-town parks include **Marine Park,** off Pascal Avenue, at the head of the harbor; **Walker Park,** on Sea Street, west side of the harbor; **Mary-Lea Park,** overlooking the harbor next to the Rockport Opera House; and **Cramer Park,** alongside the Goose River just west of Pascal Avenue. At Marine Park are the remnants of 19th-century lime kilns, an antique steam engine, picnic tables, a boat-launching ramp, and a polished granite sculpture of André, a harbor seal adopted by a local family in the early 1960s. André had been honorary harbormaster, ringbearer at weddings, and the subject of several books and a film—and even did the honors at the unveiling of his statue—before he was fatally wounded in a mating skirmish in 1986, at the age of 25.

CURTIS ISLAND

Marking the entrance to Camden Harbor is town-owned Curtis Island, with a 26-foot automated light tower (and adjoining keeper's house) facing into the bay. Once known as Negro Island, it's a sight (and site) made for photo ops; the views are stunning in every direction. A kayak or dinghy will get you out to the island, where you can picnic (take water; there are no facilities), wander around, gather berries, or just watch the passing fleet. Land on the Camden (west) end of the island, allowing for the tide change when you beach your boat. Respect the privacy of the keeper's house in summer; it's occupied by volunteer caretakers.

FERNALD'S NECK

Three miles of Megunticook Lake shoreline, groves of conifers, and a large swamp ("the Great Bog") are features of 328-acre Fernald's Neck Preserve, on the Camden-Lincolnville line (and the Knox-Waldo County line). Shoreline and mountain views are stupendous, even more so during fall-foliage season. The easiest trail is the 1.5-mile Blue Loop, at the northern end of the preserve; from it, you can access the 1-mile Orange Loop. From the Blue Loop, take the 0.2-mile Yellow Trail offshoot to Balance Rock for a great view of the lake and hills. Some sections can be wet; wear boots or rubberized shoes, and use insect repellent. From Route

1 in Camden, take Route 52 (Mountain St.) about 4.5 miles to Fernald's Neck Road, about 0.2 mile beyond the Youngtown Inn. Turn left and then bear left at the next fork and continue to the parking lot at the road's end. Pick up a map-brochure at the trailhead register. A map is also available at the chamber of commerce office. No dogs. Note: The preserve closes and the gate is locked at 7:30 P.M.

AVENA BOTANICALS MEDICINAL HERB GARDEN

Visitors are welcome to visit Deb Soule's one-acre medicinal herb gardens (519 Mill St., Rockport, 207/594-2403, www.avenabotanicals.com, 9 A.M.–5 P.M. Mon.–Fri., free), part of an herbal and healing arts teaching center. Pick up a garden map and guide at the entrance, then stroll the paths. More than 125 species of common and medicinal herbs are planted, and everything is labeled. Mill Street is just shy of one mile south of the intersection of Routes 17 and 90 in West Rockport. Turn left on Mill Street and continue for almost one mile. Avena is on the right, down a long dirt driveway.

Recreation Centers

More than an alpine ski area, the **Camden Snow Bowl** (207/236-3438, www.camdensnowbowl.com) is a four-season recreation area with tennis courts, public swimming in Hosmer Pond, and hiking trails as well as alpine trails for day and night skiing and riding and the only toboggan chute in Maine.

Bicycling and Sea Kayaking

Local entrepreneurs Stuart and Marianne Smith have made **Maine Sport Outfitters** (Rte. 1, Rockport, 207/236-8797 or 888/236-8796, www.mainesport.com) a major destination for anyone interested in outdoor recreation. The knowledgeable staff can lend a hand and steer you in almost any direction, for almost any summer or winter sport. Nothing seems to stump them. The store sells and rents canoes, kayaks, bikes, skis, and tents, plus all the relevant clothing and accessories. A bicycle rents for $20 per day, calm-water canoes and kayaks are $30–40 per day. Sea kayaks are $50 per day single, $65 per day tandem.

Maine Sport Outdoor School (800/722-0826, a division of Maine Sport) has a full schedule of canoeing, kayaking, and camping trips. A two-hour guided Camden Harbor tour departs at least three times daily in summer and costs $35 adult, $30 children 10–15. A four-hour guided harbor-to-harbor tour (Rockport to Camden) is offered once each day for $75 adults, $60 children, including a picnic lunch. Multiday instructional programs and tours are available. The store is a half mile north of the junction of Routes 1 and 90.

Ducktrap Kayak (2175 Rte. 1, Lincolnville Beach, 207/236-8608) runs guided coastal tours, with rates beginning at $30 per person. Rentals are also available for $20–30, depending upon type and size, and delivery can be arranged.

If you have your own boat, good saltwater launch sites include Eaton Point, at the end of Sea Street, in Camden, and Marine Park, in Rockport; for freshwater paddling, put in at Megunticook Lake, west and east sides; Bog Bridge, on Route 105, about 3.5 miles from downtown Camden; Barrett's Cove, on Route 52, also about 3.5 miles from Camden; or in Lincolnville, Norton Pond and Megunticook Lake. (You can even paddle all the way from the head of Norton Pond to the foot of Megunticook Lake, but use care navigating the drainage culvert between the two.)

Hiking

There's enough hiking in **Camden Hills State Park** to fill any vacation, but many other options exist. For instance, there's **Bald Mountain,** northwest of downtown Camden, for magnificent views of Penobscot Bay. From Route 1 at the southern end of town (between Subway and Exxon), take John Street for 0.8 mile. Turn left and go 0.2 mile to a fork. Continue on the left fork (Hosmer Pond Road) for two miles. Bear left onto Barnestown Road (passing the Camden Snow Bowl) and go 1.4 miles to the trailhead on the right, signposted Georges Highland Path Barnestown Access. Maps are available in the box; the parking lot holds half a dozen cars. The blue-blazed trail is relatively easy, requiring just over an hour round-trip; the summit views are spectacular, especially in fall. Carry a picnic and enjoy it at the top. Avoid this in late May and early June, however, when the blackflies take command. Depending on the season, you may encounter squishy areas, although trail stewards have installed some well-placed boardwalks.

The boundaries of both Camden Hills State Park and Fernald's Neck extend into Lincolnville, where the major state-park hike follows the **Ski Shelter Trail** to the **Bald Rock Trail.** From Route 1 in Lincolnville Beach, take Route 173 west about 2.5 miles to the marked parking area just beyond the junction of Youngtown Road. The 1,200-foot summit—with great views of Penobscot Bay (weather permitting)—is about two miles one-way, easy to moderate hiking. The route links with the rest of the state-park trail network, but unless you've arranged for a shuttle, it's best to do Bald Rock as a round-trip hike.

The Georges Highland Path eventually will wind through the Georges (St. George) River watershed from the source in Liberty to the outlet in Port Clyde. Spearheaded by members of the Georges River Land Trust (207/594-5166, www.grlt.org), the blue-blazed trail currently has 40 miles of connected trails in four main sections, including Ragged Mountain Area. Contact the Rockland-based land trust for an up-to-date map, or pick it up from a trailhead box.

Swimming
FRESHWATER
The Camden area is blessed with several locales for freshwater swimming—a real boon, since Penobscot Bay can be mighty chilly, even at summer's peak. **Shirttail Point,** with limited parking, is a small sandy area on the Megunticook River. It's shallow enough for young kids and has picnic tables and a play area. From Route 1 in Camden, take Route 105 (Washington Street) 1.4 miles; watch for a small sign on the right. **Barrett's Cove,** on Megunticook Lake, has more parking spaces, usually more swimmers, and restrooms, picnic tables, and grills, as well as a play area. Diagonally opposite the Camden Public Library, take Route 52 (Mountain Street) about three miles; watch for the sign on the left. To cope with the parking crunch on hot summer days, bike to the beaches. You'll be ready for a swim after the uphill stretches, and it's all downhill on the way back.

Lincolnville has several ponds (some would call them lakes). On Route 52 in Lincolnville Center is Breezemere Park, a small town-owned swimming and picnic area on **Norton Pond.** Other Lincolnville options are **Coleman Pond, Pitcher Pond,** and **Knight's Pond.**

SALTWATER
The region's best ocean swimming is **Lincolnville Beach,** where Penobscot Bay flirts with Route 1 on a sandy stretch of shorefront in the congested hamlet of Lincolnville Beach. On a hot day, the sand is wall-to-wall people; during one of the coast's legendary northeasters, it's quite a wild place.

Another place for an ocean dip is **Laite Beach Park,** on Bay View Street about 1.5 miles from downtown Camden. It edges Camden Harbor and has a strip of sand, picnic tables, a playground, and children's musical events 1–3 P.M. every Wednesday in July and August. Check the local papers or contact Camden Parks and Recreation (207/236-3438) for the schedule.

In Rockport, dip your toes in the ocean at **Walker Park,** tucked away on the west side of the harbor. From Pascal Avenue, take Elm Street, which becomes Sea Street. Walker Park is on the left, with picnic tables, a play area, and a small, pebbly beach.

Golf
On a back road straddling the Camden-

Rockport line, the nine-hole **Goose River Golf Club** (50 Park St., Rockport, 207/236-8488) competes with the best for outstanding scenery.

Day Sails and Excursions

Most day sails and excursion boats operate late May–October, with fewer trips in the spring and fall than in July and August. You can't compare a two-hour day sail to a weeklong cruise on a Maine windjammer, but at least you get a hint of what could be—and it's a far better choice for kids, who aren't allowed on most windjammer cruises.

The classic wooden schooner **Olad** (207/236-2323, www.maineschooners.com, $31 adults, $19 children under 12) does several two-hour sails daily from Camden's Public Landing, weather permitting, late May–mid-October. Captain Aaron Lincoln is a Rockland native, so he's got the local scoop on the all the sights.

Another historic Camden day sailer is the 57-foot, 18-passenger schooner **Surprise** (207/236-4687, www.camdenmainesailing.com, $35) built in 1918 and skippered by congenial educator Jack Moore and his wife, Barbara. Between May and October, they do daily two-hour sails, departing from Camden's Public Landing. Minimum age is 12.

The 49-passenger **Appledore** (207/236-8353, www.appledore2.com), built in 1978 for round-the-world cruising, sails from Bay View Landing beginning around 10 A.M. 3–4 times daily June–October. Most cruises last two hours and cost $35 adults, $25 children. Cocktails, wine, and soft drinks are available.

Over in Rockport, the schooner **Heron** (207/236-8605 or 800/599-8605, www.woodenboatco.com) is a 65-foot John Alden-designed wooden yacht launched in 2003. Sailing options include a lobster-roll lunch sail ($65), lighthouse sail ($45), and sunset sails with hors d'oeuvres ($55).

For a short cruise—but a great way to see Camden and Rockport and their lighthouses and shorelines—head down to the Camden Public Landing and buy a ticket for the 30-passenger converted lobster boat **Betselma** (207/236-4446, www.betselma.com). Reservations usually aren't needed. Retired schooner captain Les Bex knows these waters, the wildlife, and the history. He does about eight hour-long trips daily, beginning at 10:30 A.M. June–September, for $10 adults, $5 children under 12. The last trip is at 7:30 P.M. He also does two two-hour trips—one in the morning, one in the afternoon—for $20 adults, $10 children under 12. A three-hour combo ($30 adults, $15 children) also is available. Pets are welcome.

If the kids are bombarding you with FAQs about lobsters, here's the solution. Take a two-hour trip aboard Captain Alan Philbrick's **Lively Lady Too** (207/236-6672, www.livelyladytoo.com, $25 adults, $5 children under 15), berthed at Camden's Bay View Landing. He hauls in a trap, takes out a lobster, explains all its parts, and generally provides all the answers. As a former biology teacher, he's a whiz at natural history, so there's also information about seabirds, seals, and lots more. Trips depart Monday–Saturday.

ACCOMMODATIONS

The region is loaded with lodgings—from basic motels to cottage complexes to elegant inns and bed-and-breakfasts. Many of Camden's most attractive accommodations (especially bed-and-breakfasts) are on Route 1 (variously disguised as Elm St., Main St., and High St.), heavily trafficked in summer. If you're extra-sensitive to nighttime noises, request a room facing away from the street. Rates noted here are for peak season.

Camden
BED-AND-BREAKFASTS

A baker's dozen of Camden's finest bed-and-breakfasts have banded together in the **Camden Bed and Breakfast Association** (www.camdeninns.com), with an attractive brochure and website. Some of them are described here. Rates reflect peak season.

The 1874 ◖ **Camden Harbour Inn** (83

Most of the rooms at the Camden Harbour Inn have at least a glimpse of Camden's harbor.

Bayview St., 207/236-4200 or 800/236-4200, www.camdenharbourinn.com, $300–700) underwent a masterful renovation and restoration by new Dutch owners, partners Raymond Brunyanszki and Oscar Verest, reopening in 2007 as a boutique bed-and-breakfast complete with 21st-century amenities. It retains the bones of a 19th-century summer hotel, but the decor is contemporary European, with worldly accent pieces and velour furnishings in purples, reds, and silvers. Guest rooms, some with fireplaces, patios, decks, or balconies, have at least a glimpse of Camden's harbor or Penobscot Bay. All have air-conditioning, Wi-Fi, flat-screen TV, refrigerator, and king-size bed. Service is five-star, right down to chocolates and slippers at turndown. At breakfast, included, the menu includes choices such as lobster Benedict as well as a buffet with fresh baked items, smoked salmon, and other goodies. Snacks are always available. And their restaurant, Natalie's, is one of the state's best. The owners also speak Dutch, German, some French, and rudimentary Indonesian and Thai.

The (**Hartstone Inn** (41 Elm St., 207/236-4259 or 800/788-4823, www.hartstoneinn.com, $125–275) is Michael and Mary Jo Salmon's imposing mansard-roofed Victorian close to the heart of downtown. Although some rooms face the street (and these are insulated with triple-pane windows), most do not, and all have air-conditioning. Once inside, you're away from it all. Even more removed are rooms in two other buildings under the Hartstone's umbrella. Suites in the Manor House, tucked behind the main inn, have contemporary decor. Rooms and suites in The Hideaway, in a residential neighborhood about a block away, have country French flair. All are elegant (Wi-Fi, air-conditioning); some have fireplaces and whirlpools. Be *sure* to make reservations for dinner. And then, there's the incredible breakfast. If you get hooked, the Salmons organize culinary classes during the winter, and you can even arrange for a one-on-one cooking experience with Michael.

Opened to guests in 1901, the **Whitehall Inn** (52 High St./Rte. 1, 207/236-3391 or 800/789-6565, www.whitehall-inn.com, $149–199) retains its century-old genteel air. Lovely gardens, rockers on the veranda, a tennis court, and attentive service all add to the appeal of this historic country inn. Ask to see the Millay Room, commemorating famed poet Edna St. Vincent Millay, who graduated from Camden High School and first recited her poem "Renascence" to Whitehall guests in 1912. It also played a role in *Peyton Place,* and enlarged movie photos are displayed throughout. Spread out between the main inn and the annex are 45 comfortable, unpretentious rooms, all with flat-screen TV, Internet access, and imported linens; a few share baths. Rates include a full menu breakfast. The dining room, Vincent's, is open to the public for breakfast (7–10 A.M. daily) and dinner (6–9 P.M. Wed.–Mon.). Also on the premises is Gossip, a bar serving pub fare. It's open mid-May–late October.

Claudio and Roberta Latanza, both natives of Italy, became the fourth innkeepers at the **Camden Maine Stay** (22 High St./Rte. 1, 207/236-9636, www.mainestay.com, $155–290) in 2009. Like their predecessors, they do everything right, from the comfortable yet elegant decor to the delicious breakfasts and afternoon snacks to the welcoming window candles and garden retreats. The stunning residence, built in 1802, faces busy Route 1 and is just a bit uphill from downtown, but inside and out back, behind the carriage house and barn, you'll feel worlds away.

In the heart of downtown Camden, **The Lord Camden Inn** (24 Main St./Rte. 1, 207/236-4325 or 800/336-4325, www.lordcamdeninn.com, $199–299) is a hotel alternative in a historic four-story downtown building (with elevator). Top-floor rooms have harbor-view balconies. Rates include a breakfast buffet. Pooches are pampered in pet-friendly rooms for $25 per night, including bed, biscuits, bowls, and local dog info.

One of Maine's most unusual (and priciest) bed-and-breakfasts, **Norumbega** (61 High St./Rte. 1, 207/236-4646 or 877/363-4646, $195–525, www.norumbegainn.com) is an 1886 turreted stone castle overlooking Camden's outer harbor. Provided your wallet can stand the crunch, splurge for a night (or two) here—if only to feel like temporary royalty. Twelve rooms and suites, most named after European castles, are strikingly decorated, filled with antiques, and have all the expected amenities. Rates include a full breakfast.

ECLECTIC PROPERTIES

A hybrid of an inn, bed-and-breakfast, motel, and cottage, **The High Tide Inn on the Ocean** (Rte. 1, 207/236-3724 or 800/788-7068, www.hightideinn.com, $75–230), three miles north of town, has enough variety for every budget—all in an outstanding seven-acre oceanfront setting with a private pebbly beach. Accommodations are a bit rustic, and some are dated. The two-story, eight-unit "Oceanfront" motel unit is closest to the water and farthest from Route 1. Rates include continental breakfast with fabulous popovers on the water-view porch. Pets can be accommodated in some rooms.

Step back in time at family-owned **Beloin's on the Maine Coast** (245 Belfast Rd./Rte. 1, 207/236-3262, www.beloins.com, $80–175). Don't judge this place from the roadside motel; down the road is another motel and cottages with spectacular oceanfront settings. Agnes Beloin keeps everything tidy, but it's all a bit old-fashioned and rustic (think 1950s). All rooms have TV and phone, some have refrigerators or kitchenettes, and all guests have access to a private sand beach. A two-bedroom shorefront cottage is $160–240. Extra guests in rooms are $5 per night; pets are $10 per stay.

MOTEL

It's a short stroll into Merryspring Gardens from the **Cedar Crest Motel** (115 Elm St./Rte. 1, 207/236-4839, www.cedarcrestmotel.com, $129–144), a nicely maintained property on 3.5 wooded and landscaped acres on the southern edge of downtown. Each of the 37 rooms has air-conditioning, Wi-Fi, phone, and TV. Some have mini-fridges. On the premises are a guest computer, outdoor heated pool, playground, laundry, and restaurant serving all meals and live jazz on Friday evenings.

CAMPING

Camden Hills State Park (Belfast Rd./Rte. 1, 207/236-3109, $3 adults, $1 children 5–11,

$25 nonresidents, $15 residents for basic site; $37.45 nonresidents, $26.75 residents with water and electric) has a 112-site camping area and is wheelchair-accessible. Pets are allowed, showers are free, and the sites are large.

Rockport
MOTELS AND COTTAGE COLONIES
One of the area's spiffiest motels also has terrific Penobscot Bay views. In the Glen Cove section of Rockport (three miles south of downtown Rockport, three miles north of downtown Rockland, next door to Penobscot Bay Medical Center), the **Glen Cove Motel** (Rte. 1, Glen Cove, 207/594-4062 or 800/453-6268, www.glencovemotel.com, $89–299) sits on a 17-acre bluff with a lovely trail leading to the rocky shore. Many of the 34 units boast water views; all have air-conditioning, phone, Wi-Fi, cable TV, and refrigerator. A continental breakfast is included. The pool is heated. Request a room set back from Route 1.

Step back in time at the oceanfront ◖ **Oakland Seashore Motel & Cottages** (112 Dearborn Ln., 207/594-8104, www.oaklandseashorecabins.com, $77–122), a low-key throwback on 70 mostly wooded acres that dates back more than a century. It was originally a recreational park operated by a trolley company, but its heyday passed with the arrival of the automobile. In the late 1940s, shorefront cabins were added, and in the 1950s the dance pavilion was renovated into a motel. The rooms and cabins are simple, comfortable, clean, and right on the ocean's edge; some have kitchenettes, a few have full kitchens. Bathrooms are tiny. No phones or TVs. The grounds are gorgeous, with big shade trees, grassy lawns, and well-placed benches and chairs, and there's a rocky beach that's ideal for launching a kayak. Note: This place isn't for those who need attentive service or fluffy accommodations, but it's a gem for those who appreciate quiet simplicity with a big view.

Clean rooms, a convenient location, lovely ocean views from most rooms, and reasonable prices have made the Beale family's **Ledges by the Bay** (930 Rte. 1, Glen Cove, 207/594-894, www.ledgesbythebay.com, $89–169) a favorite among budget-conscious travelers. Rooms have air-conditioning, TV, Wi-Fi, and phone; most have private balconies. Other pluses include private shorefront, small heated pool, and light continental breakfast. Pets are welcome in some rooms. Kids under 13 stay free in parents' room.

The family-owned and -operated all-suites **Country Inn** (8 Country Inn Way/Rte. 1, 207/236-2725 or 888/707-3945, www.countryinnmaine.com, $179–219 d) is an especially good choice for families, thanks to an indoor pool, play areas, guest laundry, and fitness room. Rooms are divided between a main inn and cottage suites. Some units have fireplaces, whirlpool tubs, and microwaves; all have air-conditioning, phone, fridge, Wi-Fi, and TV. A continental breakfast buffet, afternoon snacks, and evening chocolate-chip cookies are included. Kids 6–16 are $5 per night; those older are $10. On-site massage and yoga classes are available.

Lincolnville
BED-AND-BREAKFASTS
Private, secluded, and surrounded by 22 acres of gardens, the oceanfront shingle-style **Inn at the Ocean's Edge** (Rte. 1, Lincolnville Beach, 207/236-0945, www.innatoceansedge.com, $280–475) is splurge worthy. Every room has a king-size bed, fireplace, and whirlpool tub for two, as well as TV, air-conditioning, Wi-Fi, and superb ocean views. The grounds are lovely, with an infinity pool and chairs placed just so to take in the views. There's also a good restaurant on the premises. Rates include breakfast; packages with dinner are available.

Even more private and secluded is **The Inn at Sunrise Point** (Rte. 1, Lincolnville, Camden, 207/236-7716 or 800/435-6278, www.sunrisepoint.com, $200–525), an elegant retreat with all the whistles and bells you'd expect at these rates. The three handsome rooms in the main lodge, four separate cottages, two lofts, and two suites are all named after Maine authors or artists. Breakfast in the conservatory is divine.

The views from the summit of Ducktrap Mountain, at Point Lookout Resort, take in the panorama of Penobscot Bay.

MOTEL

The family-run **Mount Battie Inn** (2158 Atlantic Hwy./Rte. 1, Lincolnville, 207/236-3870 or 800/224-3870, www.mountbattie.com, $160–180) has 22 charming motel-style rooms with air-conditioning, TV, phone, Wi-Fi, fridge, and continental breakfast, including home-baked treats.

Another family-run gem, the **Ducktrap Motel** (12 Whitney Rd., Lincolnville, 207/789-5400 or 877/977-5400, www.ducktrapmotel.com, $85–115) is set back from Route 1 and screened by trees. Both the grounds and the rooms are meticulously maintained. All rooms have TV, fridge, coffeemaker, and air-conditioning; deluxe rooms have microwaves; the cottage has an efficiency kitchen.

COTTAGE RESORT

It's hard to categorize **Point Lookout Resort and Conference Center** (Rte. 1, Lincolnville, 800/515-3611, www.visitpointlookout.com, $125–275 per cabin), but by any definition it's a good value and a tremendous property spread out on Ducktrap Mountain. Once a corporate retreat center, it was purchased by the Erickson Foundation and now doubles as an education and conference center as well as offering well-outfitted accommodations to leisure travelers. The 106 one- to three-bedroom cabins are decorated in a Ralph Lauren–does-summer-camp motif (leather chairs, comfy beds, nice linens). All have screened porches, phones, individual Wi-Fi, TV, fridges, microwaves, heat, and air-conditioning. Some have fireplaces, a second bathroom, and full kitchen. All are tucked in the woods on the 100-plus-acre property. Also on the premises are an amazing fitness-wellness center with testing programs, gym, virtual golf, squash, racquetball, a full array of equipment, and a bowling alley with video arcade; mapped hiking trails, tennis courts, softball field, and artificial turf soccer field; a casual restaurant; and full conference facilities. Use of most facilities is free for guests. The views over Penobscot Bay from the summit are stupendous.

FOOD

Call to verify days and hours of operation.

Local Flavors

ROCKPORT

The best source for health foods, homeopathic remedies, and fresh, seasonal produce is **Fresh Off the Farm** (495 Rte. 1, 207/236-3260, 8 A.M.–7 P.M. Mon.–Sat., 9 A.M.–5:30 P.M. Sun.), an inconspicuous red-painted roadside place that looks like an overgrown farmstand (it is). Watch for one of those permanent-temporary signs highlighting latest arrivals (Native Blueberries, Native Corn, etc.). The shop is 1.3 miles south of the junction of Routes 1 and 90.

At the southern entrance to Rockport, a sprawling red building is the home of **The Rockport Marketplace and The State of Maine Cheese Company** (461 Commercial St./Rte. 1, 207/236-8895 or 800/762-8895, 9 A.M.–5 P.M. Mon.–Sat., noon–4 P.M. Sun.). Inside are locally made varieties of cows'-milk hard cheeses, all named after Maine locations (Aroostook Jack, Allagash Caraway, St. Croix Black Pepper, and so on) as well as hundreds of Maine-made products, from food to crafts. Among the items are blueberry chutneys, maple syrup, designer breads, great jams—a one-stop-shopping (and tasting) site.

At the junction of Routes 1 and 90, a colorfully painted barn is the home of **The Market Basket** (Rte. 1, 207/236-4371, 7 A.M.–6:30 P.M. Mon.–Sat., 9 A.M.–4 P.M. Sun.), the best takeout source for creative sandwiches, homemade soups, cheeses, exotic condiments, pastries, wine (large selection), beer, and entrées-to-go. The market will also do boat provisioning. In winter, it sponsors weeklong cooking classes.

A combination market, farm, and café, with regular tastings, lectures, and events, **Farmers Fare** (Rte. 90 at Cross St., Rockport, 207/236-3273, www.farmersfare.com, 7 A.M.–6 P.M. Mon.–Sat., 9 A.M.–3 P.M. Sun.) focuses on what's fresh and mostly local. Go for lunch or Sunday brunch, and while there, pick up all kinds of farm-produced products.

CAMDEN

The **Camden Farmers Market** (3:30–5:30 P.M. Wed. mid-June–late Sept. and 9 A.M.–noon Sat. early May–late Oct.), one of the best in the state, holds forth at the Knox Mill Complex on Washington Street. It continues through the winter inside the Knox Mill.

The **Camden Bagel Cafe** (Brewster Mill, 26 Mechanic St., 207/236-2661, 6:30 A.M.–2 P.M. Mon.–Sat., 7:30 A.M.–2 P.M. Sun.) has a hugely loyal clientele, drawn by *real* coffee, fresh bagels, fast service, daily newspapers, and a casual air. No credit cards.

Good coffee is a draw at the **Camden Deli** (37 Main St., 207/236-8343, 7 A.M.–10 P.M. daily), in the heart of downtown, but its biggest asset is the windowed seating overlooking the Megunticook River waterfall. The view doesn't get much better than this (go upstairs for the best angle). Made-to-order sandwiches and wraps, homemade soups, veggie burgers, and subs all add to the mix.

Since the early 1970s, **Scott's Place** (85 Elm St./Rte. 1, 207/236-8751, 10:30 A.M.–4 P.M. Mon.–Fri., to 3 P.M. Sat.), a roadside lunch stand near Reny's at the Camden Marketplace, has been dishing up inexpensive ($2–10) burgers and dogs, nowadays adding veggie burgers and salads. Call ahead and it'll be ready.

Peek behind the old-fashioned facade at **Boynton-McKay Food Company** (30 Main St., 207/236-2465, 7 A.M.–5 P.M. Tues.–Sat., 8 A.M.–4 P.M. Sun., kitchen closes 3 P.M. daily) and you'll see an old-fashioned soda fountain, early-20th-century tables, antique pharmacy accessories, and a thoroughly modern café menu. Restored and rehabbed in 1997, Boynton-McKay had been *the* local drugstore for more than a century. The new incarnation features bagels, creative salads, homemade soups, superb wrap sandwiches, an espresso bar, and the whole works from the soda fountain. It's open for breakfast and lunch.

Facing downtown Camden's five-way intersection, **French and Brawn** (1 Elm St., 207/236-3361, 6 A.M.–8 P.M. Mon.–Sat., 8 A.M.–8 P.M. Sun.) is an independent market that earns the description *super*. Ready-made sandwiches, soups, and other goodies complement the oven-ready takeout meals, high-cal frozen desserts, esoteric meats, and a staff with a can-do attitude.

LINCOLNVILLE
No question, the **Northport Diner** (Rte. 1, Northport, 207/338-1524, 5 A.M.–2 P.M. daily) looks like a dive from the exterior, but this is the kind of home-cookin' gem chowhounds love to stumble upon and devour. It's a homey Mom-and-Pop operation (literally, just Pop in the kitchen and Mom out front), where the breads, muffins, doughnuts, and biscuits are all homemade; the portions are generous and prices low. Little, if anything, is more than $10, and most choices are less than $6. Breakfast is served all day, and the crabmeat omelet is alone worth the stop.

Family Favorites
CAMDEN
Elm Street Grille (Cedar Crest Motel, 115 Elm St./Rte. 1, 207/236-4839, www.cedarcrestmotel.com) is a favorite for great breakfasts, lunch, and dinner Tuesday–Sunday. The pizzas get high marks. It's all very reasonably priced and served in a comfortable dining room, with a handful of seats on a deck. On Friday nights, there's live jazz.

In the heart of Camden, **Cappy's** (1 Main St., 207/236-2254, www.cappyschowder.com, 11 A.M.–midnight daily, $10–21) is small, a bit cramped, reliably good (it's been here for more than 25 years), and very popular with locals and out-of-towners alike, despite being a bit pricey. In summer, request a table in the 2nd-floor Crow's Nest, where you'll be less squished; microbrew tastings are held here 4–6 P.M. daily in season. It's a burger-and-sandwich menu with some heartier seafood choices; clam chowder is a specialty. During summer, Cappy's operates a bakery with takeout pastries, sandwiches, and other goodies underneath, facing on the alley that runs down to the public parking lot.

LINCOLNVILLE
French flair without the attitude is why **Chez Michel** (Rte. 1, Lincolnville Beach, 207/789-5600, 4:30–9 P.M. Tues.–Sat., 11:30 A.M.–9 P.M. Sun., $18–25) is a perennial favorite, even for families (kids' menu). Try for one of the window tables with water views. Early-bird specials are served before 5:45 P.M.

Casual Dining
CAMDEN AND ROCKPORT
Chef-owner Brian Hill has created one of the region's hottest restaurants with ◖ **Francine Bistro** (55 Chestnut St., Camden, 207/230-0083, www.francinebistro.com, 5:30–10 P.M. Tues.–Sat.). The well-chosen menu (entrées $24–30) is short and focused on whatever's fresh and (usually) locally available that day. In addition to the dining room, there's also seating at the bar and, when the weather cooperates, on the front porch.

Down on the harbor is the informal, art-filled **Atlantica** (1 Bay View Landing, Camden, 207/236-6011 or 888/507-8514, www.atlanticarestaurant.com, 11:30 A.M.–2 P.M. and 5–9 P.M. daily, $25–36), two floors of culinary creativity with an emphasis on seafood. In summer, try for a table on the deck hanging over the water. Be forewarned: Service can be iffy.

The Waterfront Restaurant (Bay View St., Camden, 207/236-3747, 11:30 A.M.–9:30 P.M. daily, $16–26) has the biggest waterside dining deck in town, but you'll need to arrive early to snag one of the tables. Lunches are the most fun, overlooking lots of harbor action; at high tide, you're eye to eye with the boats. Most folks rave about the place, but I've found it inconsistent.

Food as art is the idea behind the **Gallery Café** (297 Commercial St./Rte. 1, Rockport, 207/230-0061, www.prismglassgallery-cafe.com, 11 A.M.–3 P.M. and 5–9 P.M. Wed.–Sat., 10 A.M.–3 P.M. and 4–8 P.M. Sun., $15–24), a restaurant that's part of **Prismglass,** a fine-art glass gallery and working studio representing more than 50 glass artists. The Italian-leaning menu changes seasonally. Brunch is $8–14.

LINCOLNVILLE

Appropriately named, **The Edge** (Inn at the Ocean's Edge, Rte. 1, Lincolnville Beach, 207/236-4430, www.innatoceansedge.com, 4–8:30 P.M. daily, $16–30) provides a front-row seat on Penobscot Bay, whether you're in the cozy dining room or on the deck. The menu features familiar foods with creative touches and an emphasis on fresh and local. Sunday night is pizza night, with fancy pies.

Fine Dining
CAMDEN

Reservations are a must for chef Michael Salmon's five-course fixed-price extravaganzas at the **Hartstone Inn** (41 Elm St., 207/236-4259 or 800/788-4823, www.hartstoneinn.com, $45). Michael, named Caribbean chef of the year when they lived in Aruba, has cooked at the Beard House by invitation. Even Julia Child dined here. The menu changes weekly to use the freshest ingredients.

Since opening in 2007 to rave reviews, **Natalie's at the Camden Harbour Inn** (83 Bayview St., 207/236-4200, www.natalies-restaurant.com, 5–9:30 P.M. daily) has become one of the state's top tables. Chef Lawrence Klang's French-accented menu, which complements the dining room, was designed to be reminiscent of the Left Bank in Paris a century ago. Instead of looking out at the Seine, you're gazing over Camden Harbor. Entrées begin in the high $20s, a five-course tasting menu is $65, and a four-course grand lobster menu reflects market prices. Lighter fare is served in the bar and lounge.

LINCOLNVILLE

For a romantic, classic French experience, head a bit inland to **Youngtown Inn and Restaurant** (581 Youngtown Rd., 207/763-4290 or 800/291-8438, www.youngtowninn.com, 6–9 P.M. Tues.–Sun., $22–28), where chef-owner Manuel Mercier draws on his Parisian heritage and European training. Upstairs are six guestrooms ($160–175, with breakfast; $250 with breakfast and dinner).

The Lobster Pound Restaurant is a huge barn of a place, right on Lincolnville Beach.

Lobster in the Rough

Lincolnville's best-known landmark is **The Lobster Pound Restaurant** (Rte. 1, Lincolnville Beach, 207/789-5550, www.lobsterpoundmaine.com, 11:30 A.M.–8 P.M. daily, to 9 P.M. in July and Aug., $12–35). About 300 people—some days, it looks like more than that—can pile into the restaurant and enclosed patio, so be sure to make reservations on summer weekends. Despite the crowds, food and service are reliably good. Lobster, of course, is king, but the huge menu will satisfy everyone.

INFORMATION AND SERVICES
Information

For planning, contact **Camden-Rockport-Lincolnville Chamber of Commerce** (207/236-4404 or 800/223-5459, www.visitcamden.com). Also handy is a directory published by the **Lincolnville Business Group** (www.lincolnville.org).

Check out **Camden Public Library** (Main St./Rte. 1, Camden, 207/236-3440, www.camden.lib.me.us) or **Rockport Public Library** (1 Limerock St., Rockport, 207/236-3642, www.rockport.lib.me.us).

Public Restrooms

Public restrooms are available at Camden's Public Landing, near the chamber of commerce, and at the Camden Public Library. In Rockport, there are restrooms at Marine Park. In Lincolnville, there are restrooms at the ferry terminal.

Belfast

With a population of about 6,400, Belfast is relatively small as cities go, but it's officially cool: *Budget Travel* magazine named it one of the top 10 coolest towns in America. Even before that, Belfast was one of those off-the-beaten-track destinations popular with tuned-in travelers. Chalk that up to its status as a magnet for leftover back-to-the-landers and enough artistic types to earn the city a nod for cultural cool. Belfast has a curling club, a food co-op and a green store, meditation centers, an increasing number of art galleries and boutiques, dance and theater companies, the oldest shoe store in America, and half a dozen different 12-step self-help groups. It even has a poet laureate.

This eclectic city is a work in progress, a study in Maine-style diversity. It's also a gold mine of Federal, Greek Revival, Italianate, and Victorian architecture. Take the time to stroll the well-planned backstreets, explore the shops, and hang out at the gussied-up waterfront.

Separating Belfast from East Belfast, the Passagassawakeag River (Puh-sag-gus-uh-WAH-keg) fortunately is known more familiarly as "the Passy." The Indian name has been translated as both "place of many ghosts" and the rather different "place for spearing sturgeon by torchlight." You choose. No matter, you can cross it via a pedestrian bridge.

Many travelers make Belfast a day stop on their way between Camden and Bar Harbor. Truly, Belfast is worth more time than that. Spend a full day or two here, and it's likely you'll be charmed, like many of the other urban refugees, into resettling here.

SIGHTS
Historic Walking Tour

No question, the best way to appreciate Belfast's fantastic architecture is to tour by ankle express. At the Belfast Area Chamber of Commerce, pick up the well-researched *Belfast Historic Walking Tour* map-brochure. Among more than 40 highlights on the mile-long self-guided route are the 1818 Federal-style **First Church,** handsome residences on **High** and **Church Streets,** and the 1840 **James P. White House** (corner of Church St. and Northport Ave., now an elegant bed-and-breakfast), New England's finest Greek Revival residence. Amazing for a community of this size, the city actually has three distinct National Historic Districts: Belfast Commercial Historic District (47 downtown buildings), Church Street Historic District (residential), and Primrose Hill Historic District (also residential). Another walking tour is presented by the Belfast Historical Society's **Museum in the Streets,** comprising two large panels and 30 smaller ones highlighting historic buildings and people. Signs are in English and French.

Bayside

Continuing the focus on architecture, just south of Belfast, in Northport, is the Victorian enclave of Bayside, a neighborhoody sort of place with small, well-kept gingerbreaded cottages cheek-by-jowl on pint-size lots. Formerly known as the Northport Wesleyan Grove Campground, the village took shape in the mid-1800s as a summer retreat for Methodists. In the 1930s, the retreat was disbanded and the main meeting hall was razed, creating the waterfront park at the heart of the village. Today, many of the colorfully painted homes are rented by the week, month, or summer season, and their tenants are more likely to indulge in athletic rather than religious pursuits. The camaraderie remains, though, and a stroll (or cycle or drive) through Bayside is like a visit to another era. Bayside is four miles south of Belfast, just east of Route 1. If you want to join the fun, try **Bayside Cottage Rentals** (539 Bluff Rd., Northport, 207/338-5355, www.baysidecottagerentals.com).

Temple Heights

Continue south on Shore Road from Bayside to **Temple Heights Spiritualist Camp** (Shore Rd., Northport, 207/338-3029, www.templeheightscamp.org), yet another religious enclave—this one still going. Founded in 1882, Temple Heights has become a shadow of its former self, reduced primarily to the funky 12-room Nikawa Lodge on Shore Road ($35 d, $25 s, shared bath, some with ocean view), but the summer program continues, thanks to prominent mediums from all over the country. Even a temporary setback in 1996—when the camp president was suspended for allegedly putting a hex on Northport's town clerk—failed to derail the operation. Camp programs, mid-June–Labor Day, are open to the public; a schedule is published each spring. Spiritualist church services, séances, and group healing sessions are free; Saturday-morning workshops are $20. Better yet, sign up for a 1.5-hour or longer **group message circle,** when you'll sit with a medium and a dozen or so others and receive insights—often uncannily on target—from departed relatives or friends. Message circles occur at 7:30 P.M. Wednesday and Saturday (arrive a half hour early). Suggested donation is $15 per person and reservations are necessary. Private half-hour readings can be arranged for a donation of $40.

ENTERTAINMENT AND EVENTS
Entertainment

It's relatively easy to find nightlife in Belfast—not only are there theaters and a cinema, but there usually are a couple of bars open at least until midnight, and sometimes later. Some spots also feature live music, particularly on weekends.

If you don't feel like searching out a newspaper to check the entertainment listings, just go to the **Belfast Co-op Store** (123 High St., 207/338-2532) and study the bulletin board. You'll find notices for more activities than you could ever squeeze into your schedule.

Open mic nights, jazz jams, classes, and lectures pepper the calendar for **Waterfall Arts** (265 High St., 207/338-2222, www.waterfallarts.org).

Just south of Belfast, the funky **Blue Goose Dance Hall** (Rte. 1, Northport, 207/338-3003) is the site for folk concerts, contra dances, auctions, and other events. Check local papers or the Belfast Co-op Store bulletin board.

About a dozen galleries participate in Belfast

OFF THE BEATEN PATH IN LIBERTY

Seventeen miles west of Belfast, off Route 3, is Liberty, a tiny town with a funky tool store, quirky museum, a bargain T-shirt shop, and a great state park. Everything is seasonal, running roughly mid-May through mid-October or so. Call before visiting if you want to be sure everything's open.

It's a store! It's a museum! It's amazing! More than 10,000 "useful" tools – plus used books and prints and other tidbits – fill the three-story **Liberty Tool Company** (Main St., 207/589-4771). Drawn by nostalgia and a compulsion for handmade adzes and chisels, thousands of vintage-tool buffs arrive at this eclectic emporium each year; few leave empty-handed. Nor do the thousands of everyday home hobbyists looking to pick up a hammer or find a missing wrench to fill out a set. Nor do the antiques-seekers, who browse the trash and treasures on the upper floors. The collection is beyond amazing, especially in its organization. Owner Skip Brack brings back vanloads of finds almost every week, and after sorting and cleaning, many make it into this store.

The best-of-the-best make it into Brack's **Davistown Museum** (Main St., 207/589-4900, www.davistownmuseum.org), on the 3rd floor of the building housing Liberty Graphics, across the street. The museum houses not only a history of Maine and New England hand tools, but also local, regional, Native American, and environmental artifacts and information and an amazing collection of contemporary art, highlighted by works by artists such as Louise Nevelson (who used to buy tools across the street), Melitta Westerlund, and Phil Barter.

Downstairs is **Liberty Graphics Outlet Store** (1 Main St., 207/589-4035), selling the eco-sensitive company's overstocks, seconds, and discontinued-design T-shirts. Outstanding silk-screened designs are done with water-based inks, and many of the shirts are organic cotton; prices begin at $5.

Just down Main Street is the old **Liberty Post Office,** a unique octagonal structure that looks like an oversize box. It was built in 1867

You'll find practically every tool possible, and then some, at Liberty Tool Company.

as a harnessmaker's shop and later used as the town's post office.

Two miles west of downtown, **Lake St. George State Park** (Rte. 3, 207/589-4255, $6 nonresident adults, $4 resident adults, $1 children 5-11) is a refreshing find. This 360-acre park has wooded picnic sites with grills along the lake, a beach, rental boats, playground, volleyball and basketball courts, and five miles of hiking trails. Also available are campsites, $25 for nonresidents, $15 residents. Afterward, head to **John's Ice Cream** (Rte. 3, 207/589-3700) for amazing flavors handcrafted (homemade is too pedestrian to describe it) on the premises.

If you're up for more inland exploring, weave your way along the **Georges River Scenic Byway,** a 50-mile auto route along the St. George River (a.k.a. Georges River) from its inland headwaters to the sea in Port Clyde. The official start is at the junction of Routes 3 and 220 in Liberty, but you can follow the trail in either direction, or pick it up anywhere along the way. Road signs are posted, but it's far better to obtain a map-brochure at a chamber of commerce or other information locale. Or contact the architects of the route, **The Georges River Land Trust** (207/594-5166, www.grlt.org).

Arts' **Friday Gallery Walk,** held every Friday night in July and August, and every first Friday September–December.

An old-fashioned downtown cinema—recently restored to its art deco splendor—shows first-run films for moderate ticket prices. The **Colonial Theatre** (163 High St., 207/338-1930, www.colonialtheatre.com) has three screens, each with 1–2 showings a night and matinees Saturday, Sunday, and sometimes Wednesday. It's open all year.

Check local papers for the schedule of the **Belfast Maskers** (43 Front St., 207/338-9668, www.belfastmaskerstheater.com), a community theater group that never fails to win raves for its interpretations of contemporary and classical dramas. In winter wear an extra pair of socks; the floor is drafty.

Also worth checking out is the **Northport Music Theater** (851 Rte. 1, Northport, 207/338-8383, www.northportmusictheater.com, $20–25), a 128-seat theater presenting shows mid-June–late August.

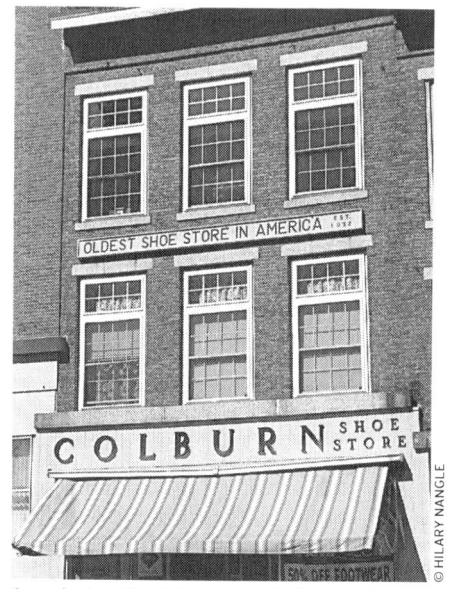

America's oldest shoe store is in downtown Belfast.

Events

The Belfast Garden Club sponsors **Open Garden Days** once a week mid-May–mid-September at the homes of club members and friends in and around Belfast. Gardens are open 10 A.M.–3 P.M. rain or shine; a $3 per person donation is requested to benefit local beautification projects. Check local newspapers or ask at the chamber of commerce for the schedule.

Every Friday evening during July and August, more than 20 mostly downtown galleries open their doors for the **Friday Gallery Walk.**

In early July, soon after the Fourth of July, the **Arts in the Park** festival gets underway at Heritage Park, on the Belfast waterfront. It's a weekend event, with two days of music, juried arts and crafts, children's activities, and lots of food booths.

The **Belfast Bay Festival,** usually the third week of July, has music, carnival rides, fireworks, food, and more.

SHOPPING

It's easy and fun to shop in downtown Belfast, a town that has so far managed to keep the big boxes away, providing fertile ground for entrepreneurs. Downtown shops reflect the city's population, with galleries and boutiques, thrift and used-goods stores, and eclectic shops.

Books

Mr. Paperback (1 E. Belmont Ave., 207/338-2084), in the Reny's Plaza, is also home to an excellent café, **Bell the Cat** (207/338-2084, 9 A.M.–8 P.M. Mon.–Sat., to 6 P.M. Sun.).

Specialty Shops

Even if shoes aren't on your shopping list, stop in at "the oldest shoe store in America." Founded in the 1830s(!), **Colburn Shoe Store** (81 Main St., 207/338-1934 or 877/338-1934) may be old, but it isn't old-fashioned.

Brambles (69 Main St., 207/338-3448) is

a gardener's delight, with fun, whimsical, and practical garden-themed merchandise.

Wooden toys are just one reason to visit **Out of the Woods** (48 Main St., 207/338-2692), which specializes in Maine-made wood products.

Just over the Belfast bridge is **Cherished Home** (31 Searsport Ave./Rte. 1, 207/338-4111), where Genie Francis (a.k.a. Laura of the famed Luke and Laura on the soap opera *General Hospital*) sells a nice selection of home-oriented merchandise.

About two miles east of Belfast's bridge, on the right, is the small roadside shop of **Mainely Pottery** (181 Searsport Ave./Rte. 1, 207/338-1108). Since 1988, Jeannette Faunce and Jamie Oates have been marketing the work of more than two dozen Maine potters, each with different techniques, glazes, and styles. It's the perfect place to select from a wide range of reasonably priced work.

The Green Store

Calling itself a "general store for the 21st century," The Green Store (71 Main St., 207/338-4045) carries a huge selection of environmentally friendly products. Whether you're thinking of going off the grid, need a composting toilet, or just want natural-fiber clothing or other natural-living products, this is the place. A very knowledgeable staff can answer nearly any question on environmentally sustainable lifestyles.

RECREATION

Belfast is rich in parks and picnic spots. One of the state's best municipal parks is just on the outskirts of downtown. Established in 1904, **Belfast City Park** (87 Northport Ave., 207/338-1661, free) has lighted tennis courts, an outdoor pool, a pebbly beach, plenty of picnic tables, an unusually creative playground, lots of green space for the kids, and fantastic views of Islesboro, Blue Hill, and Penobscot Bay. For more action, right in the heart of Belfast, head for **Heritage Park,** at the bottom of Main Street, with front-row

Kayakers, sailboats, and cruise ships share Belfast's harbor.

seats on waterfront happenings. Bring a picnic, grab a table, and watch the yachts, tugs, and lobster boats. Every street between the two parks that ends at the ocean is a public right of way.

Golf

Just south of Belfast is the nine-hole **Northport Golf Club** (581 Bluff Rd., Northport, 207/338-2270), established in 1916.

Bicycling

The **Belfast Bicycle Club** (www.belfastbicycleclub.org) invites folks on group rides. Check the website for a current schedule.

Excursion Boats

Sail aboard the Friendship sloop *Amity* (evenings 207/469-0849, daytime 207/323-1443, www.friendshipsloopamity.com), based at the Belfast Public Landing, for 90-minute morning ($20) or 2.5-hour afternoon ($30) sails; age 15 and younger are half price. The classic

Friendship sloop, built in 1901 in Friendship, was originally used for lobstering. Now beautifully restored, it carries up to six passengers. Home-baked cookies and hot coffee and tea are served on all cruises. Captain Stephen O'Connell, a former journalist, explains the boat's history and its role in lobstering and regales passengers, when asked, with tales of his experiences living in exotic locations around the world.

Take a day trip to Castine aboard the **Good Return,** operated by Belfast Bay Cruises (207/322-5530, www.belfastbaycruises.com), departing from Thompson Wharf (between Belfast Maskers theater and the pedestrian bridge). Captain Melissa Terry, a fifth-generation descendent of a whaling captain from New Bedford, Massachusetts, is a Maine Maritime Academy graduate who enjoys sharing her love of the sea. The 4.5-hour Castine Lunch Cruise ($30 adults, $17 children 5–15) provides time for exploring Castine and lunch (on your own); an extended 7.25-hour Castine trip is the same fee. Other options include a 1.5-hour educational lobstering cruise, during which traps are hauled ($25 adults, $12.50 children), and a 1.25-hour harbor cruise ($15 adults, $7 children).

If you don't have your own kayak, **Water Walker** (152 Lincolnville Ave., 207/338-6424, www.kayak-tour-maine.com) has a full range of options. Owner Ray Wirth, a Registered Maine Guide and ACA-certified open-water instructor, will arrange customized trips from a few hours to multiple days, as well as provide instruction. Two-hour Belfast Harbor tours are $35 per person; subtract $10 if you have your own boat.

Winter Sports

The Scottish national sport of curling has dozens of enthusiastic supporters at Maine's only curling rink, the **Belfast Curling Club** (Belmont Ave., Rte. 3, 207/338-9851, www.belfastcurlingclub.org), an institution here since the late 1950s. Leagues play regularly on weeknights, and the club holds tournaments *(bonspiels)* and open houses several times during the season, which runs early November–early April.

ACCOMMODATIONS
Bed-and-Breakfasts and Inns

On a quiet side street, **The Jeweled Turret** (40 Pearl St., 207/338-2304 or 800/696-2304, www.jeweledturret.com, $115–159) is one of Belfast's pioneer bed-and-breakfasts. Carl and Cathy Heffentrager understand the business and go out of their way to make guests comfortable. The 1898 Victorian inn is loaded with handsome woodwork and Victorian antiques—plus an astonishing stone fireplace. Carl can even fix your bike, if necessary, and he's up on all the local byways.

The White House (1 Church St., 207/338-1901 or 888/290-1901, www.mainebb.com, $175–250), the handsomest manse in Belfast, is the star of the Church Street Historic District. Built in the mid-19th century, the Greek Revival building is elegant inside and out—parlors, library, and guest rooms are accented with plaster ceiling medallions; it features marble fireplaces and a magnificent stairway. New owners Diana and Santiago Rich have added fancy linens, Wi-Fi, plasma TVs, and other upscale touches. A giant copper beech tree dominates the parklike grounds and gardens. Box lunches are available.

Over three years, beginning in 2005, professional innkeepers Ed and Judy Hemmingsen renovated adjacent mid-19th-century row houses into an elegant boutique hotel, the **C Belfast Bay Inn & Luxury Suites** (72 Main St., 207/338-5600, www.belfastbayinn.com, $198–350). The two rooms and six suites differ in size and design, some with fireplaces, others with balconies, but all have original art, expanded wet bars, and quality furnishings that invite relaxation. In-room spa services are available. A full breakfast is served to each room. The Hemmingsens delight in surprising guests with unexpected extras.

Motels

The 61 rooms at the oceanfront **Belfast**

Harbor Inn (91 Searsport Ave., 207/338-2740 or 800/545-8576, www.belfastharborinn.com, $59–159) have TV, air-conditioning, free Wi-Fi and local calls; there's an outdoor heated pool—a real plus for families, as is the laundry. Pets are allowed in some rooms for $10 per night. Rates include a continental breakfast buffet. If you can swing it, request an ocean-view room.

Campground

Every one of the 44 mostly open sites at the **Moorings Oceanfront RV Resort** (191 Searsport Ave./Rte. 1, 207/338-6860, www.mooringscamp.com) has an ocean view and hookups. Views are fabulous, and the rocky beach has a pocket of sand; swimming is only for the hardy. The downsides: Many sites feel crowded, and there's often a wait for showers. Sites in midsummer are $42–58 (two adults plus three kids under 17). Facilities include laundry, play area, kayak launch, game room, Wi-Fi, and on-site restaurant.

FOOD

Call to verify days and hours of operation.

Local Flavors

Wraps are fast food at **Bay Wrap** (20 Beaver St., 207/338-9757, www.baywrap.com, 11 A.M.–7 P.M. Mon.–Fri., to 4 P.M. Sat.). There's no limit to what the staff can stuff into various flavors of tortillas. Eat here or get them to go. Another plus: **John's Ice Cream,** one of Maine's best homemade treats, is available here, too.

The **Belfast Co-op Store** (123 High St., 207/338-2532, www.belfast.coop, 7:30 A.M.–8 P.M. daily) is an experience in itself. You'll have a good impression of Belfast after one glance at the clientele and the bulletin board. Open to members and nonmembers alike (with lower prices for members), the co-op is a full-service organic and natural foods grocery, with a deli-café serving lunches daily and weekend brunches.

The **Belfast Farmers Market** (Washington St. parking lot downtown, 9 A.M.–1 P.M. Fri.) provides the perfect opportunity for stocking up for a picnic. In addition to plentiful veggies, you'll find breads, meats, cheeses, sweets, and other goodies.

Ethnic Fare

Don't be put off by the lackluster exterior of **Seng Thai** (160 Searsport Ave./Rte. 1, 207/338-0010, 11 A.M.–9 P.M. Tues.–Sun.), a small, low building across from the Comfort Inn. Inside the ambience is pleasant, the service is good, everything's available for takeout if you prefer, and best of all, it's decent Thai food (entrées $8–14).

Casual Dining

A longtime standby for creative (including vegetarian) world cuisine, **Darby's Restaurant and Pub** (155 High St., 207/338-2339, www.darbysrestaurant.com, 11:30 A.M.–3:30 P.M. and 5–9 P.M. daily) served tofu before tofu was cool. This place has been providing food and drink since just after the Civil War; the tin ceilings and antique bar are reminders of that. Entrées $11–20.

Fresh food prepared in creative ways has earned **Chase's Daily** (96 Main St., 207/338-0555, 7 A.M.–5 P.M. Tues.–Sat., to 8 P.M. Fri., 8 A.M.–2 P.M. Sun.) a devoted local following. The emphasis is on vegetarian fare, and most of the produce comes from the Chase family farm in nearby Freedom. Most choices are in the $7–12 range; dinner entrées $15–22. The restaurant doubles as an art gallery, farmers market, and bakery. It's not the place for a quiet dinner, as the space is large and tends to be loud.

Industrial chic, casual, and laid-back best describe ◖ **Three Tides** (2 Pinchy La., on Marshall Wharf, 207/338-1707, www.3tides.com, 4 P.M.–1 A.M. Tues.–Sat., to 9 P.M. Sun.). Grab a booth inside, a seat at the bar, or a table on the deck overlooking the working harbor, and then choose from the tapas-style menu ($3.50–12). You might even play a game of bocce while waiting. Beers and ales are brewed on the premises. Also part of the operation is

LB, a lobster pound, so lobster is almost always on the menu.

It doesn't look like much from the outside, but **Papa J's and the Lobster Bar** (193 Searsport Ave., 207/338-6464, 4–10 P.M. Tues.–Sat.) is warm and welcoming inside, with nice water views, a casual style, and—most important—well-prepared food ($12–25) complemented by a surprisingly good wine list. Order the lobster and feta pizza; you won't be disappointed.

Lobster in the Rough

Young's Lobster Pound (2 Fairview St., 207/338-1160, 8 A.M.–8 P.M. daily May–Nov.) is a classic eat-on-the-dock lobster place overlooking the bay. Dress down, relax, and pile into the crustaceans. BYOB. No credit cards. From downtown, cross the bridge to East Belfast and turn right at Jed's Restaurant. Continue to the end of the street.

INFORMATION AND SERVICES
Information

The **Belfast Area Chamber of Commerce** (16 Main St., 207/338-5900, www.belfastmaine.org) produces a regional guide.

Check out **Belfast Free Library** (106 High St., 207/338-3884, www.belfast.lib.me.us).

Marshall Wharf is home to both a lobster pound and a brewery, both adjacent to the Three Tides restaurant, where you can order from either.

Public Restrooms

Facilities are at the waterfront Public Landing, in the railroad station, at the Waldo County Court House, and at the Waldo County General Hospital.

Searsport Area

Five miles northeast of downtown Belfast, you're in the heart of Searsport, a name synonymous with the sea, thanks to an enduring oceangoing tradition that's appropriately commemorated here in the state's oldest maritime museum. The seafaring heyday occurred in the mid-19th century, but settlers from the Massachusetts Colony had already made inroads here 200 years earlier. By the 1750s, Fort Pownall, in nearby **Stockton Springs,** was a strategic site during the French and Indian War (the American phase of Europe's Seven Years' War).

Shipbuilding was underway by 1791, reaching a crescendo between 1845 and 1866, with six year-round shipyards and nearly a dozen more seasonal ones. By 1885, 10 percent of all full-rigged American-flag ships on the high seas were under the command of Searsport and Stockton Springs captains—a significant number bearing the name of Pendleton, Nichols, or Carver. Many of these were involved in the perilous China trade, rounding notorious Cape Horn with great regularity.

All this global contact shaped Searsport's culture, adding a veneer of cosmopolitan sophistication. Imposing mansions of seafaring families were filled with fabulous Oriental treasures, many of which eventually made their way to the Penobscot Marine Museum. Brick-lined Main Street is more evidence of the mid-19th-century wealth, and local churches reaped the benefits of residents' generosity. The Second Congregational Church, known as the Safe Harbor Church and patronized by captains and shipbuilders (most ordinary seamen attended the Methodist church), boasts recently restored Tiffany-style windows and a Christopher Wren steeple.

Another inkling of this area's oceangoing superiority comes from visits to local burial grounds: Check out the headstones at Gordon, Bowditch, and Sandy Point cemeteries. Many have fascinating tales to tell.

Today the Searsport area has a population of just under 2,600, and its major draws are the Penobscot Marine Museum, the still-handsome brick Historic District, several bed-and-breakfasts, a couple of special state parks, and wall-to-wall antiques shops and flea markets.

The Maine Historic Preservation Commission considers the buildings in Searsport's Main Street Historic District the best examples of their type outside of Portland—a frozen-in-time mid-19th-century cluster of brick and granite structures. The ground floors of most of the buildings are shops or restaurants; make time to stop in and admire their interiors.

SIGHTS
(Penobscot Marine Museum

Exquisite marine paintings, historical photographs, ship models, boats, and unusual China-trade *objets* are just a few of the 10,000 treasures at the Penobscot Marine Museum (5 Church St., at Rte. 1, Searsport, 207/548-2529, www.penobscotmarinemuseum.org, 10 A.M.–5 P.M. Mon.–Sat., noon–5 P.M. Sun., $8 adults, $3 children 7–15, or $18 per family), Maine's oldest maritime museum—founded in 1936. Allow several hours to explore the exhibits, housed in five separate buildings on the museum's downtown campus. For a start, you'll see one of the nation's largest collections of paintings by marine artists James and Thomas Buttersworth. And the 1830s Fowler-True-Ross House is filled with exotic artifacts from foreign lands. Call or check the website for the schedule of lectures, concerts, and temporary exhibits. This isn't a very sophisticated museum, but it is a treasure. It's open late May–mid-October.

(Fort Knox

Looming over Bucksport Harbor, the *other* Fort Knox (Rte. 174, Prospect, 207/469-7719, www.fortknox.maineguide.com, 9 A.M.–sunset May 1–Nov. 1, $4.50 nonresident adults, $3 residents, $1 children 5–11) is a 125-acre state historic site just off Route 1. Named for Major General Henry Knox, George Washington's first secretary of war, the sprawling granite fort was begun in 1844. Built to protect the upper Penobscot River from attack, it was never finished and never saw battle. Still, it was, as guide Kathy Williamson said, "very

Construction on Fort Knox began in 1844. Today Rodman cannons are among the prizes at the sprawling granite fort.

well thought out and planned, and that may have been its best defense." Begin your visit at the Visitor and Education Center, operated by the Friends of Fort Knox, a nonprofit group that has partnered with the state to preserve and interpret the fort. Guided tours are available Memorial Day–Labor Day, and well worth it, as guides point out some of the fort's distinguishing features, including two complete Rodman cannons. Wear rubberized shoes and bring a flashlight to explore the underground passages; you can set the kids loose. The fort hosts Civil War reenactments several times a summer, a Renaissance Fair, a paranormal-psychic fair, and other events (check the website). The Halloween Fright at the Fort is a ghoulish event for the brave. The grounds are accessible all year. Bring a picnic; views over the river to Bucksport are fabulous.

Penobscot Narrows Bridge and Observatory

Do not miss the Penobscot Narrows Bridge and Observatory (9 A.M.–5 P.M. late May–Nov. 1, to 6 P.M. in July and Aug., $7.50 nonresident adults, $5 resident adults, $3 children 5–11, includes fort admission), accessible via Fort Knox. The observatory tops the 420-foot-high west tower of the new bridge spanning the Penobscot River. It's one of only three such structures in the world and the only one in the States. You'll zip up in an elevator, and when the doors open you're facing a wall of glass (yes, it's a bit of a shocker, downright terrifying for anyone with a serious fear of heights). Ascend two more flights (elevator available), and you're in the glass-walled observatory; the views on a clear day extend from Mt. Katahdin to Mount Desert Island. Even when it's hazy, it's still a neat experience.

BlueJacket Shipcrafters

Complementing the collections at the museum are the classic and contemporary models built by BlueJacket Shipcrafters (160 E. Main St./Rte. 1, Searsport, 800/448-5567, www.bluejacketinc.com), which boasts Maine's largest selection of ship models and nautical gifts.

The Penobscot Narrows Bridge and Observatory tower rises out of Fort Knox.

Even if you're not a hobbyist, stop in to see the incredibly detailed models on display. Shipcrafters is renowned for building one-of-a-kind museum-quality custom models—it's the official modelmaker for the U.S. Navy—but don't despair, there are kits here for all abilities (and budgets). It's easy to find: Just look for the inland lighthouse on Route 1.

SHOPPING

The word "shopping" in Searsport usually applies to antiques—from 25-cent flea-market collectibles to well-used tools to high-end china, furniture, and glassware. The town has more than a dozen separate businesses—and some of those are group shops with multiple dealers. Searsport vies with Wells and Wiscasset as Maine's "Antiques Capital."

More than two dozen dealers supply the juried inventory for Bob and Phyllis Sommer's **Pumpkin Patch** (15 W. Main St./Rte. 1, Searsport, 207/548-6047)—with a heavy emphasis on Maine antiques. Specialties include quilts (at least 80 are always on hand), silver, paint-decorated furniture, Victoriana, and nautical and Native American items.

In excess of 70 dealers sell their antiques and collectibles at **Searsport Antique Mall** (149 E. Main St./Rte. 1, Searsport, 207/548-2640), making it another worthwhile stop for those seeking oldies but goodies.

The **Waldo County Craft Co-op** (307 E. Main St./Rte. 1, Searsport, 207/548-6686) features the work of about 30 Mainers: quilts, jams, bears, dolls, jewelry, baskets, pottery, floorcloths, and lots else.

Are you a hooker? Thirteen rooms full of hooked rugs, and supplies, fill **Searsport Rug Hooking** (396 E. Main St./Rte. 1, Searsport, 207/548-6100, www.searsportrughooking.com), in the midst of antiques shops and flea markets at the eastern end of town. The mother-daughter team of Christine Sherman and Julie Mattison, along with a talented staff, not only sell rugs, patterns, wool, and all the other supplies and necessities of the craft, they also design the patterns, dye the wools, teach, and demonstrate.

If you're a fan of jams and jellies, a must-stop is **Colleen's** (Rte. 1, Searsport, 207/548-6613). Colleen forages for wild berries for her wild strawberry and wild raspberry jams. Then there's her rose jelly, made not from hips but petals. And her maple spread, and . . .

A local fixture in Stockton Springs since 1960, **The Book Barn** (E. Main St., Stockton Springs, 207/567-3351) is jam-packed with used and antiquarian books.

RECREATION
Parks
MOOSE POINT STATE PARK

Here's a smallish park with a biggish view—183 acres wedged between Route 1 and a dramatic Penobscot Bay panorama. Moose Point State Park (Rte. 1, Searsport, 207/548-2882, $3 nonresident adults, $2 resident adults, $1 children 5–11) is 1.5 miles south of downtown Searsport. Bring a picnic, let the kids hang out and play (there's no swimming, but good tide-pooling at low tide), or walk through the woods or along the meadow trail. It's officially open late May–October 1, but since it's alongside the highway the park is accessible, weather permitting, all year.

MOSMAN PARK

Southeast of busy Route 1, the four-acre town-owned Mosman Park has picnic tables, a traditional playground, lots of grassy space, a pocket-size pebbly beach, seasonal toilets, and fabulous views of the bay. Turn off Route 1 at Water Street and continue to the end.

SEARS ISLAND

After almost two decades of heavy-duty squabbling over a proposed cargo port on Searsport's 936-acre Sears Island (www.protectsearsisland.org), the state bought the island for $4 million in November 1997. The squabbling continued, but in 2009 a conservation easement was created that will protect 601 acres on one of the largest uninhabited islands on the East Coast for posterity. The island is a fine place for bird-watching, picnicking, walking, fishing, and cross-country skiing. It's linked to the mainland by a causeway. From downtown Searsport, continue northeast on Route 1 two miles to Sears Island Road (on your right). Turn and go 1.2 miles to the beginning of the island, where you can pull off and park before a gate (cars aren't allowed on the island). An easy 1.5-mile walk will take you to the other side of the island, overlooking Mack Point (site of a rather unattractive cargo port) and hills off to the left. Bring a picnic and binoculars—and a swimsuit if you're hardy enough to brave the water.

FORT POINT STATE PARK

Continuing northeast on Route 1 from Sears Island will get you to the turnoff for Fort Point State Park (Fort Point Rd., Stockton Springs, 207/567-3356, $3 nonresident adults, $2 resident adults, $1 children 5–11) on Cape Jellison's eastern tip. Within the 154-acre park are the earthworks of 18th-century **Fort Pownall** (a British fortress built in the French and Indian War), **Fort Point Light** (a square 26-foot 19th-century tower guarding the mouth of the Penobscot River) and adjacent bell tower, shoreline trails, and a 200-foot pier where you can fish or bird- or boat-watch. (Bird-watchers can spot waterfowl—especially ruddy ducks, but also eagles and osprey.) Bring picnic fixings, but stay clear of the keeper's house—it's private. At the Route 1 fork for Stockton Springs, bear right onto Main Street and continue to Mill Road, in the village center. Turn right and then left onto East Cape Road, then another left onto Fort Point Road, which leads to the parking area. Officially, the park is open late May–Labor Day, but it's accessible all year, weather permitting.

Bicycling

Birgfeld's Bicycle Shop (184 E. Main St./Rte. 1, Searsport, 207/548-2916 or 800/206-2916), in business since the 1970s, is a mandatory stop for any cyclist, novice or pro. Local information on about 15 biking loops, supplies, maps, weekly group rides with the **Belfast Bicycle Club** (www.belfastbicycleclub.org), sales (also skateboards and scooters), and excellent repair services are all part of the Birgfeld's mix.

An especially good ride in this area is the **Cape Jellison** loop in Stockton Springs. Park at Stockton Springs Elementary School and do the loop from there. Including a detour to Fort Point, the ride totals less than 10 miles from downtown Stockton Springs.

ACCOMMODATIONS

Searsport's gorgeous and monstrous homes seem likely prospects as inns, and indeed many have tried, but few succeed. Most only last a season or two before reverting to private homes.

Bed-and-Breakfasts

The **1794 Watchtide** (190 W. Main St./Rte. 1, Searsport, 207/548-6575 or 800/698-6575, www.watchtide.com, $140–190) occupies a sprawling late-18th-century sea captain's home formerly known as The College Club Inn. Each of the four rooms and one suite has a historic-name connection; the Eleanor Roosevelt Suite acknowledges visits by former first ladies in decades past. All have air-conditioning, TVs, and mini-fridges. Two rooms have whirlpool tubs. Rooms in the back have the nicest views and are most quiet. Breakfasts are fabulous. Collapse on the 60-foot sun porch, overlooking the bay, and you may never want to leave.

A budget find for vegetarians and vegans, **Elm Cottage** (5 Elm St., Searsport, 207/548-2941, www.elmcottageinsearsport.com, $85–90), an 1840 cape, has two rooms, one with water view, tucked under the eaves. The full vegetarian breakfast can be tailored to meet restrictive diets. Reiki is offered, and there's Wi-Fi.

Motel

The **Yardarm** (172 E. Main St./Rte. 1, Searsport, www.searsportmaine.com, $65–125), a small motel set back from the road, is next door to BlueJacket Shipcrafters. Each of the 18 pine-paneled units has TV, air-conditioning, Wi-Fi, and phone; suites (perfect for families) have a dinette, microwave, and small fridge. A continental breakfast is served in a cheery breakfast room in the adjacent farmhouse. Two rooms are pet friendly. It's open May–late October.

Here's a find. **Bait's Motel** (215 E. Main St./Rte. 1, Searsport, 207/548-7299, www.baitsmotel.com, $79–119) doesn't look like much from the exterior, but inside the recently renovated rooms are outfitted with quality comfortable furniture, down duvets and pillows, and nice toiletries. Add fridges, cable TV, free local calls and Wi-Fi, and individually controlled heat and air-conditioning. Standard rooms are pet friendly. It's adjacent to Angler's Restaurant.

Campground
How can you beat 1,100 feet of tidal oceanfront and unobstructed views of Islesboro, Castine, and Penobscot Bay? **Searsport Shores Camping Resort** (216 W. Main St./Rte. 1, Searsport, 207/548-6059, www.campocean.com) gets high marks for its fabulous setting. About 100 good-size sites (including walk-in oceanfront tenting sites) go for $39–68 a day. Facilities include a private beach, small store, free showers, laundry, play areas, recreation hall, nature trails, and volleyball court. Request a site away from organized-activity areas. Bring a sea kayak and launch it here. Leashed pets are allowed. In early September, the campground hosts Fiber Arts College, a weekend of classes, demonstrations, and camaraderie for spinners, hookers, weavers, and the like.

FOOD
Call to verify days and hours of operation.

The ◖ **Anglers Restaurant** (215 E. Main St./Rte. 1, Searsport, 207/548-2405, www.anglersrestaurant.net, 11 A.M.–8 P.M. daily) is probably the least assuming and one of the most popular restaurants around. Expect hearty New England cooking, hefty portions, local color, no frills, and a bill that won't dent your wallet. Big favorites are the chowders and stews and lobster rolls. Dinner entrées are $9–14, although lobsters are higher. The "minnow menu" for smaller appetites runs $6–13. Desserts are a specialty: The gingerbread with whipped cream is divine; kids love the "bucket o' worms." If it's not too busy, and you've ordered a lobster, ask owner Buddy Hall if he'll demonstrate hypnotizing it. It's adjacent to the Bait's Motel, 1.5 miles northeast of downtown Searsport.

Good home cooking with an emphasis on fried food has made **Just Barb's** (Main St./Rte. 1, Stockton Springs, 207/567-3886, 6 A.M.–8 P.M. daily) a dandy place for an unfussy meal at a low price. Fried clams and scallop stew are both winners; finish up with a slab of pie or shortcake. The $7.99 all-you-can-eat fish fry is available daily after 11 A.M.

INFORMATION AND SERVICES
The **Belfast Area Chamber of Commerce** (207/338-5900, www.belfastmaine.org) and **Waldo County Marketing Association** (800/870-9934, www.waldocountymaine.com) have information about the Belfast area.

Searsport's small self-serve info center is in a shed-like building on Route 1 (at Norris St.), across from the Pumpkin Patch antiques shop.

Check out the **Carver Memorial Library** (Mortland Rd. at Union St., Searsport, 207/548-2303, www.carver.lib.me.us).

Bucksport Area

The new Penobscot Narrows Bridge provides an elegant entry to the Bucksport area, a longtime rough-and-ready river port and papermaking town that's slowly gentrifying. Bucksport is no upstart. Native Americans first gravitated to these Penobscot River shores in summers, finding here a rich source of salmon for food and grasses for basketmaking. In 1764, it was officially settled by Colonel Jonathan Buck, a Massachusetts Bay Colony surveyor who modestly named it Buckstown and organized a booming shipping business here. His remains are interred in a local cemetery, where his tombstone bears the distinct outline of a woman's leg; this is allegedly the result of a curse by a witch Buck ordered executed, but in fact it's probably a flaw in the granite. (The monument is across Route 1 from the Hannaford supermarket, on the corner of Hinks Street.)

Just south of Bucksport, at the bend in the Penobscot River, Verona Island is best known as the mile-long link between Prospect and Bucksport. Just before you cross the bridge from Verona to Bucksport, hang a left and then a quick right to a small municipal park with a boat launch and broad views of Bucksport Harbor (and the paper mill). In the Buck Memorial Library is a scale model of Admiral Robert Peary's Arctic exploration vessel, the *Roosevelt*, built on this site.

Bucksport has a nice riverfront walkway, a historical theater, and the best views of Fort Knox. Route 1 east of Bucksport leads to **Orland,** with an idyllic setting on the banks of the Narramissic River. It's also the site of a unique service organization called H.O.M.E. (Homeworkers Organized for More Employment). East Orland (officially part of Orland) claims the Craig Brook National Fish Hatchery and Great Pond Mountain (you can't miss it, jutting from the landscape on the left as you drive east on Route 1).

SIGHTS

Alamo Theatre

Phoenix-like, the 1916 Alamo Theatre (85 Main St., Bucksport, 207/469-0924 or 800/639-1636, event line 207/469-6910, www.alamotheatre.org) has been retrofitted for a new life—focusing on films about New England produced and/or revived by the unique Northeast Historic Film (NHF), which is headquartered here. Stop in, survey the restoration, visit the displays (donation requested), and browse the Alamo Theatre Store for antique postcards, T-shirts, toys, and reasonably priced videos on ice harvesting, lumberjacks, maple sugaring, and other traditional New England topics. A half mile west of Route 1, it's open 9 A.M.–4 P.M. Monday–Friday all year. The Alamo has also become an active cinema, screening classic and current films regularly in the 120-seat theater, usually on weekends. Each summer there's also a silent film festival.

Bucksport Waterfront Walkway

Stroll the one-mile paved walkway from the Bucksport/Verona Bridge to Webber Docks. Along the way are historical markers, picnic tables, a gazebo, a restroom, and expansive views of the harbor and Fort Knox.

H.O.M.E.

Adjacent to the flashing light on Route 1 in Orland, H.O.M.E. (207/469-7961, www.home-coop.net) is tough to categorize. Linked with the international Emmaus Movement founded by a French priest, H.O.M.E. (Homeworkers Organized for More Employment) was started in 1970 by Lucy Poulin, still the guiding force, and two nuns at a nearby convent. The quasi-religious organization shelters refugees and the homeless, operates a soup kitchen and a car-repair service, runs a day-care center, and teaches work skills in a variety of hands-on cooperative programs. Seventy percent of its income comes from sales of crafts, produce, and services. At the Route 1 store (corner of Upper Falls Rd., 9 A.M.–4:30 P.M. daily) you can buy handmade quilts, organic produce, maple syrup, and jams—and support a worthwhile effort. You can also tour the crafts workshops on the property.

Craig Brook National Fish Hatchery

For a day of hiking, picnicking, swimming, canoeing, and a bit of natural history, pack a lunch and head for 135-acre Craig Brook National Fish Hatchery (306 Hatchery Rd., East Orland, 207/469-2803), on Alamoosook Lake. Turn off Route 1 six miles east of Bucksport and continue 1.4 miles north to the parking area just above the visitors center. The visitors center (8:30 A.M.–3:30 P.M. Mon.–Fri., 8 A.M.–3:30 P.M. Sat.–Sun. in summer, free) offers interactive displays on Atlantic salmon (don't miss the downstairs viewing area), maps, and a restroom. The grounds are accessible 6 A.M. to sunset daily year-round. Established in 1889, the U.S. Fish and Wildlife Service hatchery raises sea-run Atlantic salmon for stocking six Maine rivers. The birch-lined shorefront has picnic tables, a boat-launching ramp, an Atlantic salmon display pool, additional parking, and a spectacular cross-lake view. Watch for eagles, osprey, and loons. Also on the premises is the small **Atlantic Salmon Museum** (noon–3 P.M. Thurs., Sat., and Sun. or by arrangement with the hatchery), housed in a circa-1896 ice house and operated by the Friends of Craig Brook. Inside are salmon and fly-fishing artifacts and memorabilia.

SHOPPING

Locals come just as much for the coffee and conversation as the selection of new and used reads at **BookStacks** (71 Main St., Bucksport, 207/469-8992).

RECREATION
Great Pond Mountain Conservation

The Great Pond Mountain Conservation Trust (207/469-6772, www.greatpondtrust.org) acts as conscientious local steward for Great Pond Mountain and Great Pond Wildlands. It also hosts hikes and other activities.

Encompassing two parcels of land and nearly 4,300 acres, the Great Pond Wildlands is a jewel. The larger parcel totals 3,420 acres and surrounds Hothole Valley, including Hothole Brook, prized for its trout, and shoreline on Hothole Pond. The smaller, 875-acre tract includes two miles of frontage on the Dead River (not to be confused with the Dead River of rafting fame in northwestern Maine) and reaches up Great Pond Mountain and down to the ominously named Hell Bottom Swamp. The land is rich with wildlife: black bear, moose, bobcat, and deer, just to name a few species, plus with the pond, swamp, and river it's ideal for bird-watching. With 14 miles of woods roads lacing the land, it's prime territory for walking, mountain biking, and snowshoeing, and the waterways invite fishing and paddling. Avoid the area during hunting season. Snowmobiling is permitted; ATVs are banned. Access to the Dead River tract is from the Craig Brook National Fish Hatchery; follow Don Fish Road to the Dead River Gate and Dead River Trail. The South Gate to Hothole Pond Tract is on Route 1, just southwest of Route 176. You can drive in along Valley Road about 2.5 miles to a parking area.

The biggest rewards for the 1.8-mile easy-to-moderate hike up 1,038-foot **Great Pond Mountain** are 360-degree views and lots of space for panoramic picnics. On a clear day, Baxter State Park's Katahdin is visible from the peak's north side. In fall, watch for migrating hawks. Access to the mountain is via gated private property beginning about a mile north of Craig Brook National Fish Hatchery on Hatchery Road, East Orland. Roadside parking is available near the trailhead, but during fall-foliage season you may need to park at the hatchery. Pick up a brochure from the box at the trailhead, stay on the trail, and respect the surrounding private property.

Canoeing

If you've brought a canoe, **Silver Lake,** just

two miles north of downtown Bucksport, is a beautiful place for a paddle. There's no development along its shores, and the bird-watching is excellent. No swimming ($500 fine); this is Bucksport's reservoir. To get to the public launch, take Route 15 north off Route 1 after crossing the Verona-Bucksport Bridge. Go 0.5 mile and turn right on McDonald Road, which becomes Silver Lake Road, and follow it 2.1 miles to the launch site.

Golf

Bucksport Golf Club (Duck Cove Rd., Rte. 46, 1.5 miles north of Rte. 1, 207/469-7612, mid-Apr.–Sept.), running 3,397 yards, prides itself on having Maine's longest nine-hole course.

River Cruise

See Fort Knox and the bridges from the water and learn about the region's history and lore on a narrated trip aboard *Lil' Toot* with **Bucksport Harbor Tours** (96 Main St., Bucksport, 207/469-7498, www.littletoottours.com). Wildlife sightings, including osprey, eagles, and seals, are a possibility. The 75-minute tours depart from the Bucksport Town Dock four times on Friday, Saturday, and most Sundays in July and August. An evening cruise lasts two hours. Buy tickets ($15–20 adults, $7.50–10 children 2–12) at **Bittersweet Gift Shop** (81 Main St., Bucksport).

ACCOMMODATIONS
Inns and Bed-and-Breakfasts

The **Orland House** (10 Narramissic Dr., Orland, 207/469-1144, www.orlandhousebb.com, $85–125), Alvion and Cindi Kimball's elegant yet comfortable 1820 Greek Revival home, overlooks the Narramissic River. It's been beautifully restored, preserving the architectural details but adding plenty of creature comforts. Cindi heads the local chamber of commerce, so she's a wealth of info.

Location, location, location. If only the six simple rooms at the old-timey **Alamoosook Lakeside Inn** (off Rte. 1, Orland, 207/469-6393 or 866/459-6393, www.alamoosooklakesideinn.com, $125) actually overlooked the lake, then it would be the perfect rustic lakeside lodge. The property is gorgeous, and the location well-suited for exploring the area, but the rooms are so-so, with tiny bathrooms. All have

For a different perspective on Fort Knox and the Penobscot Narrows Bridge, book a trip aboard the *Lil' Toot* out of Bucksport.

windows and doors opening onto a long sun porch overlooking the lake. Now the upside: The lodge has a quarter mile of lakefront, and guests have access to canoes and kayaks. Paddle across the lake to the fish hatchery for a hike up Great Pond Mountain. A full breakfast is served; free Wi-Fi. It's open year-round.

Motels

In downtown Bucksport, the **Fort Knox Inn** (64 Main St., Bucksport, 207/469-3113 or 800/528-1234, $115–199) is a four-story Best Western nudged right up to the harbor's edge. Forty modern rooms have phones, air-conditioning, free Wi-Fi, and cable-satellite TV. Be sure to request a water view, or you'll be facing a parking lot.

Camping

The rivers, lakes, and ponds between Bucksport and Ellsworth make the area especially appealing for camping, and sites tend to be cheaper than in the Bar Harbor area. During July and August, especially on weekends, reservations are wise.

Six miles east of Bucksport, across from Craig Pond Road, is Back Ridge Road, leading to **Balsam Cove Campground** (286 Back Ridge Rd., East Orland, 207/469-7771 or 800/469-7771, www.balsamcove.com, $22–42). From Route 1, take Back Ridge Road 1.5 miles to the left turn for the campground on the shores of 10-mile-long Toddy Pond. Facilities on the 50 acres include 60 wooded waterfront or water-view tent and RV sites, a one-room rental cabin ($54–68), on-site rental trailers ($65–80), a dump station, a store, laundry, free showers, boat rentals, and freshwater swimming. Open late May to late September. Dogs are welcome on camping sites for $2 per day.

The same season holds for 10-acre **Whispering Pines Campground** (Rte. 1, East Orland, 207/469-3443, www.campmaine.com/whisperingpines/, $36 for two people, $2 per child over age 7), also on Toddy Pond, but with access directly from Route 1. Facilities include 50 tent and RV sites (request one close to the pond), free use of canoes and rowboats, freshwater swimming, a playground, free showers, and a recreation hall. Whispering Pines is 6.5 miles east of Bucksport.

FOOD

MacLeod's (Main St., Bucksport, 207/469-3963, 11 A.M.–9 P.M. Tues.–Sat.) is Bucksport's most popular and enduring restaurant. Some tables in the pleasant dining room have glimpses of the river and Fort Knox. The wide-ranging menu has choices for all tastes and budgets. Reservations are wise for Saturday nights.

In what passes as downtown Orland (hint: don't blink), **Orland Market and Pizza** (Rte. 175/91 Castine Rd., Orland, 207/469-9999, www.orlandmarket.com, 7 A.M.–9 P.M. daily) is a delight. Established in 1860, the old-fashioned country store has a little of this and a bit of that along with breakfast sandwiches, hot and cold sandwiches, grilled foods, salad, and all kinds of pizza. Call or drop by to find out the day's homemade specials, perhaps lasagna or spaghetti and meatballs. Smoked ribs are the specialty every other Thursday, weather permitting.

INFORMATION AND SERVICES

The **Bucksport Bay Area Chamber of Commerce** (52 Main St., Bucksport, 207/469-6818, www.bucksportchamber.org) is right next to the municipal office in downtown Bucksport. Office hours are 9 A.M.–5 P.M. Monday–Friday, but the side door is always open for access to an extensive array of brochures, newspapers, and other publications, plus bulletin board notices. The local *Enterprise* newspaper and the Bucksport Chamber of Commerce produce a very helpful annual, *The Guide,* covering Bucksport, Orland, and Verona Island.

Public Restrooms

In Bucksport, public restrooms next to the town dock (behind the Bucksport Historical Society) are open spring, summer, and fall. Restrooms are open year-round in the Bucksport Municipal Office (weekdays) on Main Street.

BLUE HILL PENINSULA AND DEER ISLE

The Blue Hill Peninsula, once dubbed "The Fertile Crescent," is unique. Few other Maine locales harbor such a high concentration of artisans, musicians, and on-their-feet retirees juxtaposed with top-flight wooden-boat builders, lobstermen, and umpteenth-generation Mainers. Perhaps surprisingly, the mix seems to work.

Anchored by the towns of Bucksport to the east and Ellsworth to the west, the peninsula comprises several enclaves with markedly distinct personalities. Blue Hill, Castine, Orland, Brooklin, Brooksville, and Sedgwick are stitched together by a network of narrow, winding country roads. Thanks to the mapmaker-challenging coastline and a handful of freshwater ponds and rivers, there's a view of water around nearly every bend.

You can watch the sun set from atop Blue Hill Mountain; tour the home of the fascinating Jonathan Fisher; stroll through the village of Castine (charming verging on precious), whose streets are lined with dowager-like homes; visit *WoodenBoat* magazine's world headquarters in tiny Brooklin; and browse top-notch studios and galleries throughout the peninsula. Venture a bit inland of Route 1, and you find lovely lakes for paddling and swimming and another hill to hike.

After weaving your way down the Blue Hill Peninsula and crossing the soaring pray-as-you-go bridge to Little Deer Isle, you've entered the realm of island living. Sure, bridges and causeways connect the points, but the farther down you drive, the more removed from civilization you'll feel. The pace slows; the population

© TOM NANGLE

HIGHLIGHTS

◖ **Parson Fisher House:** More than just another historic house, the Parson Fisher House is a remarkable testimony to one man's ingenuity (page 83).

◖ **Blue Hill Mountain:** It's a relatively easy hike for fabulous 360-degree views from the summit of this local landmark (page 85).

◖ **Flash! In the Pans Community Steel Band:** Close your eyes while listening to this phenomenal steel-pan band, and you just might think you're on a Caribbean island rather than in Maine (page 92).

◖ **Holbrook Island Sanctuary State Park:** Varied hiking trails and great bird-watching are the rewards for finding this off-the-beaten-path preserve (page 95).

◖ **Castine Historic Tour:** A turbulent history detailed on signs throughout town makes Castine an irresistible place to tour on foot or bike (page 98).

◖ **Sea Kayaking:** Hook up with "Kayak Karen" to see Castine from the water (page 101).

◖ **Haystack Mountain School of Crafts:** Arrange your schedule to visit the spectacular architect-designed campus of this renowned oceanfront school (page 107).

◖ **Art and Craft Galleries:** The Haystack crafts school has inspired dozens of world-class artisans to set up shop on Deer Isle (page 111).

◖ **Guided Island Tours:** Join Captain Walter Reed for a boat tour amidst the islands customized to your interests (page 116).

◖ **Acadia National Park:** Tipping sparsely populated **Isle au Haut** is a remote section of the national park, perfect for a day trip or longer (page 121).

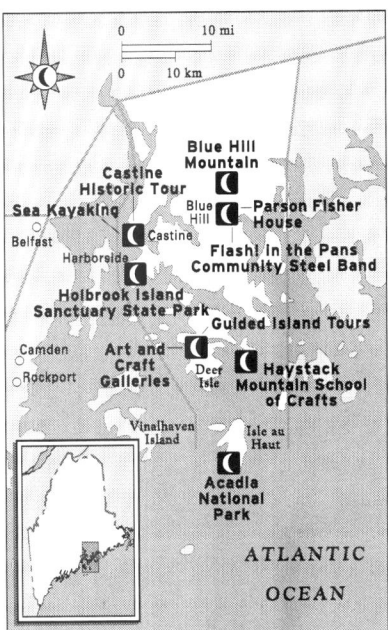

LOOK FOR ◖ TO FIND RECOMMENDED SIGHTS, ACTIVITIES, DINING, AND LODGING.

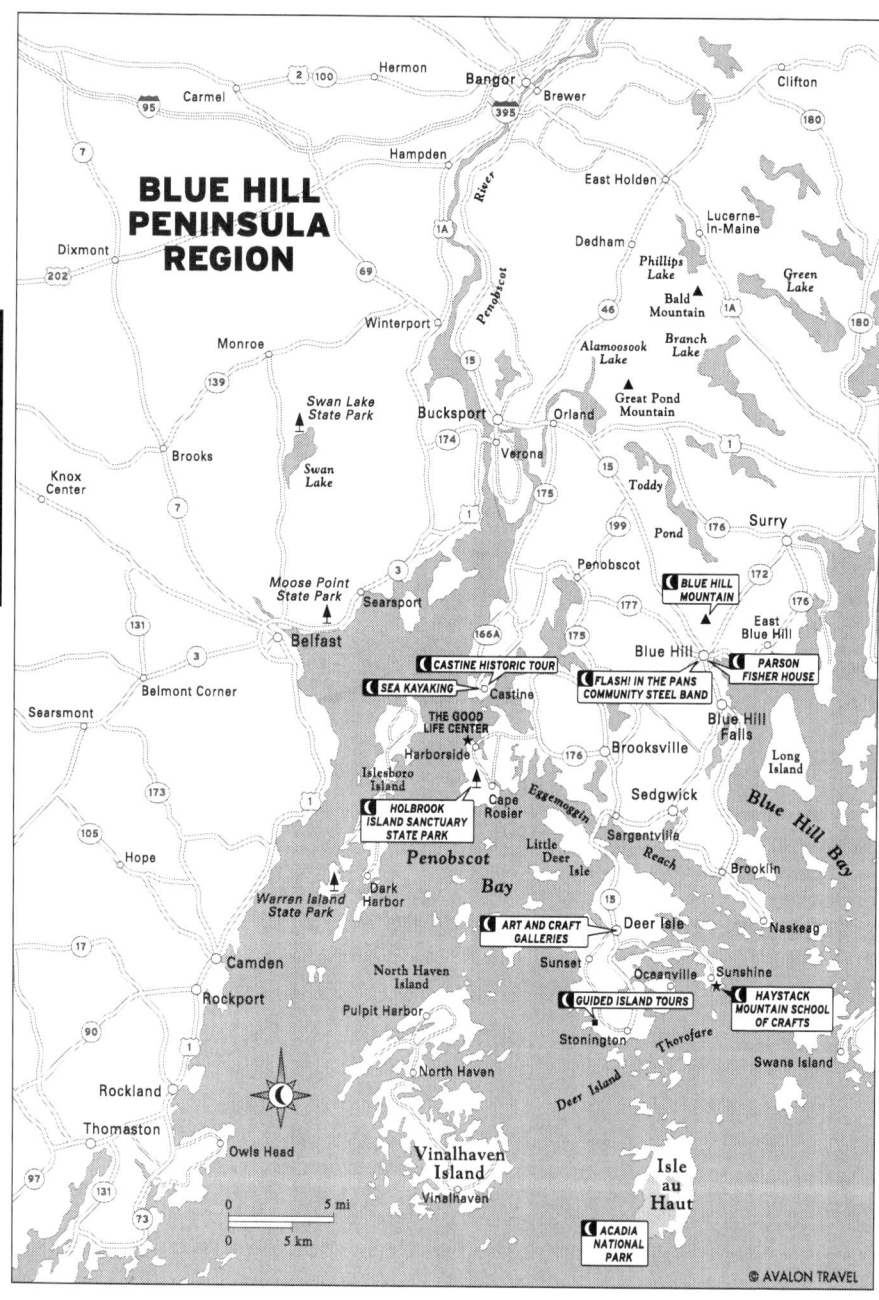

dwindles. Fishing and lobstering are the mainstays; lobster boats rest near many homes and trap fences edge properties. If your ultimate destination is the section of Acadia National Park on Isle au Haut, the drive down Deer Isle serves to help disconnect you from the mainland. To reach the park's acreage on Isle au Haut, after wending your way through Little Deer Isle and Deer Isle, you'll board the Isle au Haut ferryboat for the trip down Merchant Row to the island.

PLANNING YOUR TIME

To truly enjoy this region, you'll want to spend at least three or four days here, perhaps splitting your lodging between two or three locations. The region is designed for leisurely exploring; you won't be able to zip from one location to another. Traveling along the winding roads, discovering galleries and country stores, and lodging at traditional inns are all part of the experience.

Arts fans will want to concentrate their efforts in Blue Hill, Deer Isle, and Stonington. Outdoor-oriented folks should consider Deer Isle, Stonington, or Castine as a base for sea kayaking or exploring the area preserves. For architecture and history buffs, Castine is a must.

No visit to this region is complete without at least a cruise by if not a visit to Isle au Haut, an offshore island that's home to a remote section of Acadia National Park. Allow at least a few hours for a ride on the mail boat, but if you can afford the time, spend a full day hiking the park's trails. Don't forget to pack food and water.

Blue Hill

Twelve miles south of Route 1 is the hub of the peninsula, Blue Hill (pop. 2,390), exuding charm from its handsome old homes to its waterfront setting to the shops, restaurants, and galleries that boost its appeal.

Eons back, Native American summer folk gave the name Awanadjo ("small, hazy mountain") to the mini-mountain that looms over the town and draws the eye for miles around. The first permanent settlers arrived after the French and Indian War, in the late 18th century, and established mills and shipyards. More than 100 ships were built here between Blue Hill's incorporation, in 1789, and 1882—bringing prosperity to the entire peninsula.

Critical to the town's early expansion was its first clergyman, Jonathan Fisher, a remarkable fellow who's been likened to Leonardo da Vinci. In 1803, Fisher founded Blue Hill Academy (predecessor of today's George Stevens Academy), then built his home (now a museum), and eventually left an immense legacy of inventions, paintings, engravings, and poetry.

Throughout the 19th century and into the 20th, Blue Hill's granite industry boomed, reaching its peak in the 1880s. Scratch the Brooklyn Bridge and the New York Stock Exchange and you'll find granite from Blue Hill's quarries. Around 1879, the discovery of gold and silver brought a flurry of interest, but little came of it. Copper was also found here, but quantities of it, too, were limited.

At the height of industrial prosperity, tourism took hold, attracting steamboat-borne summer boarders. Many succumbed to the scenery, bought land, and built waterfront summer homes. Thank these summer folk and their offspring for the fact that music has long been a big deal in Blue Hill. The Kneisel Hall Chamber Music School, established in the late 19th century, continues to rank high among the nation's summer music colonies. New York City's Blue Hill Troupe, devoted to Gilbert and Sullivan operettas, was named for the longtime summer home of the troupe's founders.

SIGHTS
◖ Parson Fisher House
Named for a brilliant Renaissance man who

arrived in Blue Hill in 1794, the Parson Fisher House (Rte. 15/176, 44 Mines Rd., 207/374-2459, www.jonathanfisherhouse.org, 1–4 P.M. Thurs.–Sat. early July–mid-Oct., $5) immerses visitors in period furnishings and Jonathan Fisher lore. And Fisher's feats are breathtaking: He was a Harvard-educated preacher who also managed to be an accomplished painter, poet, mathematician, naturalist, linguist, inventor, cabinetmaker, farmer, architect, and printmaker. In his spare time, he fathered nine children. Fisher also pitched in to help build the yellow house on Tenney Hill, which served as the Congregational Church parsonage. Now it contains intriguing items created by Fisher, memorabilia that volunteer tour guides delight in explaining, including a camera obscura. Don't miss it.

Historic Houses

A few of Blue Hill's elegant houses have been converted to museums, inns, restaurants, and even some offices and shops, so you can see them from the inside out. To appreciate the private residences, you'll want to walk, bike, or drive around town. Also ask at the Holt House about village walking tours.

In downtown Blue Hill, a few steps off Main Street, stands the **Holt House** (3 Water St., 207/326-8250, www.bluehillhistory.org, 1–4 P.M. Tues. and Fri., 11 A.M.–2 P.M. Sat., July–mid-Sept., $3 adults, free children 12 and under), home of the Blue Hill Historical Society. Built in 1815 by Jeremiah Holt, the Federal-style building contains restored stenciling, period decor, and masses of memorabilia contributed by local residents. In the carriage house are even more goodies, including old tools, a sleigh, carriages, and so forth.

Walk or drive up Union Street (Route 177), past George Stevens Academy, and wander **The Old Cemetery,** established in 1794. If gnarled trees and ancient headstones intrigue you, there aren't many good-sized Maine cemeteries older than this one.

Bagaduce Music Lending Library

At the foot of Greene's Hill in Blue Hill is one of Maine's more unusual institutions, a library where you can borrow from a collection of more than one million scores and pieces of sheet music (3 Music Library La., Rte. 172, 207/374-5454, www.bagaducemusic.org, 10 A.M.–3 P.M. Mon.–Fri. or by appointment). Somehow this seems so appropriate for a community that's a magnet for music lovers. Annual membership is $10 ($5 for students); fees range $1–4 per piece.

Scenic Routes

Parker Point Road (turn off Route 15 at the Blue Hill Library) takes you from Blue Hill to Blue Hill Falls the back way, with vistas en route toward Acadia National Park. For other great views, drive the length of **Newbury Neck,** in nearby Surry, or head west on Route 15/176 toward Sedgwick, Brooksville, and beyond.

ENTERTAINMENT

Variety and serendipity are the keys here. Check local calendar listings and tune in to radio station WERU (89.9 and 102.9 FM, www.weru.org), the peninsula's own community radio; there might be announcements of concerts by local resident pianist Paul Sullivan or the Bagaduce Chorale, or maybe a contra dance or a tropical treat from Flash! In the Pans Community Band (www.flashinthepans.org). The George Stevens Academy has a free Tuesday evening lecture series in July and August.

Music

Since 1922, chamber-music students have been spending summers perfecting their skills and demonstrating their prowess at the **Kneisel Hall Chamber Music School** (Pleasant St., Rte. 15, 207/374-2811, www.kneisel.org). Faculty concerts run Friday evenings and Sunday afternoons late June–late August. The concert schedule is published in the spring, and reserved-seating tickets ($30 inside, $20 on the veranda outside, nonrefundable) can be ordered by phone. Other opportunities to hear the students and faculty exist, including young artist concerts, children's concerts, open rehearsals, and more. Kneisel Hall is about a half mile from the center of town.

The Blue Hill Congregational Church is the site for the **Vanderkay Summer Music Series** (207/374-2891), which ranges from choral music from the Middle Ages to gospel. Tickets are $15.

Chamber music continues in winter thanks to the volunteer **Blue Hill Concert Association** (207/326-4666, www.bluehillconcerts.org), which presents five concerts between January and March at the Congregational Church. Recommended donation is $20.

EVENTS

WERU's annual Full Circle Fair is usually held in mid-August at the Blue Hill Fairgrounds (Rte. 172, north of downtown Blue Hill). Expect world music, good food, crafts, and socially and environmentally progressive talks.

On Labor Day weekend, the **Blue Hill Fair** (Blue Hill Fairgrounds, Rte. 172, 207/374-9976) is one of the state's best agricultural fairs.

SHOPPING

Boutiques, antiques, galleries, and even two downtown bookstores make shopping a pleasure in Blue Hill.

Antiques

Blue Hill Antiques (8 Water St., 207/374-2199 or 207/326-4973) specializes in 18th- and 19th-century French and American furniture—it attracts a high-end clientele. The same patrons seek out neighboring Brad Emerson's **Emerson Antiques** (33 Water St., 207/374-5140), concentrating on early Americana, such as hooked rugs and ship models.

Books

Blue Hill's literate population manages to support two full-service, year-round independent bookstores.

Ever-helpful Bonnie Myers provides free advice on the region with a money-back guarantee at **North Light Books** (Main St., 207/374-5422). It's a delight to browse, the children's book selection is terrific, and out back is Blue Hill Hearth, with all sorts of treats.

Around the corner is **Blue Hill Books** (26 Pleasant St., Rte. 15, 207/374-5632, www.bluehillbooks.com), which organizes an "authors series" during the summer.

Wine

Blue Hill Wine Shop (138 Main St., 207/374-2161), tucked into a converted horse barn, carries more than 1,000 wines, plus teas, coffees, and blended tobaccos and unusual pipes for diehard, upscale smokers. Monthly wine tastings (usually 2:30–6 P.M. last Saturday of the month) are always an adventure.

PARKS AND RECREATION
◖ Blue Hill Mountain

Mountain seems a fancy label for a 943-footer, yet Blue Hill Mountain stands alone, visible from Camden and even beyond. On a clear day, head for the summit and take in the wraparound view encompassing Penobscot Bay, the hills of Mount Desert, and the Camden Hills. Climb the fire tower and you'll see even more. In mid-June, the lupines along the way are breathtaking; in fall, the colors are spectacular—with reddened blueberry barrens added to the variegated foliage. Go early in the day; it's a popular easy-to-moderate hike. A short loop on the lower slopes takes only half an hour. Take Route 15 (Pleasant Street) to Mountain Road. Turn right and go 0.8 mile to the trailhead (on the left) and the small parking area (on the right). You can also walk (uphill) the mile from the village.

Blue Hill Heritage Trust

This fine organization (101 Union St., 207/374-5118, www.bluehillheritagetrust.org, 8 A.M.–5 P.M. Mon.–Fri.) works hard at preserving the region's landscape. It also presents a Walks 'n' Talks series, with offerings such as kayaking by preservation land along Eggemoggin Reach, a full-moon hike up Blue Hill Mountain, and walks through other trust properties, such as 700-acre Kingdom Woods

GALLERY HOPPING IN BLUE HILL

Perhaps it's Blue Hill's location near the renowned Haystack Mountain School of Crafts. Perhaps it's the way the light plays off the rolling countryside and onto the twisting coastline. Perhaps it's the inspirational landscape. Whatever the reason, numerous artists and artisans call Blue Hill home, and top-notch galleries are abundant.

Judith Leighton knows contemporary art, and her **Leighton Gallery** (24 Parker Point Rd., 207/374-5001, www.leightongallery.com) is a real treat. The airy two-story-plus-basement space, in a converted barn on the Parker Point Road, is filled with a great selection. Be sure to visit the equally spectacular and extremely peaceful backyard sculpture garden. The **Liros Gallery** (14 Parker Point Rd., 207/374-5370 or 800/287-5370, www.lirosgallery.com) has been dealing in Russian icons since the mid-1960s. Prices are high, but the icons are fascinating. The gallery also carries Currier and Ives prints, antique maps, and 19th-century British and American paintings. From here, it's a short walk to **Blue Hill Bay Gallery** (Main St., 207/374-5773, www.bluehillbaygallery.com), which represents contemporary artists in various media and has a permanent collection of earlier works.

Don't miss the spacious, well-lit intown gallery of **Jud Hartmann** (Main St. at Rte. 15, 207/359-2544, www.judhartmanngallery.com), who makes limited-edition bronze sculptures of the Woodland tribes of the northeast. Hartmann often can be seen working on his next model in the gallery – a real treat. He's a wealth of information about his subjects, and he loves sharing the fascinating – even mesmerizing – stories he's uncovered during his meticulous research.

Also on Main Street are three other fun, artsy gallery-shops. **Handworks Gallery** (Main St., 207/374-5613, www.handworksgallery.org) sells a range of fun, funky, utilitarian and fine-art crafts by more than 50 Maine artists and craftspeople, including jewelry, furniture, rugs, wall hangings, and clothing. Browse **North Country Textiles** (Main St., 207/374-2715, www.northcountrytextiles.com) for fine handwoven throws, rugs, clothing, and table linens as well as other fine crafts.

Pottery is abundant in Blue Hill. **Rackliffe Pottery** (Rte. 172, 207/374-2297 or 888/631-3321, www.rackliffepottery.com), noted for its vivid blue wares, also makes its own glazes and has been producing lead-free pottery since 1969.

About two miles from downtown is another don't-miss. **Mark Bell Pottery** (Rte. 15, 207/374-5881), in a tiny building signaled only by a small roadside sign, is the home of exquisite award-winning porcelain by the eponymous potter. It's easy to understand why his wares were displayed at the Smithsonian Institution's Craft Fair as well as other juried shows across the country. The delicacy of each vase, bowl, or other item is astonishing, and the glazes are gorgeous. Twice each summer he has kiln openings – they're must-attend events for collectors and fans. Call for details.

Conservation Preserve and Cooper Farm at Caterpillar Hill. Many include talks by knowledgeable folks on complementary topics.

Blue Hill Town Park

At the end of Water Street is a small park with a terrific view. It has a small pebble beach, picnic tables, portable toilet, and a playground.

MERI Center

A great way to raise kids' environmental consciousness is to enroll them in summer activities sponsored by the MERI Center for Marine Studies (55 Main St., 207/374-2135, www.meriresearch.org). MERI (the Marine Environmental Research Institute), a nonprofit marine-ecology organization, schedules **island excursions** and **"eco-cruises"** geared to different age groups ($20–60); cruises are limited to 12 passengers. The MERI Center has a touch tank, a marine lending library, and exhibit space. A Thursday-evening Ocean

Environment lecture series is offered once or twice monthly. On Fridays during fall, winter, and spring, MERI offers a movie night, with refreshments, during which it screens marine-related films. It's free, but a $3 donation is appreciated. MERI is open Monday–Friday year-round and also Saturdays in July and August.

Outfitter

The Activity Shop (61 Ellsworth Rd., 207/374-3600, www.theactivityshop.com) rents bicycles for $35 per week and Old Town canoes and kayaks at rates beginning at $25 per day, including delivery within a reasonable area.

ACCOMMODATIONS
Inns and Bed-and-Breakfasts

If you're trying to imagine a classic country inn, **The Blue Hill Inn** (Union St., Rte. 177, 207/374-2844 or 800/826-7415, www.bluehillinn.com, $175–205, mid-May–late Oct.) would be it. Sarah Pebworth graciously welcomes guests to her antiques-filled inn, open since 1840 and located steps from Main Street's shops and restaurants. Ten air-conditioned rooms and a suite have real chandeliers, four-poster beds, down comforters, fancy linens, and braided and Oriental rugs; three have wood-burning fireplaces. Rear rooms overlook the extensive cutting garden, with chairs and a hammock. A three-course breakfast is served by candlelight in the elegant dining room (also available to the public, $12.95). Afternoon refreshments with sweets and superb hors d'oeuvres are served 6–7 P.M. in two elegant parlors or the garden. Also available are two year-round accommodations in the elegant Cape House ($270–295).

What's old is new at **Barncastle** (125 South St., 207/374-2330, www.barncastlehotel.com, $125–175), a late-19th-century shingle-style cottage that's listed on the National Register. It opens to a two-story foyer with a split stairway and balcony. Rooms and suites open off the balcony, and all are spacious, minimally decorated, and have contemporary accents,

The Blue Hill Inn is a classic country inn.

including flat-screen TVs, Wi-Fi, fridge, and microwave. Rates include a continental breakfast. Downstairs are a games room with pool table and a tavern, serving lighter fare.

Two miles north of town, at Marcia and Jim Schatz's **Blue Hill Farm Country Inn** (Rte. 15, 207/374-5126, www.bluehillfarminn.com, $95–115), a huge refurbished barn serves as the gathering spot for guests. If the weather is lousy, you can plop down in front of the oversize woodstove and start in on cribbage or other games. Antique sleigh-runner banisters lead to the barn's seven 2nd-floor rooms—all with private baths, skylights, hooked rugs, and quilts. A wing of the farmhouse has seven more rooms with shared baths. Breakfast is generous continental. On the inn's 48 acres are well-cleared nature trails, an 18th-century cellar hole, and a duck pond. It's open year-round.

FOOD

As always, hours are listed for peak season; call to verify days and hours of operation before making a special trip.

Local Flavors

Picnic fare and pizza are available at **Merrill & Hinckley** (11 Union St., 207/374-2821, 6 A.M.–9:30 P.M. Mon.–Fri., 7 A.M.–10 P.M. Sat., 8 A.M.–9 P.M. Sun.), a quirky 150-year-old family-owned grocery and general store.

The **Blue Hill Co-op and Cafe** (4 Ellsworth Rd., Rte. 172, 207/374-2165, cafe 207/374-8999, 7 A.M.–9 P.M. daily) sells organic and natural foods. Breakfast items, sandwiches, salads, and soups—many with ethnic flavors—are available in the café.

Tucked behind North Light Books is **Blue Hill Hearth** (58 Main St., 207/610-9090, 8 A.M.–7 P.M. Mon.–Fri., 9 A.M.–3 P.M. Sat.–Sun.). The breads are outstanding, but you can also pick up ready-made sandwiches, soups, and irresistible baked goods, including 15 different types of chocolate chip cookies. Vegan options are available, and these are made using completely separate utensils.

Local gardeners, farmers, and craftspeople peddle their wares at the **Blue Hill Farmers Market** (9–11:30 A.M. Sat. and 3–5 P.M. Wed. late May–mid-Oct.). It's a particularly enduring market, well worth a visit. Demonstrations by area chefs and artists are often on the agenda. From late May to late August, the Saturday market is at the Blue Hill Fairgrounds, then it moves to the First Congregational Church. The Wednesday market is at the church.

Here's a double hit: **Bird Watcher's Store & Cafe** (37 Water St., 207/374-3740, 9 A.M.–5 P.M. Mon.–Sat.). Half the store is a café, serving baked goods, soups, salads, and sandwiches; the other half is a store catering to bird-watchers. Choose from tables inside on the water-view deck, or just take it down the street to the park.

The chowder earns raves at **The Pantry** (27 Water St., 207/374-2229, 8 A.M.–2 P.M. Mon.–Fri., 8 A.M.–2 P.M. Sat.–Sun.), a no-frills source of inexpensive meals.

Pop into **Millbrook Company** (103 Main St., 207/359-8344, 8 A.M.–7 P.M. Mon.–Thurs., 8 A.M.–8 P.M. Fri., 1–8 P.M. Sat., 1–6 P.M. Sun.) for baked goods and wonderful homemade ice creams in flavors such as blueberry pear.

Family Favorites

The first choice for families or anyone looking for a casual but very good meal is **The Blue Moose** (50 Main St., 207/374-3274, www.thebluemooserestaurant.com, 10 A.M.–3 P.M. and 5–9 P.M. Mon.–Fri., 7:30 A.M.–3 P.M. and 5–9 P.M. Sat.–Sun.), which has two menus and welcomes kids. Most choices are in the $9–21 range, reflecting pub fare and small and large portions available for most dishes. Kids' menu ranges $6–7. It's open daily for breakfast, lunch, and dinner.

Very popular with local folks is **Marlintini's Grill** (83 Mines Rd., 207/374-2500, 11:30 A.M.–9 P.M. daily, bar stays open until 1 A.M.). Inside, half is a sports bar, the other half a restaurant. You can sit in either, but the bar side can get raucous. Best bet: the screened-in porch. The menu ranges from soups, salads, and burgers to fried seafood, ribeye, and nightly homestyle specials; there's a kids' menu, too. The portions are big; the service is good; the food is okay.

Just south of town is **Barncastle** (125 South St., 207/374-2300, www.barncastlehotel.com, 11:30 A.M.–8 P.M. daily), serving a creative selection of wood-fired pizzas in three sizes, as well as sandwiches, subs, paninis, calzones, and salads, in a lovely shingle-style cottage. There are vegetarian options. Expect to wait for a table; this is one popular spot.

Fine Dining

Here's a double header: (**Arborvine** and **The Vinery** (Main St., www.arborvine.com). For a light lunch or dinner, head to The Vinery (207/374-2441, 5:30–9 P.M. Wed.–Sun.), a piano and wine bar–bistro in a beautifully renovated barn, with live music. Entrées are $7–15. If you're up for something fancier, make reservations at the Arborvine (207/374-2119, 5:30–9 P.M. Tues.–Sun. summer, Fri.–Sun. winter), a conscientiously renovated two-century-old Cape-style house with four dining areas, each with a different feel and understated decor. Most entrées are in the $26–35 range. The wine list is small but select. Chef-owner John Hikade and his wife, Beth, operate both establishments.

Beard nominee Rich Hanson, chef-owner of the popular Cleonice in Ellsworth, is bringing new life to the historic old forge building that hangs over the river downtown. The two-level **Table A Farmhouse Bistro** (66 Main St., 207/374-5677, www.farmkitchentable.com, 11:30 A.M.–9 P.M. daily, no lunch Mon.) serves a casual bistro menu upstairs ($12–28). It's a bit more formal downstairs, where the entrées begin at $22. Request a table on the porch, and you'll be serenaded by the water rushing (or, during dry spells, at least attempting to gurgle) underneath as you dine.

Seafood

For lobster, fried fish, and the area's best lobster roll, head to **The Fish Net** (Main St., 207/374-5240, 11 A.M.–8 P.M. Sun.–Thurs., until 9 P.M. Fri.–Sat.), an inexpensive mostly take-out joint on the eastern end of town.

It's not easy to find **Perry Long's Lobster Shack and Pier** (1076 Newbury Neck Rd., Surry, 207/667-1955, 10 A.M.–7 P.M. daily), but for a classic lobster shack experience, make the effort. Expect lobster, rolls, corn, chips, mussels, and clams and a few picnic tables on the water's edge. Do call first. Oh, and save room for the homemade ice cream sandwiches.

INFORMATION AND SERVICES
Information

The **Blue Hill Peninsula Chamber of Commerce** (207/374-3242, www.bluehillpeninsula.org) has information on Blue Hill and the surrounding area. You can also find information (although some is outdated) at www.bluehillme.com. One interesting feature on this site is a section on wildlife sightings.

At the **Blue Hill Public Library** (5 Parker Point Rd., 207/374-5515, www.bluehill.lib.me.us), ask to see the armored vest, which *may* have belonged to Magellan. The library also sponsors a summer lecture series.

Public Restrooms

Public buildings with restrooms are the Blue Hill Town Hall (Main Street), Blue Hill Public Library (Main Street), and Blue Hill Memorial Hospital (Water Street).

Brooklin/Brooksville/Sedgwick

Nestled near the bottom of the Blue Hill Peninsula and surrounded by Castine, Blue Hill, and Deer Isle, this often-missed area offers superb hiking, kayaking, and sailing, plus historic homes and unique shops, studios, lodgings, and personalities.

The best-known town is Brooklin (pop. 841), thanks to two magazines: the *New Yorker* and *WoodenBoat*. Wordsmiths extraordinaire E. B. and Katharine White "dropped out" to Brooklin in the 1930s and forever afterward dispatched their splendid material for the *New Yorker* from here. (The Whites' former home, a handsome colonial not open to the public, is on Route 175 in North Brooklin, 6.5 miles from the Blue Hill Falls bridge.) In 1977, *WoodenBoat* magazine moved its headquarters to Brooklin, where its 60-acre shoreside estate attracts builders and dreamers from all over the globe. Nearby Brooksville (pop. 911) drew the late Helen and Scott Nearing, whose *Living the Good Life* made them role models for back-to-the-landers. Their compound now verges on "must-see" status. Buck's Harbor, a section of Brooksville, is the setting for *One Morning in Maine*, one of Robert McCloskey's beloved children's books. Oldest of the three towns is Sedgwick (pop. 1,175, incorporated in 1789), which once included all of Brooklin and part of Brooksville. Now wedged *between* Brooklin and Brooksville, it includes the hamlet of Sargentville, the Caterpillar Hill scenic overlook, and a well-preserved complex of historic buildings. The influx of pilgrims—many of them artists bent on capturing the spirit that has proved so enticing to creative types—continues in this area.

SIGHTS
WoodenBoat Publications
On Naskeag Point Road, 1.2 miles from downtown Brooklin (Rte. 175), a small sign marks the turn to the world headquarters of the *WoodenBoat* empire (Naskeag Point Rd., Brooklin, 207/359-4651, www.woodenboat.com). Buy magazines, books, clothing, and all manner of nautical merchandise at the handsome new store, stroll the grounds, or sign up for one of the dozens of one- and two-week spring, summer, and fall courses in seamanship, navigation, boatbuilding, sailmaking, marine carving, and more. Special courses are geared to kids, women, pros, and all-thumbs neophytes; the camaraderie is legendary, and so is the cuisine. School visiting hours are 8 A.M.–5 P.M. Monday–Saturday June–October.

Historical Sights
Now used as the museum/headquarters of the Sedgwick-Brooklin Historical Society, the 1795 **Reverend Daniel Merrill House** (Rte. 172, Sedgwick, 207/359-8086, 2–4 P.M. Sun. July–Aug., or by appt., donations welcomed) was the parsonage for Sedgwick's first permanent minister. Inside the house are period furnishings, old photos, toys, and tools; a few steps away are a restored 1874 schoolhouse, an 1821 cattle pound (for corralling wandering bovines), and a hearse barn. Pick up a brochure during open hours and guide yourself around the buildings and grounds. The **Sedgwick Historic District,** crowning Town House Hill, comprises the Merrill House and its outbuildings, plus the imposing 1794 Town House and the 23-acre Rural Cemetery (the oldest headstone dates from 1798) across Route 172.

The Good Life Center
Forest Farm, home of the late Helen and Scott Nearing, is now the site of The Good Life Center (372 Harborside Rd., Harborside, 207/326-8211, www.goodlife.org). Advocates of simple living and authors of 10 books on the subject, the Nearings created a trust to perpetuate their farm and philosophy. Resident stewards lead tours (usually 1–4 P.M. Thurs.–Mon. late June–early Sept., but call ahead), $5 donation suggested. Ask about the schedule for the

Shop for all things wooden boat related at the *WoodenBoat* school's shop.

traditional Monday-night meetings (7 P.M.), featuring free programs by gardeners, philosophers, musicians, and other guest speakers. Occasional work parties, workshops, and conferences are also on the docket. The farm is on Harborside Road, just before it turns to dirt. From Route 176 in Brooksville, take Cape Rosier Road, go eight miles, passing Holbrook Islands Sanctuary. At the Grange Hall, turn right and follow the road 1.9 miles to the end. Turn left onto Harborside Road and continue 1.8 miles to Forest Farm, across from Orrs Cove.

Four Season Farm

About a mile beyond the Nearings' place is Four Season Farm (609 Weir Cove Rd., Harborside, 207/326-4455, www.fourseasonfarm.com, 1–5 P.M. Mon.–Sat., June–Sept.), the lush organic farm owned and operated by internationally renowned gardeners Eliot Coleman and Barbara Damrosch. Both have written numerous books and articles and starred in TV gardening shows. Coleman is a driving force behind the use of the word "authentic" to mean "beyond organic," demonstrating a commitment to food that is local, fresh, ripe, clean, safe, and nourishing. He's successfully pioneered a "winter harvest," developing environmentally sound and economically viable systems for extending fresh vegetable production from October through May in cold-weather climates. The farm is a treat for the eyes as well as the taste buds—you've never seen such gorgeous produce. Ask about dinners on the farm and other events. Also here is the **Cape Rosier Artist Collective,** a gallery showing works by local artisans.

Scenic Routes

No one seems to know how **Caterpillar Hill** got its name, but its reputation comes from a panoramic vista of water, hills, and blueberry barrens—with a couple of convenient picnic tables where you can stop for lunch, photos, or a ringside view of sunset and fall foliage. From the 350-foot elevation, the views take in Walker Pond, Eggemoggin Reach, Deer Isle, Swans Island, and even the Camden Hills. The signposted rest area is on Route 175/15, between Brooksville and Sargentville, next to

The Flash! In the Pans Community Steel Band performs somewhere on the peninsula nearly every Monday night.

a gallery; watch out for the blind curve when you pull off the road. If you want to explore on foot, the one-mile Cooper Farm Trail loops through the blueberry barrens and woods. From the scenic overlook, walk down to and out Cooper Farm Road to the trailhead.

Between Sargentville and Sedgwick, Route 175 offers nonstop views of Eggemoggin Reach, with shore access to the Benjamin River just before you reach Sedgwick village.

Two other scenic routes are **Naskeag Point,** in Brooklin, and **Cape Rosier,** the westernmost arm of the town of Brooksville. Naskeag Point Road begins off Route 175 in "downtown" Brooklin, heads down the peninsula for 3.7 miles past the entrance to WoodenBoat Publications, and ends at a small shingle beach (limited parking) on Eggemoggin Reach. Here you'll find picnic tables, a boat launch, a seasonal toilet, and a marker commemorating the 1778 Battle of Naskeag, when British sailors came ashore from the sloop *Gage,* burned several buildings, and were run off by a ragtag band of local settlers. Cape Rosier's roads are poorly marked, perhaps deliberately, so keep your DeLorme atlas handy. The Cape Rosier loop takes in Holbrook Island Sanctuary, Goose Falls, the hamlet of Harborside, and plenty of water and island views. Note that some roads are unpaved, but they usually are well maintained.

ENTERTAINMENT AND EVENTS
⊙ Flash! In the Pans Community Steel Band

If you're a fan of steel-band music, the Flash! In the Pans Community Steel Band (207/374-2172, www.flashinthepans.org) usually performs somewhere on the peninsula on Monday nights (7:30–9 P.M.) mid-June–early September. Local papers carry the summer schedule for the nearly three-dozen-member band, which deserves its devoted following. Admission is usually a small donation to benefit a local cause. It's worth every penny to join the fun.

Brooksville Open Mic Nights
Meet locals, savor soup and bread, and share your talents at the Tinder Hearth open mic nights (207/326-9266, www.tinderhearth.org, 5–8 P.M. Sun.), held in the barn during the warmer months. Check Tinder Hearth's website for other programs and workshops.

Eggemoggin Reach Regatta
Wooden boats are big attractions hereabouts, so when a huge fleet sails in for this regatta (usually the first Saturday in August, but the schedule can change), crowds gather. Don't miss the parade of wooden boats. The best locale for watching the regatta itself is on or near the bridge to Deer Isle or near the Eggemoggin Landing grounds on Little Deer Isle. For details, see www.erregatta.com.

SHOPPING
Most of these businesses are small, owner-operated shops, which means they're often catch as catch can. If you want to be sure, call ahead.

Antiques
When you need a slate sink, a clawfoot tub, brass fixtures, or a Palladian window, **Architectural Antiquities** (52 Indian Point La., Harborside, 207/326-4938, www.archantiquities.com), on Cape Rosier, is just the ticket—a restorer's delight. Prices are reasonable for what you get, and they'll ship your purchases. Open all year by appointment; ask for directions when you call. Antiques dating from the Federal period through the turn of the 20th century are the specialties at **Sedgwick Antiques** (775 N. Sedgwick Rd./Rte. 172, Sedgwick, 207/359-8834). Early furniture, handmade furniture, and a full range of country accessories and antiques can be found at **Thomas Hinchcliffe Antiques** (26 Cradle Knolls La., off Rte. 176, West Sedgwick, 207/326-9411). Painted country furniture, decoys, and unusual nautical items are specialties at Peg and Olney Grindall's **Old Cove Antiques** (106 Caterpillar Rd./Rte. 15, Sargentville, 207/359-2031 or 207/359-8585), a weathered-gray shop across from the Eggemoggin Country Store.

Artists' and Artisans' Galleries
Small studio-galleries pepper Route 175 (Reach Road) in Sedgwick and Brooklin; most are marked only by small signs, so watch carefully. First up is **Eggemoggin Textile Studio** (off Rte. 175/Reach Rd., Sedgwick, 207/359-5083, www.chrisleithstudio.com), where the incredibly gifted Christine Leith weaves scarves, wraps, hangings, and pillows with hand-dyed silk and wool; the colors are magnificent. You might catch her at work on the big loom in her studio shop, a real treat.

Continue along the road to find **Reach Road Gallery** (Reach Rd., Sedgwick, 207/359-8803), where Holly Meade sells her detailed woodblock prints as well as prints from the children's books she's illustrated.

Only a few doors down is **Mermaid Woolens** (Reach Rd., Sedgwick, 207/359-2747, www.mermaidwoolens.com), source of Elizabeth Coakley's wildly colorful hand knits—vests, socks, and sweaters. They're pricey but worth every nickel. She also does seascape paintings. Clever woman.

Continue over to Brooklin, where Virginia G. Sarsfield handcrafts paper products, including custom lampshades, calligraphy papers, books, and lamps, at **Handmade Papers** (Rte. 175 at Center Harbor Rd., Brooklin, 207/359-8345, www.handmadepapersonline.com). She shares the address with Ken Carpenter's **Maine Hooked Rugs** (207/359-9878, www.mainehookedrugs.com).

Just a bit farther is **Naskeag Gallery** (Rte. 175, Brooklin, 207/359-4619), where talented glass artist Sihaya Hopkins has a studio gallery.

In Brooksville, more treasures await on Route 176. You'll need to watch carefully for the sign marking the long drive to **Paul Heroux and Scott Goldberg Pottery** (2032 Coastal

E. B. WHITE: SOME WRITER

Since the mid-1940s, every child has heard of E. B. White – author of the memorable *Stuart Little*, *Charlotte's Web*, and *Trumpet of the Swan* – and every college kid for decades has been reminded to consult his *Elements of Style* – but how many realize that White and his wife, Katharine, were living not in the Big City but in the hamlet of North Brooklin, Maine? It was Brooklin that inspired Charlotte and Wilbur and Stuart, and it was Brooklin where the Whites lived very full, creative lives.

Abandoning their desks at the *New Yorker* in 1938, Elwyn Brooks White and Katharine S. White bought an idyllic saltwater farm on the Blue Hill Peninsula and moved here with their young son, Joel, who became a noted naval architect and yachtbuilder in Brooklin before his untimely death in 1997. Andy (as E. B. had been dubbed since his college days at Cornell) produced 20 books, countless essays and letters to editors, and hundreds (maybe thousands?) of "newsbreaks" – those wry clipping-and-commentary items sprinkled through each issue of the *New Yorker*. Katharine continued wielding her pencil as the magazine's standout children's-book editor, donating many of her review copies to Brooklin's Friend Memorial Library, one of her favorite "causes." (The library also has two original Garth Williams drawings from *Stuart Little*, courtesy of E. B., and a lovely garden dedicated to the Whites.) Katharine's book, *Onward and Upward in the Garden*, a collection of her *New Yorker* gardening pieces, was published in 1979, two years after her death.

Later in life, E. B. sagely addressed the young readers of his three award-winning children's books:

Are my stories true, you ask? No, they are imaginary tales, containing fantastic characters and events. In real life, a family doesn't have a child who looks like a mouse; in real life, a spider doesn't spin words in her web. In real life, a swan doesn't blow a trumpet. But real life is only one kind of life – there is also the life of the imagination. And although my stories are imaginary, I like to think that there is some truth in them, too – truth about the way people and animals feel and think and act.

E. B. White died on October 1, 1985, at the age of 86. He and Katharine and Joel left large footprints on this earth, but perhaps nowhere more so than in Brooklin.

Rd./Rte. 176, Brooksville, 207/326-9062). The small gallery is a treat for pottery fans.

Continue southwest on Route 176 and watch closely for signs for **Bagaduce Forge** (140 Ferry Rd., Brooksville, 207/326-9676); this isn't easy to find. Joseph Meltreder is both blacksmith and farrier, and his small forge, with big views, is the real thing. He turns out whimsical pieces. Especially fun are the nail people—you'll know them when you see them.

Wine and Gifts

Three varieties of English-style hard cider are specialties at **The Sow's Ear Winery** (Rte. 176 at Herrick Rd., Brooksville, 207/326-4649), a minuscule operation in a funky gray-shingled building. Winemaker Tom Hoey also produces sulfite-free blueberry, chokecherry, and rhubarb wines; he'll let you sample it all. Ask to see his cellar, where everything happens. No credit cards.

Nautical books, T-shirts, gifts, food (including homemade bread and key lime pie), and boat gear line the walls and shelves of the shop at **Buck's Harbor Marine** (on the dock, South Brooksville, 207/326-8839, www.bucksharbor.com).

PARKS, PRESERVES, AND RECREATION
Holbrook Island Sanctuary State Park
In the early 1970s, foresighted benefactor Anita Harris donated to the state 1,230 acres in Brooksville that would become the Holbrook Island Sanctuary (207/326-4012, www.state.me.us/doc/parks, free). From Route 176, between West Brooksville and South Brooksville, head west on Cape Rosier Road, following brown-and-white signs for the sanctuary. Trail maps and bird checklists are available in boxes at trailheads or at park headquarters. The easy Backshore Trail (about 30 minutes) starts here, or go back a mile and climb the steepish trail to **Backwoods Mountain** for the best vistas. Other attractions include shorefront picnic tables and grills, four old cemeteries, and super bird-watching during spring and fall migrations. Leashed pets are allowed, but no bikes on the trails and no camping. Officially open May 15–October 15, but the access road and parking areas are plowed for cross-country skiers.

Swimming
A small, relatively little-known beach is Brooklin's **Pooduck Beach**. From the Brooklin General Store (Route 175), take Naskeag Point Road about half a mile, watching for the Pooduck Road sign on the right. Turn right and drive to the end. You can also launch a sea kayak into Eggemoggin Reach here.

Bicycling
Bicycling in this area is hazardous. Roads here are particularly narrow and winding, with poor shoulders. If you're determined to pedal, consider either the Naskeag scenic route or around Cape Rosier, where traffic is light.

Sailing
Captain LeCain Smith sails *Perelandra* (Buck's Harbor, 207/326-4279), a 44-foot steel-hulled ketch, in the waters of Penobscot Bay. Rates begin at $40 per person for a two-hour sail and increase to $100 per person for a full day. The boat holds a maximum of six passengers.

Ensign-class Antares day sailboats are available for rental at **Buck's Harbor Marine** (on the dock, South Brooksville, 207/326-8839, www.bucksharbor.com). The full-keel boats rent for $135 per day. Buck's Harbor also charters bareboat sail and power yachts to qualified skippers.

Picnicking
You can take a picnic to the **Bagaduce Ferry Landing,** in West Brooksville off Route 176, where there are picnic tables and cross-river vistas toward Castine.

ACCOMMODATIONS
Cottage Colony
The fourth generation manages the **Hiram Blake Camp** (220 Weir Cove Rd., Harborside, 207/326-4951, www.hiramblake.com, Memorial Day–late Sept.), but other generations pitch in and help with gardening, lobstering, maintenance, and kibitzing. Thirteen cottages and a duplex line the shore of this 100-acre property, which has been in family hands since before the Revolutionary War. The camp itself dates from 1916. Don't bother bringing reading material: The dining room has ingenious ceiling niches lined with countless books. Guests also have the use of rowboats. The rate includes home-cooked breakfasts and dinners served family style; lobster is always available at an additional charge. Much of the fare is grown in the expansive gardens. Other facilities include a dock, a recreation room, a pebble beach, and an outdoor chapel. There's a one-week minimum (beginning Sat. or Sun.) in July and August, when cottages go for $600–2,850 a week (including breakfast, dinner, and linens). Off-season rates (no meals or linens, but cottages have cooking facilities) are $630–895 a week. The best chances for getting a reservation are in June and September. Dogs are welcome. No credit cards accepted.

Bed-and-Breakfasts
The **Dragonflye Inn** (Naskeag Point Rd.,

Brooklin, 207/359-808, www.dragonflyinn.com, $175), an 1874 mansard-roofed Victorian in what passes as downtown Brooklin, is a casual put-your-feet-up kind of place, with a special invitation issued to WoodenBoat school students, gallery fans (lots of work by local artisans), and kayakers. Owner Joe Moore's goal is sustainability: Towels and linens are made from organic cotton; soaps and shampoos are local and all natural; cleaning products are all natural, biodegradable, and earth friendly. Breakfast is light continental.

Best known for its restaurant and pub, **The Brooklin Inn** (Rte. 175, Brooklin, 207/359-2777, www.brooklininn.com, $105–135 with breakfast; add $10 for a one-night stay) also has five comfortable bedrooms; two share a bath. It's open year-round.

FOOD

As always, hours are listed for peak season; call to verify days and hours of operation.

Cooking Classes

In summer, chef Terence Janericco (617/426-7458, or, after July 1, 207/359-2068, www.terencejanericcocookingclasses.com), author of a dozen cookbooks, moves his cooking school from Boston to Brooklin. The demonstration-only three-hour classes are $70 per person, which includes dining on the foods prepared.

Local Flavors

Competition is stiff for lunchtime seats at the **Morning Moon Cafe** (junction of Rte. 175 and Naskeag Point Rd., Brooklin, 207/359-2373, 7 A.M.–2 P.M. Thurs.–Sun.), mostly because WoodenBoat staffers consider it an annex to their offices. "The Moon" is a friendly hangout for coffee, pizza, or great sandwiches and salads.

Across the street from the Morning Moon Cafe, the **Brooklin General Store** (1 Reach Rd., junction of Rte. 175 and Naskeag Point Rd., Brooklin, 207/359-8817, 5 A.M.–7 P.M. Mon.–Sat., 7 A.M.–5 P.M. Sun.), vintage 1872, carries groceries, beer and wine, newspapers, take-out sandwiches, and local chatter.

In North Brooksville, where Route 175/176 crosses the Bagaduce River, stands the **Bagaduce Lunch,** named an "American Classic" by the James Beard Foundation in 2008. Owners Judy and Mike Astbury buy local fish and clams. Check the tide calendar and go when the tide is changing; order a clam roll or a hamburger, settle in at a picnic table, and watch the reversing falls. If you're lucky, you might sight an eagle, osprey, or seal. The food is so-so, but the setting is tops. The popular takeout stand (outdoor tables only) is open 11 A.M.–7 or 8 P.M. daily, but closes at 3 P.M. Wednesday, from early May to mid-September.

Lunch is the specialty at **Buck's Harbor Market** (Rte. 176, South Brooksville, 207/326-8683, 7 A.M.–7 P.M. Mon.–Fri., 8 A.M.–7:30 P.M. Sat., 8 A.M.–6 P.M. Sun., year-round), a low-key, marginally yuppified general store popular with yachties in summer.

Ethnic Fare

El El Frijoles (41 Caterpillar Rd./Rte. 15, Sargentville, 207/359-2486, www.elelfrijoles.com, 11 A.M.–8 P.M. Wed.–Sun.) gets good marks for its California-style empanadas, burritos, and tacos. It's a small, somewhat funky operation housed in a barn behind Coast to Coast Fine Arts.

Casual Dining

Behind the Buck's Harbor Market is **Buck's Restaurant** (6 Cornfield Hill Rd., Brooksville, 207/326-8688, 5:30–8:30 P.M. daily, $15–24), an outpost of fiery colors calmed down by white tablecloths. Respected chefs Jonathan Chase and Nancy McMillan create comfort foods with a dash of creativity.

All the meat and produce is organic and most is sourced locally at **The Brooklin Inn** (Rte. 175, Brooklin, 207/359-2777, www.brooklininn.com, 5:30–9 P.M. daily, $19–40). The chef tries to know "who raised, grew, picked, or caught all the food," and all the fish are wild, free swimming, and locally caught. A children's menu is available.

Downstairs an **Irish pub** (5:30–10 P.M. daily) serves burgers, Guinness stew, pizza, and, on Fridays, all the fresh baked haddock you can eat for $10.

Country Inn Dining
The chef seems to change annually at **The Lookout** (455 Flye Point Rd., off Rte. 175, North Brooklin, 207/359-2188, www.thelookoutinn.biz, 5:30–8 P.M. Wed.–Sun., $18–24). The inn and restaurant, at the tip of Flye Point, have a knockout view of Herrick Bay (as long as there's no fog). It's been owned and operated by Flye family descendants for more than 110 years (judging from the look of the place, little has changed in that period); ask around about its current reputation.

INFORMATION AND SERVICES
The best source of information about the region is the **Blue Hill Peninsula Chamber of Commerce** (207/374-2281, www.bluehillpeninsula.org).

Libraries
Friends Memorial Library (Rte. 175, Brooklin, 207/359-2276) has a lovely Circle of Friends Garden, with benches and a brick patio. It's dedicated to the memory of longtime Brooklin residents E. B. and Katharine White. Also check out **Free Public Library** (1 Town House Rd., Rte. 176, Brooksville, 207/326-4560) and Sedgwick Village Library (Main St., Sedgwick, 207/359-2177).

Castine

Castine (pop. 1,343) is a gem—a serene New England village with a tumultuous past. It tips a cape, surrounded by water on three sides, including the entrance to the Penobscot River, which made it a strategic defense point. Once beset by geopolitical squabbles, saluting the flags of three different nations (France, Britain, and Holland), its only crises now are local political skirmishes. This is an unusual community, a National Historic Register enclave that many people never find. The town celebrated its bicentennial in 1996. Today a major presence is Maine Maritime Academy, yet Castine remains the quietest imaginable college town. Students in search of a party school won't find it here; naval engineering is serious business.

What visitors discover is a year-round community with a busy waterfront, an easy-to-conquer layout, a handful of traditional inns, wooded trails on the outskirts of town, an astonishing collection of splendid Georgian and Federalist architecture, and water views nearly every which way you turn. If you're staying in Blue Hill or even Bar Harbor, spend a day here. Or book a room in one of the town's lovely inns, and use Castine as a base for exploring here and beyond. Either way, you won't regret it.

HISTORY
Originally known as Fort Pentagoet, Castine received its current name courtesy of Jean-Vincent d'Abbadie, Baron de St.-Castin. A young French nobleman manqué who married a Wabanaki princess named Pidiwamiska, d'Abbadie ran the town in the second half of the 17th century and eventually returned to France.

A century later, in 1779, occupying British troops and their reinforcements scared off potential American seaborne attackers (including Colonel Paul Revere), who turned tail up the Penobscot River and ended up scuttling their more than 40-vessel fleet—a humiliation known as the Penobscot Expedition and still regarded as one of America's worst naval defeats.

When the boundaries for Maine were finally set in 1820, with the St. Croix River marking the east rather than the Penobscot River, the last British Loyalists departed, some floating their homes north to St. Andrews, in New Brunswick, Canada, where they can still be seen today. For a while, peace and prosperity became the bywords for Castine—with lively commerce in fish and salt—but it all collapsed during the California Gold Rush and the Civil War trade embargo, leaving the town down on its luck.

Of the many historical landmarks scattered around town, one of the most intriguing must be the sign on "Wind Mill Hill," at the junction of Route 166 and State Street:

On Hatch's Hill there stands a mill. Old Higgins he doth tend it. And every time he grinds a grist, he has to stop and mend it.

In smaller print, just below the rhyme, comes the drama:

Here two British soldiers were shot for desertion.

Castine has quite a history indeed.

SIGHTS
Castine Historic Tour

To appreciate Castine fully, you need to arm yourself with the Castine Merchants Association's visitors brochure-map (all businesses and lodgings in town have copies) and follow the numbers on bike or on foot. With no stops, walking the route takes less than an hour, but you'll want to read dozens of historical plaques, peek into public buildings, shoot some photos, and perhaps even do some shopping.

Highlights of the tour include the late-18th-century **John Perkins House,** moved to Perkins Street from Court Street in 1969 and restored with period furnishings. It's open in July and August for guided tours (2–5 P.M. Sun. and Wed., $5).

Next door, **The Wilson Museum** (107 Perkins St., 207/326-8545, www.wilsonmuseum.org, 2–5 P.M. Tues.–Sun. late May–late Sept., free), founded in 1921, contains an intriguingly eclectic two-story collection of prehistoric artifacts, ship models, dioramas,

You can tour the John Perkins House, which is adjacent to the Wilson Museum.

baskets, tools, and minerals assembled over a lifetime by John Howard Wilson, a geologist-anthropologist who first visited Castine in 1891 (and died in 1936). Among the exhibits are Balinese masks, ancient oil lamps, cuneiform tablets, Zulu artifacts, pre-Inca pottery, and assorted local findings.

Open the same days and hours as the Perkins House are the **Blacksmith Shop,** where a smith does demonstrations, and the **Hearse House,** containing Castine's 19th-century winter and summer funeral vehicles. Both have free admission.

At the end of Battle Avenue stands the 19th-century **Dyce's Head Lighthouse,** no longer operating; the keeper's house is owned by the town. Alongside it is a public path (signposted; pass at your own risk) leading via a wooden staircase to a tiny patch of rocky shoreline and the beacon that has replaced the lighthouse.

The highest point in town is **Fort George State Park,** site of a 1779 British fortification. Nowadays, little remains except grassy earthworks, but there are interpretive displays and picnic tables.

Main Street, descending toward the water, is a feast for historic architecture fans. Artist Fitz Hugh Lane and author Mary McCarthy once lived in elegant houses along the elm-lined street (neither building is open to the public). On Court Street between Main and Green stands turn-of-the-20th-century **Emerson Hall,** site of Castine's municipal offices. Since Castine has no official information booth, you may need to duck in here (it's open weekdays) for answers to questions.

Across Court Street, **Witherle Memorial Library,** a handsome early-19th-century building on the site of the 18th-century town jail, looks out on the Town Common. Also facing the Common are the Adams and Abbott Schools, the former still an elementary school. The **Abbott School** (10 A.M.–4 P.M. Tues.–Sat., 1–4 P.M. Sun. July–Labor Day, reduced schedule spring and fall, free but donations welcome), built in 1859, has been carefully restored for use as a museum and headquarters for the **Castine Historical Society**

MAINE MARITIME ACADEMY

The state's only merchant-marine college (and one of only seven in the nation) occupies 35 acres in the middle of Castine. Founded in 1941, the academy awards undergraduate and graduate degrees in such areas as marine engineering, ocean studies, and marina management, preparing a student body of about 750 men and women for careers as ship captains, Naval architects, and marine engineers.

The academy owns a fleet of 60 vessels, including the historic research schooner *Bowdoin*, flagship of Arctic explorer Admiral Donald MacMillan, and the 499-foot training vessel *State of Maine*, berthed down the hill at the waterfront. In 1996 and 1997, the *State of Maine*, formerly the U.S. Navy hydrographic survey ship *Tanner*, underwent a $12 million conversion for use by the academy. It is still subject to deployment, and, in 2005, the school had to quickly find alternative beds for students using the ship as a dormitory when it was called into service in support of rescue and rebuilding efforts after Hurricane Katrina in New Orleans. Midshipmen conduct free 30 minute tours of the vessel on weekdays in summer (about mid-July to late August). The schedule is posted at the dock, or call 207/326-4311 to check; photo ID is required.

Weekday tours of the campus can be arranged through the admissions office (207/326-2206 or 800/227-8465 outside Maine, www.mainemaritime.edu). Campus highlights include the three-story Nutting Memorial Library in Platz Hall (open daily during the school year, weekdays in summer and during vacations); the Henry A. Scheel Room, a cozy oasis in Leavitt Hall containing memorabilia from late Naval architect Henry Scheel and his wife, Jeanne; and the well-stocked bookstore (Curtis Hall, 207/326-9333, 8 A.M.–3 P.M. Mon.–Fri.).

(207/326-4118, www.castinehistoricalsociety. org). A big draw at the volunteer-run museum is the 24-foot-long Bicentennial Quilt, assembled for Castine's 200th anniversary in 1996. The historical society, founded in 1966, organizes lectures, exhibits, and special events (some free) in various places around town.

On the outskirts of town, across the narrow neck between Wadsworth Cove and Hatch's Cove, stretches a rather overgrown canal (signposted "British Canal") scooped out by the occupying British during the War of 1812. Effectively severing land access to the town of Castine, the Brits thus raised havoc, collected local revenues for eight months, then departed for Halifax with enough funds to establish Dalhousie College (now Dalhousie University). Wear waterproof boots to walk the canal route; the best time to go is at low tide.

If a waterfront picnic sounds appealing, buy the fixings at Bah's Bakehouse and settle in on the grassy earthworks along the harborfront at **Fort Madison,** site of an 1808 garrison (then Fort Porter) near the corner of Perkins and Madockawando Streets. The views from here are fabulous, and it's accessible all year. A set of stairs leads down to the rocky waterfront.

ENTERTAINMENT AND EVENTS

Possibilities for live music include **Dennett's Wharf** (15 Sea St., 207/326-9045), where some performances require a ticket, and **The Reef** (on the wharf, tucked underneath the bank facing the parking area and harbor).

The Castine Town Band often performs free concerts on the Common. Check www.castine.org for its schedule.

The community-based **Castine Arts Association** (www.castinearts.org) presents concerts, exhibits, workshops, and other performances at various locations around town each summer.

The Wilson Museum (107 Perkins St., 207/326-8545, www.wilsonmuseum.org) frequently schedules concerts, lectures, and demonstrations.

The Trinitarian Church often brings in high-caliber musical entertainment.

Celebrate Castine (www.celebratecastine.com) is a town-wide event in mid-July.

SHOPPING
Antiques and Galleries

Tucked into the back of the 1796 Parson Mason House, one of Castine's oldest residences, **Leila Day Antiques** (53 Main St., 207/326-8786, www.leiladayantiques.com) is a must for anyone in the market for folk art, period furniture, and quilts.

Traditional American craftwork is sold at **Castine Historical Handworks** (9 Main St., Castine, 207/326-4460, www.castinehistoricalhandworks.com).

Oil paintings by local artists Joshua and Susan Adam are on view at **Adam Gallery** (140 Battle Ave., 207/326-8272, www.adamgalleryonline.com).

Books

Driving toward Castine on Route 166, watch on your right for a small sign for **Dolphin Books and Prints** (314 Castine Rd., 207/326-0888, www.dolphin-book.com), where Pete and Liz Ballou have set up their antiquarian business with more than 10,000 books as well as framed prints and art.

In downtown Castine, a block up from the waterfront, **The Compass Rose Bookstore and Café** (3 Main St., 207/326-9366 or 800/698-9366, www.compassrosebooks.com) carries an ever-expanding selection of new books, cards, games, and prints chosen by owner Sharon Biggie. In the back of the shop is a café serving hot and cold drinks (espresso, too), soup, sandwiches, and tasty baked goods.

Furniture

Bench-made Windsor chairs are the specialty at **M&E Gummel Chairworks** (600 Shore Rd., 207/326-8122, www.gummelchairworks.com). The father-and-son team use 18th-century methods when handcrafting the chairs, colonial dining tables, and bowls, one at a time in their late-19th-century barn workshop.

RECREATION
Witherle Woods
This 152-acre preserve, owned by Maine Coast Heritage Trust (maps available via email from info@mcht.org), is a popular walking area with a maze of trails and old woods roads leading to the water. Many Revolutionary War–era relics have been found here; if you see any, do *not* remove them. Access to the preserve is via a shaded old woods road on Battle Avenue, located between the water district property (at the end of the wire fence) and the Manor's exit driveway and diagonally across from La Tour Street.

C Sea Kayaking
Right near Dennett's Wharf is **Castine Kayak Adventures** (17 Sea St., 207/326-9045, www.castinekayak.com), spearheaded by Maine Guide Karen Francoeur. All skill levels are accommodated; "Kayak Karen," as she's known locally, is particularly adept with beginners, delivering wise advice from beginning to end. Three-hour half-day trips are $55; six-hour full-day tours are around $105 including lunch. Two-hour sunset tours are $40; the sunrise tour includes a light breakfast for $55. Friday nights, there are special two-hour phosphorescence tours, under the stars (weather permitting), for $55 per person. Longer trips are available for $150 per day. If you have your own boat, call Karen for advice; she knows these waters. She also offers instruction for all levels as well as a Maine Sea Kayak Guide course.

Swimming
Backshore Beach, a crescent of sand and gravel on Wadsworth Cove Road (turn off Battle Avenue at the Castine Golf Club), is a favorite saltwater swimming spot, with views across the bay to Stockton Springs. Be forewarned, though, that ocean swimming in this part of Maine is not for the timid. The best

Kayaking provides a different perspective on Castine's harbor.

time to try it is on the incoming tide, after the sun has had time to heat up the mud. At mid- to high tide, it's also the best place to put in a sea kayak.

Golf
The nine-hole **Castine Golf Club** (200 Battle Ave., 207/326-8844, www.castinegolfclub.com) dates to 1897, when the first tee required a drive from a 30-step-high mound. It was redesigned in 1921 by Willie Park Jr.

EXCURSION BOATS
Glide over Penobscot Bay aboard the wooden motorsailor **Guildive** (207/701-1421, www.guildivecruises.com), captained by Kata Kana and Zander Parker. The two-hour sails coast $30–35 adults, $25 children under 12, and depart Dennett's Wharf four times daily, including a sunset BYOB cocktail cruise.

Several times weekly, Captain Melissa Terry's **Belfast Bay Cruises** (207/322-5530, www.belfastbaycruises.com, $15 adults, $6 children 5–15) offers a one-hour Castine Harbor Tour aboard the *Good Return*, passing by Dyce's Head Lighthouse and Holbrook and Nautilus Islands. Also ask about a day trip to Belfast ($30 adult, $17 children).

ACCOMMODATIONS
Inns

Castine is blessed with three fine traditional inns. This is not the place to come if you require in-room phones, air-conditioning, or fancy bathrooms. Rather, the pace is relaxed and the accommodations reflect the easy elegance of a bygone era.

The three-story Queen Anne–style **Pentagöet Inn** (26 Main St., 207/326-8616 or 800/845-1701, www.pentagoet.com, May–late Oct., $115–245 peak) is the perfect Maine summer inn, right down to the lace curtains billowing in the breeze, the soft floral wallpapers, and the intriguing curiosities that accent, but don't clutter, the rooms. Congenial innkeepers Jack Burke, previously with the foreign service, and Julie Van de Graaf, a pastry chef, took over the century-old inn in 2000 and have given it new life, upgrading rooms and furnishing them with Victorian antiques, adding handsome gardens, and carving out a niche as a dining destination. Their enthusiasm for the area is contagious. The inn's 16 rooms are spread out between the main house (with Wi-Fi service) and the adjoining house. A hot buffet breakfast and afternoon refreshments are provided. Jack holds court in Passports Pub (chock-full of vintage photos and prints and exotic antiques) every afternoon, advising guests on activities and opportunities. Borrow one of the inn's bikes and explore around town or simply walk—the Main Street location is convenient to everything Castine offers. Better yet, just sit on the wraparound porch and take it all in.

Once the summer "cottage" of Arthur Fuller, a South Boston Yacht Club commodore, **The Manor Inn** (Battle Ave., 207/326-4861 or 877/626-6746, www.manor-inn.com, $115–275) overlooks town and harbor from

The yellow Victorian Pentagöet Inn stands out in a town of white houses.

five mostly wooded acres elevated above Battle Avenue. Though the atmosphere is informal, there are lots of elegant architectural touches. Nancy Watson and Tom Ehrman, innkeepers here since 1998, continue to improve the inn each year. The 14 2nd- and 3rd-floor rooms are an eclectic mix: Some have canopied beds and fireplaces, some are especially family friendly. A separate guest building has a TV and games as well as Nancy's yoga studio; guests are welcome to join her morning Iyengar classes (Mon., Wed., Fri., $12 drop-ins). Wi-Fi is available. The trailhead for Witherle Woods is close by. The inn is often the site of weddings and receptions; ask before you book unless you don't mind being the odd man out. It's open mid-February–late December. Well-behaved pets are $25 per stay.

FOOD

As always, hours are listed for peak season; call to verify days and hours of operation.

Local Flavors

Since 1920, locals have been buying lunch and ice cream at **Castine Variety** (1 Main St., 207/326-8625, 7 A.M.–8 P.M.). Go for the vintage feeling and the inexpensive breakfasts, lunches, and ice cream.

Another institution is ◖ **The Breeze** (Town Dock, 207/326-9200, 9 A.M.–7 P.M. daily), a waterfront takeout stand with reliably good basics like burgers, fried clams, and ice cream. You can't beat the location or the view.

When everything else in town is closed, your best bet for late-night eats is **The Reef** (8 Sea St., on the wharf, tucked underneath the bank facing the parking area and harbor, 207/326-4040, 11 A.M.–1 A.M. daily). The hand-tossed gourmet pizzas are available in three sizes. There are plenty of pub-style favorites, too. The atmosphere is more bar than restaurant, with a pool table in the back and a small stage area for live entertainment.

Casual Dining

Here's a doubleheader: **Bah's Bakehouse** (26 Water St., 207/326-9510, www.bahsworld.com, 7 A.M.–3 P.M. daily) and, sharing the same location, **Stella's Jazz Nocturnal** (207/326-9710, 5:30–11 P.M. Tues.–Sun., food service to 10 P.M.). Upstairs is Bah's, a higgledy-piggledy eatery of three rooms and a deck at the end of an alleyway tucked between Main and Water Streets. Its slogan is "creative flour arrangements," and creative it is. Stop here for coffee, cold juices, pastries, interesting snacks and salads, homemade soups, wine or beer, good sandwiches, and, if you're lucky, fish cakes. Be forewarned: If it's crowded, go elsewhere—the kitchen is quickly overwhelmed and service can be slow to frustrating. Underneath the deck is Stella's ($9–18), an intimate dining room and lounge where live jazz is performed Thursday through Sunday.

On a warm summer day, it's hard to find a better place to while away a few hours than **Dennett's Wharf** (15 Sea St., 207/326-9045, www.dennettswharf.com, 11 A.M.–midnight daily, May–Columbus Day), and that's likely what you'll do here, as service can be slow. Next to the town dock, it's a colorful barn of

Dennett's Wharf hangs over Castine Harbor and is a good spot for a brew and a burger.

a place with outside deck and front-row windjammer-watching seats in summer. Best advice is to keep your order simple.

The Pine Cone Pub at the Manor Inn (76 Battle Ave., 207/326-4861, from 5 A.M. Tues.–Sat.) serves a light menu, with such choices as Caesar salad and fish-and-chips.

Fine Dining

Jazz music plays softly and dinner is by candlelight at the ◖ **Pentagoet** (26 Main St., 207/326-8616 or 800/845-1701, www.pentagoet.com, opens at 6 P.M. Tues.–Sat.). In fine weather, you can dine on the porch. Choices vary from roasted *loup de mer* to slow-cooked lamb shank, or simply make a meal of small plates, such as lamb lollipops and crab cakes and a salad. Don't miss the lobster bouillabaisse or the chocolate *budino,* a scrumptious warm Italian pudding that melts in your mouth (a must for chocoholics). Most entrées are in the $18–29 range.

The bi-level dining room at **The Manor Inn** (76 Battle Ave., 207/326-4861, 6–8:30 P.M. Tues.–Sat. in summer, Thurs.–Sat. off-season) overlooks the gardens and lawn. Dinner is served from an extensive menu accented with Asian tastes, Indian curries, and other world flavors, accompanied by home-baked breads, and always including vegetarian choices (most entrées $16–24). Reservations are essential on weekends. It's open from Valentine's Day to late December.

INFORMATION AND SERVICES

Castine has no local information office, but all businesses and lodgings in town have copies of the Castine Merchants Association's visitors brochure-map. For additional information, go to the **Castine Town Office** (Emerson Hall, 67 Court St., 207/326-4502, www.castine.me.us, 8 A.M.–3:30 P.M. Mon.–Fri.).

Libraries

Check out **Witherle Memorial Library** (41 School St., 207/326-4375, www.witherle.lib.me.us). Also accessible to the public is the Nutting Memorial Library, in Platz Hall on the Maine Maritime Academy campus.

Public Restrooms

Castine has public restrooms on the town dock, at the foot of Main Street.

Deer Isle

"Deer Isle is like Avalon," wrote John Steinbeck in *Travels with Charley*—"it must disappear when you are not there." Deer Isle (the name of both the island and its midpoint town) has been romancing authors and artisans for decades, but it's unmistakably real to the quarrymen and fishermen who've been here for centuries. These long-timers are a sturdy lot, as even Steinbeck recognized: "I would hate to try to force them to do anything they didn't want to do."

Early-18th-century maps show no name for the island, but by the late 1800s, nearly 100 families lived here, supporting themselves first by farming, then by fishing. In 1789, when Deer Isle was incorporated, 80 local sailing vessels were scouring the Gulf of Maine in pursuit of mackerel and cod, and Deer Isle men were circling the globe as yachting skippers and merchant seamen. At the same time, in the once-quiet village of Green's Landing (now called Stonington), the shipbuilding and granite industries boomed, spurring development, prosperity, and the kinds of rough hijinks typical of commercial ports the world over.

Green's Landing became the "big city" for an international crowd of quarrymen carving out the terrain on Deer Isle and nearby Crotch Island, source of high-quality granite for Boston's Museum of Fine Arts, the Smithsonian Institution, a humongous fountain for John D. Rockefeller's New York

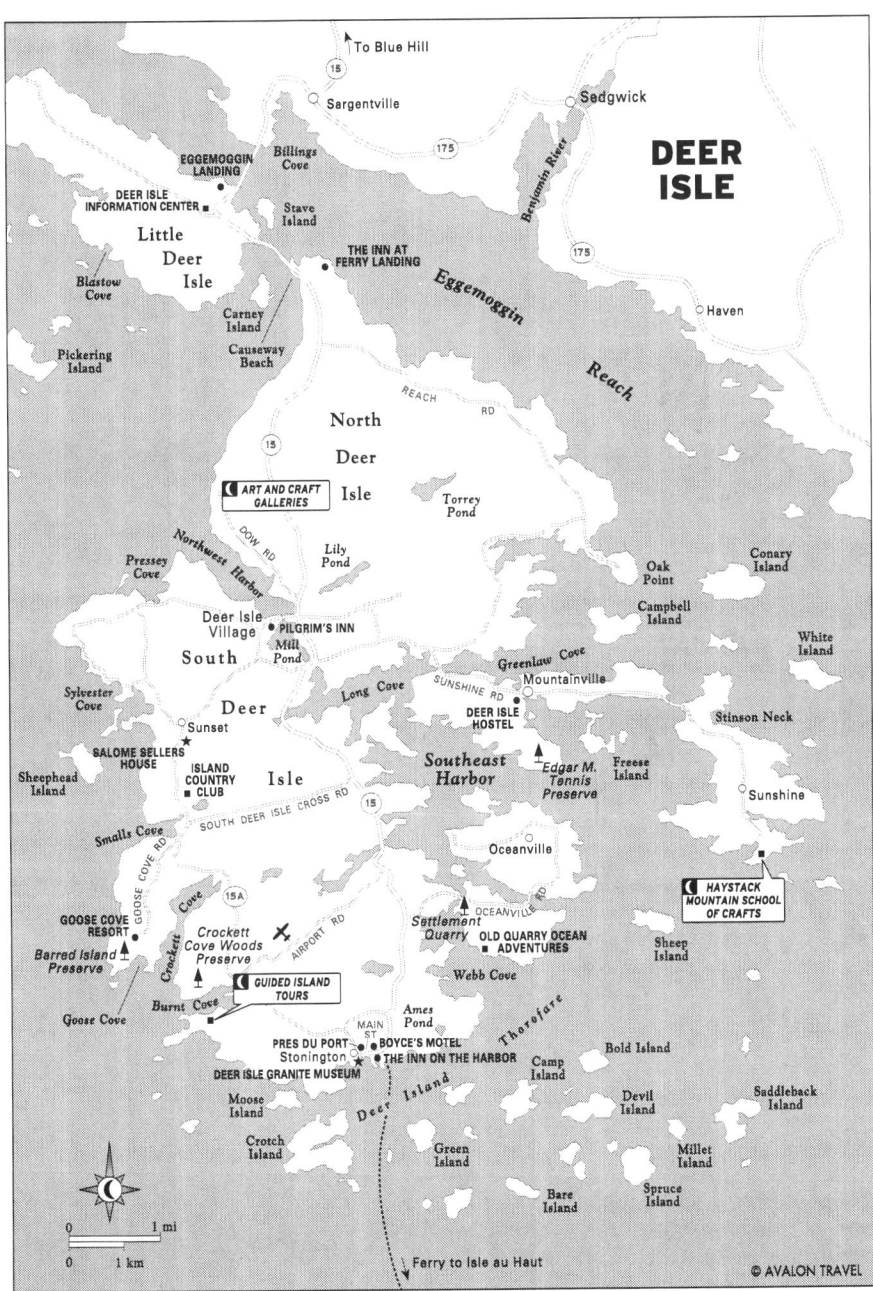

THE MAINE ISLAND TRAIL

In the early 1980s, a "trail" of coastal Maine islands was only the germ of an idea. By the end of the millennium, the **Maine Island Trail Association** (MITA, 207/596-6456, www.mita.org) counted some 4,000 members dedicated to conscientious (i.e., low- or no-impact) recreational use of about 150 public and private islands along 350 miles of Maine coastline between Kennebunkport and Machias, and it continues to grow.

More than a dozen of these islands (each year new ones are added and others are subtracted) are in the Acadia region – between Isle au Haut and Schoodic Point. In fact, one of the best island clusters along the entire trail is in the waters off Stonington on Deer Isle.

Access to the trail is only by private boat, and the best choice is a sea kayak, to navigate shallow or rock-strewn coves. Sea kayak rentals are available in Bar Harbor, Southwest Harbor, Blue Hill, Castine, and Stonington, and several outfitters offer island tours. The best source of information is the Maine Association of Sea Kayaking Guides and Instructors (MASKGI), whose members agree to adhere to the Leave No Trace philosophy.

The trail's publicly owned islands – supervised by the state Bureau of Public Lands – are open to anyone; the private islands are restricted to MITA members, who pay $45 per individual or $65 per family annually for the privilege (and, it's important to add, the responsibility). With the fee comes the *Maine Island Trail Guidebook,* providing directions and information for each of the islands. With membership comes the expectation of care and concern. "Low impact" means different things to different people, so MITA experienced acute growing pains when enthusiasm began leading to "tent sprawl."

To cope with and reverse the overuse, MITA has created an "adopt-an-island" program, in which volunteers become stewards for specific islands and keep track of their use and condition. MITA members are urged to pick up trash, use tent platforms where they exist, and move on if an island has already reached its assigned capacity (stipulated on a shoreline sign and/or in the guidebook).

A superb complement to the *Maine Island Trail Guidebook* is a copy of *Hot Showers!* by Lee Bumsted, a former MITA staff member. Recognizing the need for alternating island camping and warm beds (and hot showers), Bumsted has almost single-handedly alleviated island stress and strain. Some of the bed-and-breakfasts and inns listed in her guide give discounts to MITA members.

---

estate, and less showy projects all along the Eastern Seaboard. The heyday is long past, but the industry did extend into the 20th century (including a contract for the pink granite at President John F. Kennedy's Arlington National Cemetery gravesite). Today, Crotch Island is the site of Maine's only operating island granite quarry.

Measuring about nine miles north to south (plus another three miles for Little Deer Isle), the island of Deer Isle today has a handful of hamlets (including **Sunshine, Sunset, Mountainville,** and **Oceanville**) and two towns—**Stonington** and **Deer Isle**—with a population just under 3,000. Road access is via Route 15 on the Blue Hill Peninsula. A huge suspension bridge, built in 1939 over Eggemoggin Reach, links the Sargentville section of Sedgwick with Little Deer Isle; from there, a sinuous 0.4-mile causeway connects to the northern tip of Deer Isle.

Deer Isle remains an artisans' enclave, anchored by the Haystack Mountain School of Crafts. Studios and galleries are plentiful, although many require noodling along back roads to find them. Stonington, a rough-and-tumble fishing port with an idyllic setting, is slowly being gentrified, as each season more and more galleries and upscale shops open for the summer. Locals are holding their collective breaths, hoping that any improvements don't change the town too much (although most visitors could do without the car racing on Main Street at night). Already, real-estate prices and accompanying taxes have escalated way past the point where many a local fisherman can hope to buy, and in some cases maintain, a home.

SIGHTS

Sightseeing on Deer Isle means exploring back roads, browsing the galleries, walking the trails, hanging out on the docks, and soaking in the ambience.

◖ Haystack Mountain School of Crafts

The renowned Haystack Mountain School of Crafts (Sunshine Rd., Deer Isle, 207/348-2306, www.haystack-mtn.org) in Sunshine is open to the public on a limited basis, but if it fits in your schedule, go. Anyone can visit the school store or walk down the central stairs to the water; to see more of the campus, take a tour (1 P.M. Wed., $5), which includes a video, viewing works on display, and the opportunity to visit some studios. Beyond that, there are slide programs, lectures, demonstrations, and concerts, presented by faculty and visiting artists, starting at 8 P.M. on varying weeknights from early June to late August. Perhaps the best opportunities are the End-of-Session auctions, held on Thursday nights every two or three weeks, when you can tour the studios for free 4–6 P.M. and view the works the teachers and students have produced, then return for the auction preview at 7:30 P.M., followed by the auction at 8 P.M. It's a great opportunity to buy craftwork at often very reasonable prices.

Historic Houses and Museums

There's more to the 1830 **Salome Sellers House** (416 Sunset Rd./Rte. 15A, Sunset Village, 207/348-2897, 1–4 P.M. Wed. and Fri. July–early Sept., free but donations appreciated) than first meets the eye. A repository of local memorabilia, archives, and intriguing artifacts, it's also the headquarters of the **Deer**

Architect Edward Larrabee Barnes designed the oceanfront Haystack Mountain School of Crafts on Deer Isle.

GETTING CRAFTY

Internationally famed artisans – sculptors and papermakers, weavers and jewelers, potters and printmakers – become the faculty each summer for the unique **Haystack Mountain School of Crafts.** Founded in 1950 by Mary Beasom Bishop (1885-1972) and a group of talented Maine artisans as a studio research and study program, Haystack has grown into one of the top craft schools in the country.

Under the direction of beloved former director Francis Merritt, the school opened its first campus near Haystack Mountain, in Montville, Maine, in 1951. Ten years later, when the state unveiled plans to build a new highway (Route 3) that would bisect that campus, the school moved to its present 40-acre oceanfront location at the end of the Sunshine Road in Deer Isle. Good move.

You would be hard-pressed to find a more artistically stimulating and architecturally stunning environment. Architect Edward Larrabee Barnes's award-winning campus perfectly complements its dramatic setting. The angular cedar-shingled buildings are connected via walkways and teaching decks and a central staircase that cascades like a waterfall down the wooded hillside to the rocky coast below. The visual impression is one of spruce and ledge, glass and wood, islands and water.

One thing that makes Haystack work is its diverse student body. Students of all abilities, from beginners through advanced professionals, come from around the globe for the two- to three-week summer sessions, taking weekday classes and enjoying round-the-clock studio access to follow their creative muses. In a recent year, students ranged in age from 18 to 75, and in professions from a retired teacher to a physicist. What brings them all here, says current director Stuart Kestenbaum, is the "direct making experience." That experience draws not only those who make but also those who collect. For a collector of fine craft, he says, taking a class is a "great way to get insight into the making process; it gives a different relationship with the craft being collected." Each session also includes a range of crafts. These may include blacksmithing, drawing, metals, wood, beads, clay, fibers, printmaking, glass, weaving, mixed media, paper, and baskets.

Isle-Stonington Historical Society. Sellers, matriarch of an island family, was a direct descendent of Mayflower settlers. She lived to be 108, a lifetime spanning from 1800 to 1908, earning the record for oldest recorded Maine resident. The house contains Sellers's furnishings, and in a small exhibit space in the rear is a fine exhibit of baskets made by Maine's Native American tribes. Behind the house are the archives, heritage gardens, and an exhibit hall filled with nautical artifacts. Bringing all this to life are enthusiastic volunteer guides, many of them island natives. They love to provide tidbits about various items; seafarers' logs and ship models are particularly intriguing, and don't miss the 1920s peapod, the original lobster boat on the island. The house is just north of the Island Country Club and across from Eaton's Plumbing.

Close to the Stonington waterfront, the **Deer Isle Granite Museum** (51 Main St., Stonington, 207/367-6331) was established to commemorate the centennial of the quarrying business hereabouts. The best feature of the small museum is a 15-foot-long working model of Crotch Island, center of the industry, as it appeared at the turn of the 20th century. Flatcars roll, boats glide, and derricks move—it all looks very real. The museum is open in July and August, but it's best to call for current days and hours of operation. The recommended donation is $5 per family.

Another downtown Stonington attraction is a Lilliputian complex known as the **Miniature Village.** Some years ago, the late Everett Knowlton created a dozen and a half replicas of local buildings and displayed them on granite blocks in his yard. Since his death, they've been restored and put on display each summer in town—along with a donation box to support the upkeep. The village is set up on East Main Street (Route 15), below Hoy Gallery.

Pumpkin Island Light
A fine view of Pumpkin Island Light can be had from the cul-de-sac at the end of the Eggemoggin Road on Little Deer Isle. If heading south on Route 15, bear right at the information booth after crossing the bridge and continue to the end.

Penobscot East Resource Center
The purpose of the Penobscot East Resource Center, in Stonington (207/367-2708, www.penobscoteast.org), is "to energize and facilitate responsible community-based fishery management, collaborative marine science, and sustainable economic development to benefit the fishermen and the communities of Penobscot Bay and the Eastern Gulf of Maine." Bravo to that! It operates a **Lobster Hatchery** (Stonington Lobster Coop No. 1, 51 Indian Point Rd.), which was constructed by volunteers from the lobster industry in donated space with $25,000 raised locally and a matching grant. Lobster production began in 2006. Guided tours are offered ($10 adults, $5 children); call the resource center for the schedule.

The man behind both ventures is Ted Ames, who won a $500,000 MacArthur Foundation "genius grant" in 2005.

ENTERTAINMENT AND EVENTS
Stonington's National Historic Landmark, the 1912 **Opera House** (207/367-2788, www.operahousearts.org), is home to Opera House Arts, which hosts films, plays, lectures, concerts, family programs, and workshops year-round.

Mid-June, when lupine in various shades of pink and purple seem to be blooming everywhere, brings the **Lupine Festival** (207/348-2676 or 207/367-2420). The weekend festival includes art openings and shows, boat rides, a

The lights are on once again in Stonington's Opera House.

private garden tour, and entertainment ranging from a contra dance to movies.

July through September is the season for **First Friday,** an open-house night held on the first Friday evening of each month, with demonstrations, music, and refreshments, sponsored by the Stonington Galleries (www.stoningtongalleries.com).

Seamark Community Arts (207/348-2333, www.seamarkcommunityarts.com) hosts arts workshops for children and adults in areas such as book arts, nature crafts, pottery, drawing and painting, film and video, printmaking, basketry, textile arts, and more. The summer highlight is the themed annual auction; in 2009, local artists contributed artistic serving trays keeping with that year's theme, "At Your Service."

Mid-July brings the **Stonington Lobsterboat Races** (207/348-2804), very popular competitions held in the harbor, with lots of possible vantage points. Stonington is one of the major locales in the lobster-boat race circuit.

TED AMES, GENIUS

Ted Ames, the man behind the Penobscot East Resource Center and the Lobster Hatchery in Stonington, is a genius. In 2005, he was awarded a $500,000 MacArthur Fellowship. These prestigious "genius grants" are awarded to "talented individuals who have shown extraordinary originality and dedication in their creative pursuits and a marked capacity for self-direction." The foundation credited Ames with fusing "the roles of fisherman and applied scientist in response to increasing threats to the fishery ecosystem resulting from decades of overharvesting." Criteria for selection are: exceptional creativity, promise for important future advances based on a track record of significant accomplishment, and potential for the fellowship to facilitate subsequent creative work. No question, they found the right guy in Ted Ames.

A humble, soft-spoken man with dogged determination, Ames found little time to bask in the limelight from the award. While he certainly appreciated the money and the attention paid to his causes, the numerous interviews with TV, radio, and newspaper reporters took up valuable time, time he would rather use researching fisheries, collecting data, and devising ways to develop community-based fisheries management.

Ames is a fascinating guy, a combination of fisherman, lobsterman, and research scientist with deep Maine roots. "My family were some of the original settlers of Vinalhaven," he says. Ancestors on his father's side arrived in 1757, on the island off Rockland in Maine's mid-coast. "My mother's side came from Mount Desert." They were the original settlers on Bartlett's Island. When King George told the family to leave, they refused and stayed put. Ames grew up in a fishing family on Vinalhaven and went on to earn a master's degree in biochemistry from the University of Maine. But fishing was in his blood, and he eventually returned to the sea as a lobsterman and groundfisherman.

His years on the water gave him firsthand experience watching the changes in Maine's fisheries. He watched Maine's coastal economy change as fishing ports became more gentrified: Commercial piers gave way to oceanfront homes, and marine-related businesses gave way to fancy boutiques. His education combined with his experiences gave him tools and the insight needed to work toward developing new fisheries management practices and supporting fishing communities. He studied fishing patterns in the Gulf of Maine, noting spawning and habitat, and he complemented his research by listening to the stories and experiences of aging fishermen. By doing so, he was able to establish a fishing timeline beginning with historical patterns and following their evolution to current ones.

The Penobscot East Resource Center, which he founded with his wife, Robin, a former marine resources commissioner, and the Lobster Hatchery both are designed as research facilities as well as places for community members and others to learn more about fishing, meet commercial fishermen and women, and learn about their lifestyles in order to help support them and preserve the tradition and the economy. Ames, a master at gaining community support (due perhaps to his impeccable Maine credentials), managed to raise $25,000 from local fishing families, businesses, and individuals in an area not known for wealth.

Ames is using the unrestricted MacArthur Fellows Program money to continue his fisheries research and to develop "community-based groundfishing management to make it sustainable, so coastal fishing communities can survive into the next century. That's a challenge, but we're in the midst of it." There's no better person to be at the forefront than Ted Ames.

In early October is **Peninsula Potters Open Studios** (207/348-5681), during which more than two dozen potters welcome visitors.

Want to meet locals and learn more about the area? **Island Heritage Trust** sponsors a series of walks, talks, and tours from mid-June through mid-September. For information and reservations, call 207/348-2455.

ART AND CRAFT GALLERIES

Thanks to the presence and influence of Haystack Mountain School of Crafts, megatalented artists and artisans lurk in every corner of the island. Most galleries are tucked away on back roads, so watch for roadside signs. Many have studios open to the public where you can watch the artists at work. Here's just a sampling.

North End of Deer Isle

Although **Ronald Hayes Pearson** has died, his innovative and beautiful jewelry lives on in his eponymous studio and gallery (29 Old Ferry Rd., 207/348-2535), where artisans continue to create his designs under the watchful eye of his wife.

The nearby **Greene-Ziner Gallery** (73 Reach Rd., 207/348-2601, www.melissagreene.com) is a double treat. Melissa Greene turns out incredible painted and incised pottery (she's represented in the Smithsonian's Renwick Gallery) and Eric Ziner works magic in metal sculpture and furnishings. Your budget may not allow for one of Melissa's pots (in the four-digit range), but I guarantee you'll covet them. The gallery also displays the work of several other local artists.

Deer Isle Village Area

One of the island's premier galleries is Elena Kubler's **The Turtle Gallery** (61 N. Deer Isle Rd., Rte. 15, 207/348-9977, www.turtlegallery.com), in a handsome space formerly known as the Old Centennial House Barn (owned by the late Haystack director Francis Merritt) and the adjacent farmhouse. Group and solo shows of contemporary paintings, prints, and crafts are hung upstairs and down in the barn; works by gallery artists are in the farmhouse; and there's usually sculpture in the gardens both in front and in back. It's just north of Deer Isle Village—across from the Shakespeare School, oldest gallery on the island.

After the death of its founder, Mary Nyburg, the future of the famed **Blue Heron Gallery** (207/348-2267, www.blueherondeerisle.com) was blowing in the wind. Supporters, Haystack alumni, and friends rose to the occasion, and now the gallery is secure, even if its location moves every season. It remains a retail outlet for the work of the school's internationally renowned faculty—printmakers, blacksmiths, potters, weavers, papermakers, glassworkers, and more; seek it out.

Just a bit south is **Dockside Quilt Gallery** (33 Church St., 207/348-2531, www.docksidequiltgallery.com), where Nancy Knowlton, her daughter Kelly Pratt, and daughter-in-law Rebekah Knowlton stitch heirloom-quality quilts. Also here are Re-Bears, one-of-a-kind teddy bears handcrafted from vintage furs and fabrics by ninth-generation islander Heather Cormier. Custom quilts and bears can be ordered.

The **Deer Isle Artists Association** (13 Dow Rd., 207/348-2330, www.deerisleartists.com) is headquartered less than a mile northwest of the village. The co-op gallery features two-week exhibits of paintings, prints, drawings, and photos by local pros. Horse fans won't want to miss Penelope Plumb's upstairs gallery, **Equine Art** (207/348-6892, www.penelopeplumb.com).

The **RED DOT Gallery** (3 Main St., 207/348-2733, www.reddotgallery.net) shows the works of 10 artists creating in varied media.

Sunshine Road

Now for a bit of whimsy. From Route 15 in Deer Isle Village, take the Sunshine Road east 2.9 miles to **Peter Beerits Sculpture** (600 Sunshine Rd., 800/777-6845, www.nervousnellies.com). The meadows and woods surrounding the studio teem with whimsical wood and metal sculptures, including

Peter Beerits's whimsical sculptures accent the grounds of Nervous Nellie's.

dragons, Huns on horseback, moose, a blues joint and a western saloon, a general store, and more. The property is also home to Beerits's other enterprise, **Nervous Nellie's Jams and Jellies,** known for outstandingly creative condiments; sampling is encouraged. The best time to come is from May to early October, 9 a.m.–5 p.m., when the shop operates the ultra-casual **Mountainville Cafe,** serving tea, coffee, and delicious scones—with, of course, delicious Nervous Nellie's products. Stock up, because they're sold in only a few shops.

Stonington

Cabinetmaker Geoffrey Warner features his work as well as that of other local woodworkers in rotating shows at **Geoffrey Warner Studio** (431 N. Main St., 207/367-6555, www.geoffreywarnerstudio.com). Warner mixes classic techniques with contemporary styles and Eastern, nature-based, and Arts and Crafts accents to create some unusual and rather striking pieces.

Bright and airy **Isalos Fine Art** (Main St., Stonington, 207/367-2700, www.isalosart.com) shows the work of local artists in rotating shows.

Debi Mortenson shows her paintings, photography, and sculptures at **D Mortenson Gallery** (10 W. Main St., 207/367-5875, www.debimortenson.com) year-round.

The **g.Watson Gallery** (68 Main St., 207/367-2900) is a fine art gallery representing a number of top-notch artists working in varied media.

More paintings, many in bold, bright colors, can be found at Jill Hoy's **Hoy Gallery** (E. Main St., 207/367-2368, www.jillhoy.com).

A bit off the beaten path, but worth seeking out, is the **Siri Beckman Studio** (115 Airport Rd., 207/367-5037, www.siribeckman.com), Beckman's home studio–gallery featuring her woodcuts, prints, and watercolors.

SHOPPING

The greatest concentration of shops is in Stonington, where galleries, clothing boutiques, and eclectic shops line Main Street.

If you're in need of a good read, pop into Dockside Books & Gifts, on Stonington's waterfront.

Antiques, Books, and Gifts

In "downtown" Deer Isle Village, you'll find **The Periwinkle** (8 Main St., Deer Isle, 207/348-2256), where Neva Beck carries a fine inventory of Maine books, as well as crafts, notecards, and gifts. Look for Neva's hand-braided rugs and chair pads and her baby quilts.

The eclectic selection at **Bayside Antiques and Gifts** (131 Main St., Stonington, 207/367-8714) includes antiques, decorative accessories, and gifts, but the specialty is quality 18th- and 19th-century furniture and accessories from the northeast.

In downtown Stonington, below the Opera House, **Dockside Books & Gifts** (62 W. Main St., Stonington, 207/367-2652) carries just what its name promises, with a specialty in marine and Maine books. The rustic two-room shop has spectacular harbor views.

In 2008, Janice Glenn moved her browsers' emporium, **Old Schoolhouse Antiques at Burnt Cove** (194 Burnt Cove Rd., Stonington, 207/367-2849), to Burnt Cove, across from the grocery store. It's a funky shop jam-packed with vintage clothing, kitchenware (organized by color), textiles, cookbooks, and other collectibles, with an especially nice collection of quilts, rugs, and samplers. No credit cards.

Eclectic Shops

If you're looking for Maine pottery, weaving, metalwork, pewterware, imported tiles, or walking sticks, go directly to the **Harbor Farm Store** (Rte. 15, Little Deer Isle, 207/348-7755 or 800/342-8003, www.harborfarm.com), one of the state's best gift shops.

At the bottom of the island, **The Seasons of Stonington** (6 Thurlow's Hill Rd., Stonington, 207/367-6348) sells wine, fine foods, art, and other finds.

RECREATION
Parks and Preserves

Foresighted benefactors have managed to set aside precious acreage for respectful public use on Deer Isle. The Nature Conservancy (207/729-5181, www.nature.org) owns two properties, **Crockett Cove Woods Preserve** and **Barred Island Preserve**. The conscientious steward of other local properties is the **Island Heritage Trust** (420 Sunset Rd., Sunset, 207/348-2455, www.islandheritagetrust.org). At the office, open daily in summer and 1–4 P.M. Wednesday and Friday in winter, you can pick up notecards, photos, T-shirts, and helpful maps and information on hiking trails and nature preserves. Proceeds benefit the IHT's efforts; donations are much appreciated.

SETTLEMENT QUARRY

Here's one of the easiest, shortest walks in the area, leading to an impressive vista. From the parking lot on Oceanville Road (just under a mile off Route 15), marked by a carved granite sign, it's about five minutes to the top of the old quarry, where the viewing platform (a.k.a. the "throne room") takes in the panorama—all the way to the Camden Hills on a good day. In early August, wild raspberries are an additional enticement. Three short loop trails lead into the surrounding woods from here. A map is available in the trailhead box.

EDGAR TENNIS PRESERVE

The 145-acre Tennis Preserve, off the Sunshine Road, has very limited parking, so don't try to squeeze in if there isn't room; schedule your visit for another hour or day. But do go, and bring at least a snack if not a full picnic to enjoy on one of the convenient rocky outcroppings (be sure to carry out what you carry in, though). Allow at least 90 minutes to enjoy the walking trails, one of which skirts Pickering Cove, providing sigh-producing views. Another trail leads to an old cemetery. Parts of the trails can be wet, so wear appropriate footwear. Bring binoculars for bird-watching. The preserve is open sunrise–sunset. To find it, take the Sunshine Road 2.5 miles to the Tennis Road, and follow it to the preserve.

SHORE ACRES PRESERVE

The 38-acre preserve, a gift in 2000 from Judy Hill to the Island Heritage Trust, comprises old farmland, woodlands, clam flats, a salt marsh, and granite shorefront. Three walking trails connect in a 1.5-mile loop, with the Shore Trail section edging Greenlaw Cove. As you walk along the waterfront, look for the islands of Mount Desert rising in the distance and seals basking on offshore ledges. Do not walk across the salt marsh and try to avoid stepping on beach plants. To find the preserve, take the Sunshine Road 1.2 miles and then bear left at the fork onto the Greenlaw District Road. The preserve's parking area is just shy of one mile down the road. Park only in the parking area, not on the paved road.

CROCKETT COVE WOODS PRESERVE

Donated to the Nature Conservancy by benevolent, eco-conscious local artist Emily Muir, 98-acre Crockett Cove Woods Preserve is Deer Isle's natural gem—a coastal fog forest laden with lichens and mosses. Four interlinked walking trails cover the whole preserve, starting with a short nature trail. Pick up the helpful map-brochure at the registration box. Wear rubberized shoes or boots and respect adjacent private property. The preserve is open sunrise–sunset daily all year. From Deer Isle Village, take Route 15A to Sunset Village. Go 2.5 miles to Whitman Road and then to Fire Lane 88. The local contact phone number is 207/367-2674.

BARRED ISLAND PRESERVE

Owned by the Nature Conservancy but managed by the Island Heritage Trust, Barred Island Preserve was donated by Carolyn Olmsted, grandniece of noted landscape architect Frederick Law Olmsted, who summered nearby. A former owner of Goose Cove Lodge donated an additional 48 acres of maritime boreal fog forest. A single walking trail, one mile long, leads from the parking lot to the point. At low tide, and when eagles aren't nesting, you can continue out to Barred Island. Another trail skirts the shoreline of Goose Cove, before retreating inland and rejoining with the main trail. From a high point on the main trail, you can see more than a dozen islands, many of which are protected from development, as well as Saddleback Ledge Light, 14 miles distant. To get to the preserve, follow Route 15A to Goose Cove Road and then continue to the parking area on the right. If it's full, return another day.

HOLT MILL POND PRESERVE
The Stonington Conservation Commission administers this town-owned preserve, where more than 47 bird species have been identified (bring binoculars). It comprises four habitats: upland spruce forest, lowland spruce/mixed forest, freshwater marsh, and saltwater marsh. A self-guiding nature trail is accessible off the Airport Road (off Route 15 at the intersection with Lily's Café). Look for the Nature Trail sign just beyond the medical center. The detailed self-guiding trail brochure, available at the trailhead registration kiosk, is accented with drawings by noted artist Siri Beckman.

AMES POND
Ames Pond is neither park nor preserve, but it might as well be. On a back road close to Stonington, it's a mandatory stop in July and August, when the pond wears a blanket of pink and white water lilies. From downtown Stonington, take Indian Point Road east, just under a mile, to the pond.

CAUSEWAY BEACH AND SCOTT'S LANDING
If you're itching to dip your toes in the water, stop by Causeway Beach along the causeway linking Little Deer Isle to Deer Isle. It's popular for swimming and is also a significant habitat for birds and other wildlife. On the other side of Route 15 is Scott's Landing, with more than 20 acres of fields, trails, and shorefront.

Sporting Outfitters and Guided Trips
The biggest operation is **Old Quarry Ocean Adventures** (Stonington, 207/367-8977 or 877/479-8977, mobile 207/266-7778, www.oldquarry.com), with a broad range of outdoor adventure choices. Bill Baker's ever-expanding enterprise rents canoes, kayaks, sailboats, bikes, moorings, platform tent sites, and cabins. Bicycle rentals are $20 per day or $100 per week. Sea kayak rentals are $57 per day for a single, $67 for a tandem. Half-day rates (based on a four-hour rental) are $42 and $52, respectively. Overnight 24-hour rental is available for a 10 percent surcharge. Other options include canoes, rowboats, and sailboats; check the website for details. For all boat rentals, you must demonstrate competency in the vessel. They'll deliver and pick up anywhere on the island for a fee of $22. All-day guided tours in single kayaks are $105; tandems are $175. Half-day tours are $55 and $110, respectively. Plenty of other options are available, including sunset tours, family trips, and gourmet picnic paddles.

Overnight kayaking camping trips on nearby islands are led by a Registered Maine Guide. Rates, including meals, begin at $285 per adult for one night; three-person minimum. If you're bringing your own kayak, you can park your car ($7 per night up to two nights, $6 per night for three or more nights) and launch from here ($5 per boat for launching); they'll take your trash and any trash you find. Old Quarry is off the Oceanville Road, less than a mile from Route 15, just before you reach the Settlement Quarry preserve. It's well signposted.

Next to the restaurant of the same name, and owned by the same family, is **Finest Kind** (Center District Crossroad, about halfway between Routes 15 and 15A, 207/348-7714). Bicycle rentals here are $15 per day or $75 per week. Kayak or canoe rentals are $35 per day for a single, $45 for a tandem, including paddles, life jackets, spray skirts, delivery, and pickup.

Guided Walks
The Island Heritage Trust (402 Sunset Rd., Sunset, 207/348-2455, www.islandheritagetrust.org), along with the Stonington and Deer Isle Conservation Commissions, sponsors a Walks and Talks series. Guided walks cover topics such as Birds and Bird Calls for Beginners, The Geology of Deer Isle, and Migrating Shorebird Walk. Call for information and reservations.

Sea Kayaking

The waters around Deer Isle, with lots of islets and protected coves, are extremely popular for sea kayaking, especially off Stonington.

If you sign up with the **Maine Island Trail Association** (207/761-8225, www.mita.org, $45/year), you'll receive a handy manual that steers you to more than a dozen islands in the Deer Isle archipelago where you can camp, hike, and picnic—eco-sensitively, please. Boat traffic can be a bit heavy at the height of summer, so to best appreciate the tranquility of this area, try this in September, after the Labor Day holiday. Nights can be cool, but days are likely to be brilliant. Do remember this is a working harbor.

The six-mile paddle from Stonington to Isle au Haut is best left to experienced paddlers, especially since fishing folks refer to kayakers as "speed bumps."

For equipment rentals or guided trips, Old Quarry Ocean Adventures (Stonington, 207/367-8977 or 877/479-8977, mobile 207/266-7778, www.oldquarry.com) is especially helpful and provides many services for kayakers. Old Quarry is off the Oceanville Road, less than a mile from Route 15, just before you reach the Settlement Quarry preserve. It's well signposted.

Swimming

The island's only major freshwater swimming hole is the **Lily Pond,** northeast of Deer Isle Village. Just north of the Shakespeare School, turn into the Deer Run Apartments complex. Park and take the path to the pond, which has a shallow area for small children.

Golf and Tennis

About two miles south of Deer Isle Village, watch for the large sign (on the left) for the **Island Country Club** (Rte. 15A, Sunset, 207/348-2379, early June–late Sept.), a nine-hole public course that's been here since 1928. Also at the club are three beautifully maintained tennis courts. Note: The club's cheeseburgers and salads are among the island's best bargain lunches.

Excursion Boats

ISLE AU HAUT BOAT COMPANY

If you're not up for self-propulsion, board the *Miss Lizzie,* which from mid-June through late August departs at 2 P.M. Monday–Saturday from the Isle au Haut Boat Company (Seabreeze Ave., Stonington, 207/367-5193 or 207/367-6516, www.isleauhaut.com) dock in Stonington for a narrated one-hour trip among the islands; on morning tours, the crew hauls a string of lobster traps. Cost is $18 adults, $8 children under 12. Another option is to cruise over and back to Isle au Haut, without stepping foot off the boat, for half of the usual round-trip fare ($35 adults, $18 children). Reservations are advisable, especially in July and August. Day parking is available at the pier for $4, or find a spot in town and save the surcharge.

GUIDED ISLAND TOURS

Captain Walter Reed's Guided Island Tours (207/348-6789, www.guidedislandtours.com) aboard the *Gael* are custom designed for a maximum of four passengers. Walt is a Registered Maine Guide and professional biologist who also is a steward for Mark Island Lighthouse and several uninhabited islands in the area. He provides in-depth perspective and the local scoop. The cost is $35 per person for the first hour plus $25 per person for each additional hour; kids under 12 are half price. Reservations required; box lunches are available for an additional fee.

OLD QUARRY OCEAN ADVENTURES

Yet another aspect of the Old Quarry Ocean Adventures (Stonington, 207/367-8977 or 877/479-8977, mobile 207/266-7778, www.oldquarry.com) empire are sightseeing tours on the *Nigh Duck.* The three-hour trips, one in the morning (9 A.M.–noon) and one in the afternoon (1–4 P.M.), are $40 for adults and $24 for children under 12. Both highlight the natural history of the area as Captain Bill navigates the boat through the archipelago. Lobster traps are hauled on both trips (but not on Sunday); the morning trip visits Isle au Haut. The afternoon excursion features an island swimming break in a freshwater quarry. Also available is a 1.5-hour sunset cruise, departing half an hour before sunset, for $34 adults and $24 children under 12. And if that's not enough, Old Quarry also offers puffin, lighthouse, whale-watching, and island cruises, with rates beginning at $55 per adult, $35 per child. Of course, if none of this floats your boat, you can also arrange for a custom charter for $140 per hour.

Old Quarry also offers a number of special trips in conjunction with Island Heritage Trust. Most are noted on Old Quarry's website, but for reservations or more info, call 207/348-2455.

ACCOMMODATIONS
Inns and Bed-and-Breakfasts

Pilgrim's Inn (20 Main St., Deer Isle, 207/348-6615, www.pilgrimsinn.com, $129–239) is a beautifully restored colonial building and newer cottages overlooking the peaceful Mill Pond. The National Historic Register inn began life in 1793 as a boardinghouse named The Ark; be sure to check out the fascinating guestbook, with names dating back to 1901. A bit of a disconnect from the peacefulness is the recently added TV room (request a room far away from it, as the noise carries) and the downstairs tavern (formerly a fine-dining restaurant). It's open from early May to mid-October.

❰ **The Inn on the Harbor** (45 Main St., Stonington, 207/367-2420 or 800/942-2420, www.innontheharbor.com, $139–225) is exactly as its name proclaims—its expansive deck hangs right over the harbor. Although recently updated, the 1880s complex still has an air of unpretentiousness. Most of the 14 rooms and suites, each named after a windjammer, have fantastic harbor views and private or shared decks where you can keep an eye on lobster boats, small ferries, windjammers, and pleasure craft. (Binoculars are provided.) Streetside rooms can be noisy at night. Rates include a continental buffet breakfast. An espresso bar is open 11 A.M.–4:30 P.M. Nearby are antiques, gift, and craft shops; guest moorings

The view from the back decks at the Inn on the Harbor is first rate.

are available. The inn is open all year, but call ahead off-season, when rates are lower.

In downtown Stonington, just up the hill from the Inn on the Harbor and convenient for walking to everything (even a small sandy beach a mile away), is **Pres du Port** (W. Main St. and Highland Ave., Stonington, 207/367-5007, www.presduport.com, $125–150), a bright bed-and-breakfast run by amiable innkeeper Charlotte Casgrain. After many summers at a Deer Isle French summer camp and a career as a Connecticut French teacher, she's settled here. Three rooms have detached baths, one has a private bath; there are vanity sinks in the rooms. Children are welcome, and there's even a toy cupboard to entertain them. Adults can relax in the water-view hot tub, or climb to Charlotte's Folly, a rooftop lookout, for the extensive views. No credit cards.

Eggemoggin Reach is almost on the doorstep at **The Inn at Ferry Landing** (77 Old Ferry Rd., Deer Isle, 207/348-7760, www.ferrylanding.com, $130–178), overlooking the abandoned Sargentville–Deer Isle ferry wharf. The view is wide open from the inn's great room, where guests gather to read, play games, talk, and watch passing windjammers. Professional musician Gerald Wheeler has installed two grand pianos in the room; it's a treat when he plays. His wife, Jean, is the hospitable innkeeper, managing three water-view guest rooms and a suite. A harpsichord and a great view are big pluses in the suite. The Mooring, an annex that sleeps five, is rented by the week ($1,700, without breakfast). The inn is open all year except Thanksgiving and Christmas; Wi-Fi is available throughout.

Motels

Right in downtown Stonington, just across the street from the harbor, is **Boyce's Motel** (44 Main St., Stonington, 207/367-2421 or 800/224-2421, www.boycesmotel.com, $65–130). Eleven units all have TV, phones, and refrigerators; some have kitchens and living rooms, and one has two bedrooms. Across the street, Boyce's has a private harborfront deck for its guests. Ask for rooms well back from Main Street to lessen the noise of locals cruising the street at night. It's open year-round.

Resort

In 2009, **Goose Cove Resort** (Goose Cove Rd., Sunset, 207/348-2600, www.goosecovelodgemaine.com, $125–550) reopened the rustic cabins and guestrooms on this fabulous oceanfront property adjacent to the Barred Island Preserve. Many have ocean views, some have kitchenettes, most have either decks or granite ledge patios. There's a beach, nature trails, and the **Cocatoo Restaurant** serves lunch and dinner daily in season. The location is remote, secluded, and fabulous for those who enjoy communing with nature.

Hostels

In 2009, the rustic-bordering-on-primitive **Deer Isle Hostel** (65 Tennis Rd., Deer Isle, 207/348-2308, www.deerislehostel.com, $25 adults, $15 children under 12) opened near the Tennis Preserve. Owner Dennis Carter, a Surry, Maine, native and local stoneworker and carpenter, modeled it on The Hostel in the Forest in Brunswick, Georgia. It's completely off the grid, with a pump in the kitchen for water and an outhouse. Carter expects guests to work in the extensive organic gardens, using produce for shared meals prepared on a wood stove, the sole source of heat. The three-story timber-frame design is taken from a late-17th-century home in Massachusetts. Carter hand-cut the granite for the basement, and the timbers in the nail-free frame are hand-hewn from local blown-down spruce. Frills are limited to a sauna and a solar shower. The goal is sustainability, not profit. No credit cards.

Camping

Plan ahead if you want to camp at **Old Quarry Ocean Adventures Campground** (130 Settlement Rd., Stonington, 207/367-8977, www.oldquarry.com), with both oceanfront and secluded platform sites for tents and just three RV sites. Rates range $35–50 for two, plus $17 for each additional person, varying with location and hook-ups. Children younger than 12 are $6, under 5 are free. Leashed pets are permitted. Parking is designed so that vehicles are kept away from most campsites, but you can use a garden cart to transport your equipment between your car and your site. The campground is adjacent to Settlement Quarry Park.

FOOD
As always, hours are listed for peak season; call to verify days and hours of operation.

Local Flavors
After browsing the shops, you just might need a double-dip cone from **Harbor Ice Cream,** across the street from the Periwinkle in Deer Isle Village. Or a scoop of farm-made Smiling Hill Farm ice cream from **Stonington Cow Ice Cream,** on the main drag in Stonington.

The hickory-smoked salmon, unsliced, made by **Stonington Sea Products** (100 N. Main St., Stonington, 207/367-2400 or 888/402-2729, www.stoningtonseafood.com) was named in the May 2005 issue of the *Rosengarten Report* as one of the "25 Best Products" the noted food critic has ever recommended, describing it in terms including "Wow!" and "Bravo!" See for yourself, or try any of the company's other smoked products.

Craving sweets? Head to **Susie Q's Sweets and Curiosities** (40 School St., Stonington, 207/367-2415, 8 A.M.–3 P.M. Thurs.–Mon.). Susan Scott bakes a fine selection of cookies and pies, offers a limited selection of breakfast and lunch choices, and also carries antiques, books, quilts, toys, and other fun items. It's a Wi-Fi hotspot.

Burnt Cove Market (Rte. 15, Stonington, 207/367-2681, 6 A.M.–9 P.M. Mon.–Sat., 9 A.M.–9 P.M. Sun.) sells pizza, fried chicken, and sandwiches, plus beer and wine.

Creativity defines the menu at (**Lily's Cafe and Wine Bar** (450 Airport Rd. at Rte. 15, Stonington, 207/367-5936, 7 A.M.–5 P.M. Mon.–Thurs., to 8 P.M. Fri.), mercifully expanded in 2008. It's all very casual; order at the counter and find a table either inside, on the upstairs deck, or outside in the garden. Or assemble an haut gourmet picnic from veggie and meat sandwiches, Mediterranean salads, cheeses, and homemade soups and breads. Upstairs is the Chef's Attic, with a smattering of antiques as well as works by local artists. Alas, it's closed on weekends. Beer and wine are served. Most lunch entrées are about $9.

The Island Community Center (6 Memorial La., just off School St., Stonington) is the locale for the lively **Island Farmers Market** (10 A.M.–noon Fri. late May–late Sept.), selling smoked and organic meats, fresh herbs and flowers, produce, gelato and yogurt, maple syrup, jams and jellies, fabulous breads and baked goods, chocolates, ethnic foods, crafts, and so much more. Go early; items sell out quickly.

Family Favorites
In July or August, don't show up at **Finest Kind Dining** (70 Center District Crossroad, Deer Isle, 207/348-7714, www.finestkindenterprises.com, 5–8:30 P.M. Mon.–Sat. May–Oct.) without a dinner reservation. This log-cabin family restaurant serves home-style all-American food in a come-as-you-are setting. Pizza, pasta, prime rib, and seafood are all available, and there's a salad bar, too; most items are in the $8–20 range. And save room for dessert. The restaurant, owned by the Perez family, is halfway between Route 15 and Sunset Road (Route 15A). The enterprising Perezes also own the adjacent **Round the Island Mini Golf** (same phone, open the same months) and rent canoes, kayaks, and bicycles.

Harbor Cafe (Main St., Stonington, 207/367-5099, 6 A.M.–8 P.M. Mon.–Thurs., to 9 P.M. Fri.–Sat., to 2 P.M. Sun.) is *the* place to go for breakfast (you can eavesdrop on the local fisherfolk if you're early enough), but it's also reliable for lunch and dinner (especially on Friday nights for the seafood fry, with free seconds).

The views are top-notch from the harborfront **Fisherman's Friend Restaurant** (5 Atlantic Ave., Stonington, 207/367-2442, 11 A.M.–9 P.M. Sun.–Thurs., to 10 P.M. Fri.–Sat.). The restaurant gets high marks for respectable food, generous portions, ultra-fresh seafood, outstanding desserts, and consistency, but it seems to have lost its soul when it moved from its old digs to this larger and more modern space. Still, where else can you get lobster prepared 30 different ways? Prices are reasonable—the Friday-night fish fry, with free seconds, is $9.99. It's open from early May to late October.

Casual Dining

Families are welcome at the **Whale's Rib Tavern** (20 Main St./Sunset Rd., Deer Isle Village, 207/348-5222, 5–8:30 P.M. daily, closed Tues. in May, Sept., and Oct.), a comfy white-tablecloth tavern in the lower level of the Pilgrim's Inn. Everyone can find something that appeals and is within their budget, from burgers to beef tenderloin, fish-and-chips to scampi. Ask about the Friday-night three-course special.

You have a front seat—and a comfortable one at that—for all the harbor action at **Maritime Cafe** (27 Main St., Stonington, 207/367-2600, www.maritimecafe.com, 11:30 A.M.–3:30 P.M. and 5–8:30 P.M. daily, $18–28). Big windows frame the harbor from the dining room, and there's also lunch seating on the harborside deck. The menu emphasizes seafood (no surprise), but there are other choices and always a vegetarian selection.

In 2007 **The Cockatoo Portuguese Restaurant** (Goose Cove Rd., Sunset, 207/348-2300, noon–9 P.M. daily) opened in the lovely Goose Cove Lodge. The views are the best on the island, and there is both indoor and outdoor seating and a full bar. Chef Suzen Carter prepares fresh, fresh, fresh seafood, most of it caught by her husband, Bradley, as well as chicken and meat. She was brought up in the Azores, so Portuguese-inspired preparations are the specialty, but you can get a classic Maine shore dinner here, too. Frankly, the Portuguese paella is the way to go. An order for two includes scallops, shrimp, mussels, and clams, most still in their shells, as well as a whole lobster, all served over Mozambique rice in a fabulous and slightly spicy sauce. Unless you're really big eaters, you'll likely have leftovers. Equally delicious is the Bacalhau ha Braz, shredded codfish with onions and crispy potatoes and peppers. Everything is cooked to order, and while service and timing has improved from the interminable wait times of the place's early operation, you should go prepared for a leisurely meal. With this location and these views, sit back and relax. Most choices are $18–38, although lunch rolls (fish, crabmeat, scallop) begin at $8.

INFORMATION AND SERVICES

The **Deer Isle-Stonington Chamber of Commerce** (207/348-6124, www.deerisle-maine.com) has a summer information booth on a grassy triangle on Route 15 in Little Deer Isle, a quarter of a mile after crossing the bridge from Sargentville (Sedgwick).

Across from the Pilgrim's Inn is the **Chase Emerson Memorial Library** (Main St., Deer Isle Village, 207/348-2899). At the tip of the island is the **Stonington Public Library** (Main St., Stonington, 207/367-5926).

Public Restrooms

Public restrooms are at the Atlantic Avenue Hardware pier and at the Stonington Town Hall, Main Street; at the Chase Emerson Library in Deer Isle Village; and behind the information booth on Little Deer Isle.

Isle au Haut

Eight miles off Stonington lies 4,700-acre Isle au Haut, roughly half of which belongs to Acadia National Park. Pronounced variously as "I'll-a-HO" or "I'LL-a-ho," the island has nearly 20 miles of hiking trails, excellent birdwatching, and a tiny village.

About 60 souls call 5,800-acre Isle au Haut home year-round, most of them eking out a living from the sea. Each summer, the population temporarily swells with day-trippers, campers, and cottagers—then settles back in fall to the measured pace of life on an offshore island.

Samuel de Champlain, threading his way through this archipelago in 1605 and noting the island's prominent central ridge, came up with the name of Isle au Haut—High Island. Appropriately, the tallest peak (543 feet) is now named Mount Champlain.

More recent fame has come to the island thanks to island-based author Linda Greenlaw, of *Perfect Storm* fame, who wrote *The Lobster Chronicles*. Although that book piqued interest, Isle au Haut remains uncrowded and well off the beaten tourist track.

Most of the southern half of the six-mile-long island belongs to Acadia National Park, thanks to the wealthy summer visitors who began arriving in the 1880s. It was their heirs who, in the 1940s, donated valuable acreage to the federal government. Today, this offshore division of the national park has a well-managed 18-mile network of trails, a few lean-tos, several miles of unpaved road, and summertime passenger-ferry service to the park entrance.

In the island's northern half are the private residences of fisherfolk and summer folk, a minuscule village (including a market and post office), a five-mile paved road, and a lighthouse. The only vehicles on the island are owned by residents.

If spending the night on Isle au Haut sounds appealing (it is), you'll need to plan well ahead; it's no place for spur-of-the-moment sleepovers. (Even spontaneous day trips aren't always possible.) The best part about staying overnight on Isle au Haut is that you'll have so much more than seven hours to enjoy this idyllic island.

◖ ACADIA NATIONAL PARK

Mention Acadia National Park and most people think of Bar Harbor and Mount Desert Island, where more than three million visitors arrive each year. The Isle au Haut section of the park sees maybe 5,000 visitors a year—partly because only 48 people a day (not counting campers) are allowed to land here. But the remoteness of the island and the scarcity of beds and campsites also contribute to the low count.

Near the town landing, where the year-round mail boat and another boat dock, is the **Park Ranger Station** (207/335-5551), where you can pick up trail maps and park information—and use the island's only public facilities. (Do yourself a favor, though: Make your plans

The Isle au Haut lighthouse, built in 1907, is now listed on the National Historic Register.

by downloading Isle au Haut maps and information from the Acadia National Park website, www.nps.gov/acad.)

Hiking

Hiking on Acadia National Park trails is the major recreation on Isle au Haut, and even in the densest fog you'll see valiant hikers going for it. A loop road circles the whole island; an unpaved section goes through the park, connecting with the mostly paved non-park section. Walking on that is easy. Beyond the road, none of the park's 18 miles of trails could be labeled "easy"; the footing is rocky, rooty, and often squishy. But the park trails *are* well marked, and the views—of islets, distant hills, and ocean—make the effort worthwhile. Go prepared with proper footwear.

The most-used park trail is the four-mile one-way **Duck Harbor Trail,** connecting the town landing with Duck Harbor. (You can either use this trail or follow the island road—mostly unpaved in this stretch—to get to the campground when the summer ferry ends its Duck Harbor runs.)

Even though the summit is only 314 feet, **Duck Harbor Mountain** is the island's toughest trail. Still, it's worth the 1.2-mile one-way effort for the stunning 360-degree views from the summit. Option: Rather than return via the trail's steep, bouldery sections, cut off at the Goat Trail and return to the trailhead that way.

For terrific shoreline scenery, take **Western Head** and **Cliff Trails** at the island's southwestern corner. They form a nice loop around Western Head. The route follows the coastline, ascending to ridges and cliffs and descending to rocky beaches, with some forested sections. Options: Close the loop by returning via the Western Head Road. If the tide is out (and *only* if it's out), you can walk across the tidal flats to the quaintly named Western Ear for views back toward the island. Western Ear is private, so don't linger. The **Goat Trail** adds another four miles (round-trip) of moderate coastline hiking east of the Cliff Trail; views are fabulous and bird-watching is good, but if you're here only for a day, you'll need to decide whether there's time to do this and still catch the return mail boat. If you do have the time and the energy, you can connect from the Goat Trail to the **Duck Harbor Mountain Trail.**

OTHER RECREATION
Biking

Pedaling is limited to the 12 or so miles of mostly unpaved, hilly roads, and while it is a way to get around, frankly, the terrain is neither exciting, fun, nor view-worthy. Mountain bikes are not allowed on the park's hiking trails, and rangers try to discourage park visitors from bringing them to the island. If you're staying at the Inn at Isle au Haut, you can borrow a bike, which is handy around the "village" and for going swimming in Long Pond. You can also rent a bike (about $23 per day) on the island from the Isle au Haut Ferry Service or Old Quarry Ocean Adventures. It costs $18 round-trip to bring your own bike aboard the Isle au Haut Ferry. Both boats carry bikes *only* to the town landing, not to Duck Harbor.

Swimming

For superb **freshwater swimming,** head for Long Pond, a skinny 1.5-mile-long swimming hole running north–south on the east side of the island, abutting national park land. You can bike over there, clockwise along the road, almost five miles, from the town landing. Or bum a ride from an island resident. There's a minuscule beachlike area on the southern end with a picnic table and a float. If you're here only for the day, though, there's not enough time to do this *and* get in a long hike. Opt for the hiking—or do a short hike and then go for a swim (the shallowest part is at the southern tip).

ACCOMMODATIONS AND FOOD

Options for food are extremely limited on Isle au Haut, so if you're coming for a day trip, bring sufficient food and water.

Inn

On the east side of the island is **The Inn at**

Isle au Haut (Lighthouse Point, Isle au Haut, off-island 207/335-5141, www.innatisleauhaut.com, $300–375), a mansard-roofed waterfront Victorian home that Diana Santospago has turned into an inn. An accomplished cook, Diana whips up fabulous breakfasts, lunches, and dinners for her guests; bring your own beer or wine. Open to the public for dinner by reservation. The downstairs room with private bath is most spacious. Three rather small rooms on the 2nd floor share one bath; all but one have water views. Single-speed bikes are provided for guests, and it's an easy pedal to Long Pond for swimming or to connect with park trails. Special early- and late-summer packages at the inn include cruises, tours, and cooking classes with Linda Greenlaw. The inn is open from early June to late September.

Camping

You'll need to get your bid in early to reserve one of the five six-person lean-tos at the national park's **Duck Harbor Campground**, the only camping on Isle au Haut, open May 15 to October 15. Before April 1, contact the park for a reservation request form (Acadia National Park, 207/288-3338, www.nps.gov/acad). From April 1 on *(not before, or the park people will send it back to you)*, return the completed form, along with a check for $25, to reserve camping for up to six people for a maximum of five nights May 15–June 14, three nights June 15–September 15, and five nights again September 16–October 15. Mark the envelope "Attn: Isle au Haut Reservations." Competition is stiff in the height of summer, so list alternate dates. The park refunds the check if there's no space; otherwise, it's nonrefundable and you'll receive a "special-use permit" (*do not* forget to bring it along). There's no additional camping fee.

Unless you don't mind backpacking nearly five miles to reach the campground, try to plan your visit between mid-June and Labor Day, when the mail boat makes a stop in Duck Harbor. It's wise to call the Isle au Haut Company for the current ferry schedule before choosing dates for a lean-to reservation.

Trash policy is carry-in/carry-out, so pack a trash bag or two with your gear. Also bring a container for carting water from the campground pump, since it's 0.3 mile from the lean-tos. It's a longish walk to the general store for food—when you could be spending your time hiking the island's trails—so bring enough to cover your stay.

The three-sided lean-tos are big enough (8 by 12 feet, 8 feet high) to hold a small (two-person) tent, so bring one along if you prefer being fully enclosed. A tarp will also do the trick. (Also bring mosquito repellent—some years, the critters show up here en masse.) No camping is permitted outside of the lean-tos, and nothing can be attached to trees.

Food

Isle au Haut is pretty much a BYO place—and for the most part, that means BYO food. Although the Inn at Isle au Haut is open to the public for dinner by reservation, you need to get there and back, only possible if you're staying in a rental cottage with a car.

Thanks to the seasonal **Isle au Haut General Store** (207/335-5211, www.theislandstore.net), less than a five-minute walk from the town landing, you won't starve. The inventory isn't extensive, but it can be intriguing, due to the store manager who travels worldwide and stocks the shop with her finds. On the other hand, food probably won't be your prime interest here—the island itself is as good as it gets.

Even more intriguing is **Black Dinah Chocolatiers** (207/335-5010, www.blackdinahchocolatiers.com), just shy of a mile from the town landing. Steve and Kate Shaffer's little shop doubles as a café, serving pastries, organic coffees and teas, a few lunch-type offerings, and, of course, decadent handmade chocolates. It also has free Wi-Fi.

GETTING THERE
Isle au Haut Boat Company

The Isle au Haut Boat Company (Seabreeze Ave., Stonington, 207/367-5193, www.isleauhaut.com) generally operates five daily trips

Monday–Saturday, plus two on Sunday from mid-June to early September. Other months, there are 2–3 trips Monday–Saturday.

Round-trips from April to mid-October are $35 adults, $19 children under 12 (two bags per adult, one bag per child). Round-trip surcharges include bikes ($18), kayaks/canoes ($38 minimum), and pets ($8). If you're considering bringing a bike, be sure to inquire about on-island bike rentals ($23 per day). Weather seldom affects the schedule, but be aware that ultra-heavy seas could cancel a trip.

There is twice-daily ferry service, from mid-June to Labor Day, from Stonington to Duck Harbor, at the edge of Isle au Haut's Acadia National Park campground. For a day trip, the schedule allows you 6.5 hours on the island Monday–Saturday and 4.5 hours on Sunday. No boats or bikes are allowed on this route, and no dogs are allowed in the campground. A ranger boards the boat at the town landing and goes along to Duck Harbor to answer questions and distribute maps. Before mid-June and after Labor Day, you'll be off-loaded at the Isle au Haut town landing, about five miles from Duck Harbor. The six-mile passage from Stonington to the Isle au Haut town landing takes 45 minutes; the trip to Duck Harbor is 75 minutes.

Ferries depart from the Isle au Haut Boat Company dock (Seabreeze Ave., off E. Main St. in downtown Stonington). Parking ($9 per day outside, $11 indoors) is available next to the ferry landing.

Old Quarry Ocean Adventures

The new kid on the block offering seasonal service to Isle au Haut, Old Quarry Ocean Adventures (Stonington, 207/367-8977 or 877/479-8977, mobile 207/266-7778, www.oldquarry.com) transports passengers on the renovated *Nigh Duck*. The boat usually leaves Old Quarry at 9 A.M. and arrives at the island's town landing one hour later. It departs from the same point at 5 P.M., arriving back at Old Quarry around 6 P.M. The fee is $35 round-trip for adults, $18 for children under 12. You can add an island bike rental for an additional $20. Old Quarry also offers a taxi service to Isle au Haut for $140 per hour for up to six people.

MOON MAINE'S PENOBSCOT BAY &
THE BLUE HILL PENINSULA
Avalon Travel
a member of the Perseus Books Group
1700 Fourth Street
Berkeley, CA 94710, USA
www.moon.com

Editor and Series Manager: Kathryn Ettinger
Copy Editor: Amy Scott
Graphics and Production Coordinator:
   Lucie Ericksen
Cover Designer: Kathryn Osgood
Map Editor: Brice Ticen
Cartographers: Kat Bennett, Albert Angulo
Proofreader: Nikki Iokimedes

ISBN: 978-1-59880-549-9

Text © 2010 by Hilary Nangle.
Maps © 2010 by Avalon Travel.
All rights reserved.

Some photos and illustrations are used by permission and are the property of the original copyright owners.

Front cover photo: harborfront in Rockport
   © istockphoto.com
Title page photo: view from Monhegan Island ©
   Hilary Nangle

Printed in the United States

Moon Handbooks and the Moon logo are the property of Avalon Travel. All other marks and logos depicted are the property of the original owners. All rights reserved. No part of this book may be translated or reproduced in any form, except brief extracts by a reviewer for the purpose of a review, without written permission of the copyright owner.

Although every effort was made to ensure that the information was correct at the time of going to press, the author and publisher do not assume and hereby disclaim any liability to any party for any loss or damage caused by errors, omissions, or any potential travel disruption due to labor or financial difficulty, whether such errors or omissions result from negligence, accident, or any other cause.

ABOUT THE AUTHOR

Hilary Nangle

Perhaps it's because she was born under the sign of Aquarius, but Hilary Nangle has always had a passion for the coast. Since she first watched the sun rise out of the Atlantic while waiting for the school bus in Cape Elizabeth, the ocean has been a constant in her life.

In college, Hilary discovered her love for writing. She briefly pursued a graduate degree in Middle Eastern studies, but when she realized her intended career path would take her far from Maine, she dropped out. She subsequently became a ski and whitewater-rafting bum, an experience that introduced her to the state's back roads and ignited her wanderlust. When she tired of her parents asking when she was going to get a "real" job, she drew on her writing skills, working as an editor for the pro ski tour, managing editor for a food trade publication, features editor for a daily newspaper, and freelance writer/editor.

Hilary never tires of exploring Maine, always seeking out the offbeat and quirky. To her husband's dismay, she inherited her grandmother's shopping gene and can't pass a used bookstore, artisans' gallery, or antiques shop without browsing. She's equally curious about food – she's never met a lobster she didn't like. Hilary still divides her year between the coast and the mountains, residing with her husband, photographer Tom Nangle, and two oversized dogs, Bernie and Dooley, all of whom share her passions for long walks and Maine-made ice cream. To learn more about Hilary, please visit her website, www.HilaryNangle.com, and click on her blog, where she keeps her readers updated on what's new in Maine.